*We are convinced that
the sustainability of communities and societies
largely rests on the strength of the family
as a basic unit of society and the natural environment
for the growth and well-being of all its members,
particularly children.*

*We recognise the vital role of the family in
attaining the internationally agreed development goals
and confirm our commitment to enhance the
contribution of the families in the efforts to
achieve sustainable development goals
by promoting family-oriented policies and
prioritising the needs and priorities of the family
at the national and international levels.*

Presented by the UN Group of Friends of the Family
Bangladesh, Belarus, Comoros, Egypt, Indonesia, Iran, Iraq, Kuwait,
Kyrgyzstan, Libya, Malaysia, Nicaragua, Nigeria, Oman, Pakistan,
Qatar, the Russian Federation, Saudi Arabia, Somalia, Sudan,
Tajikistan, Turkmenistan, Yemen, Uganda and Zimbabwe

U.N. Intergovernmental Negotiations on
Post-2015 Development Agenda
New York, June 23, 2015

Immaculee,
Thank you for sharing your story!
Truly inspiring...

Family Capital and the SDGs

Implementing the
17 Sustainable Development Goals

Articles Focusing on Specific Targets of the
Sustainable Development Goals

Compiled by Susan Roylance

Debora Ruano Fletcher (Facebook name)
Sustainable Families Executive Director
and founder. Dr-Fletcher @ hotmail·com
801·201·7166

———▷ Sustainable Families Group
United Families International
World Congress of Families

— 2016 —

Family Capital and the SDGs
Implementing the 17 Sustainable Development Goals

ISBN: 978-0-692-77260-7
First printing: 2016

World Congress of Families
934 North Main Street, Rockford, IL 61103
http://www.worldcongress.org/

TABLE OF CONTENTS

TARGETS AND ARTICLES

Foreword

E. Douglas Clark

To discover the key to achieving the Sustainable Development Goals, you have to look beyond what the goals themselves say. But you don't have to look far.

It was not that long ago that UN Secretary-General, then Kofi Annan, declared the family to be "a vital partner" in achieving the Millennium Development Goals.[1] His statement was soon echoed by Bangladesh Ambassador Iftekhar Chowdhury: "The attainment of every Millennium Development Goal must begin with the family. The family is the main instrument of societal transformation."[2]

The driving force behind social progress and development

These are hardly isolated statements. Qatar's Sheikha Moza Bint Nasser referred to the family as "the driving force" behind "social progress and development,"[3] while the Doha Declaration, drafted by delegates from around the world, holds the family to be "the fundamental agent for sustainable social, economic and cultural development."[4]

The implication for the Sustainable Development Goals is unmistakable. Their attainment likewise begins and ends with the family, which, says the Universal Declaration of Human Rights, "is the natural and fundamental group unit of society and is entitled to protection by society and the State."[5]

The words merit close attention, according to Professor Richard Wilkins. "As reflected in the precise and elegant terms of the Universal Declaration, the family is not merely a construct of human will or imagination," but "has a profoundly important connection to nature... begin[ning] with the realities of reproduction" and "extend[ing] to the forces that shape civilization itself....The family, in short, is the 'natural and fundamental group unit of society.'"[6]

The fundamental nucleus of civilization

This language from the Universal Declaration resounds through more than a hundred national constitutions with their varied descriptions of the family as society's fundamental unit, element, cornerstone, or foundation; or, in language more evocative of life and growth, as the basic cell or fundamental nucleus of civilization.[7] Why it is so was explained in an address to the General Assembly on the 10th anniversary of the International Year of the Family:

> The family [is] the foundation of the social order, the bedrock of nations, and the bastion of civilization,... a universal and irreplaceable community, rooted in human nature.... As the cradle of life and love for each new generation, the family is the primary source of personal identity, self-esteem, and support for children. It is also the first and foremost school of life, uniquely suited to teach children integrity, character, morals, responsibility, service, and wisdom....The state's foremost obligation... is to respect, defend, and protect the family as an institution.[8]

The great determinant of development

Little wonder that the family is the great determinant of development, as seen most clearly in those societies most in need of development. The Regional Conference on the Family in Africa declared:

> [As] the basic and most fundamental unit of society, a dynamic unit engaged in an intertwined process of individual and group development,...the African family [is] at the core of society [and] needs to be strengthened as part of Africa's development process.... The centrality, uniqueness and indispensability of the family in society [are] unquestionable.[9]

In the case of Asia, the family's decisive role was obvious to Nobel Laureate Gary Becker. Notwithstanding the recent "revolutionary alterations" affecting societies around the world, noted Becker, Asians have managed to maintain "a strong reliance on the family. I think there is a connection there—not yet proven by economists, but I believe some day it will be proven that there is a connection—between the rapidity of the Asian economic growth and the fact that they have had this very powerful attachment to the family."[10]

Our bridge to the future

Always and everywhere it is the same: "The family is the ultimate foundation of every civilization known to history,"[11] observed historian Will Durant. Perhaps Alex Haley said it best: "The family is our refuge and our springboard; nourished on it, we can advance to new horizons. In every conceivable manner, the family is link to our past, bridge to our future."[12]

How does the family provide the bridge to achieve the Sustainable Development Goals? This book provides definitive and timely answers as we seek to transform our world for a brighter future. Read on.

E. Douglas Clark, JD, MBA
Director of International Advocacy
World Congress of Families

Endnotes

1. U.N. Secretary-General, Preparations for and Observance of the Tenth Anniversary of the International Year of the Family in 2004, ¶ 9, U.N. Doc. A/59/176 (July 23, 2004).
2. His Excellency Iftekhar Ahmed Chowdhury, in U.N. GAOR, 59th Sess., 67th plen. mtg. at 24-25, U.N. Doc. A/59/PV.67 (Dec. 6, 2004).
3. Her Highness Sheikha Mozah Bint Nasser, "Preface," in A. Scott Loveless and Thomas B. Holman, eds., *The Family in the New Millennium: World Voices Supporting the "Natural" Clan*, 1:x (3 vols.; Westport, CT: Praeger Publishers, 2007).
4. The Doha Declaration, Preamble, at World Family Policy Center, http://www.law2.byu.edu/wfpc/intl_conf_doha.html (last visited June 30, 2016).
5. G.A. Res. 217 (III) A, Universal Declaration of Human Rights (Dec. 10, 1948).
6. Richard G. Wilkins, "Preface of the NGO Working Group," in Loveless and Holman, *The Family in the New Millennium* 3:xiii.
7. See listing of constitutional provisions in World Family Declaration, n. 3, in Ave Maria International Law Journal 2016:58-65, and at http://www.worldfamilydeclaration.org/WFD (last visited June 30, 2016).
8. Wade F. Horn for the United States, U.N. GAOR, 59th Sess., 67th plen. mtg. at 2-3, U.N. Doc. A/59/PV.67 (Dec. 6, 2004).
9. Plan of Action on the Family in Africa, 13-14, from Regional Conference on the Family in Africa held at Cotonou, Benin (July 27-28, 2004), http://sa.au.int/en/sites/default/files/plan_of_action_on_the_family-16july2004.pdf (last visited June 30, 2016).
10. Gary S. Becker, "The Role of the Family in Modern Economic Life," in Loveless and Holman, *The Family in the New Millennium* 1:4.
11. Will Durant, *The Mansions of Philosophy: A Survey of Human Life and Destiny*, 395-396 (New York: Simon and Schuster, 1929).
12. Alex Haley, in Dolores Curran, *Traits of a Healthy Family*, 226 (New York: Ballantine Books, 1984).

"The family provides a crucial and irreplaceable social function. Inside a family, helpless babies are transformed from self-centered bundles of impulses, desires and emotions to fully socialized adults. The family teaches trust, cooperation, and self-restraint. The family is uniquely situated to teach these skills because people instill these qualities in their children as a side effect of loving them. Contracts and free political institutions, the formation of a free society, require these attributes that only families can inculcate. Without loving families, no society can govern itself."

> Jennifer Roback Morse
> Love & Economics, page 5
> Spence Publishing Co.
> Dallas, TX 2001

The above quote has appeared on the back of the title page in each edition of the UN Negotiating Guide (compiled by Susan Roylance and published by United Families International). We thank "Dr. J" for her insight and continued leadership in promoting the importance of parents and the family unit in today's society.

Preface

Susan Roylance

This book has been a labor of love – love for our own family and love, collectively, for the families of the world.

While governments readily recognize the needs of children and youth, there seems to be a reluctance to recognize the importance of good parents, and strong families, to raise the children and youth of the world.

The chapter on "Family Capital" promotes the value of the combined resources and talent of the family unit to nurture children and provide the necessities of life for family members, and also help achieve the important Sustainable Development Goals of the world.

None of the authors have been compensated for the contribution of their articles to this book. They have freely shared their knowledge and experience, in hopes of helping other families in their pursuit of happiness and contributing their knowledge and talents to strengthen other families, as well.

The book has been a combined effort of many people – specifically the Sustainable Families Group, and our excellent editor, Debie Rossi – without whom I could not have produced this book. We also thank: E. Douglas Clark and the World Congress of Families, for their support and vision of the importance of this book; United Families International and Big Ocean Women.

From my first day at the U.N. (April 1995), when a group of women in the Linkage Caucus laughed and jeered at me for representing "United Families of America," I have worked diligently to promote motherhood and the family unit. This book is my final effort in that saga.

If you find something of value in the pages of this book – for your family – please pass the information on to other families, that collectively we might help make the world a better place to live – sustainably.

Susan Roylance

> "Family capital" is greatly diminished when families disintegrate or fail to form, and it is maximized when adults marry and create a stable unit and environment for all members, especially children, to flourish.
>
> – Marcia Barlow

Marcia Barlow, MPA, Vice President of International Programs for United Families International (UFI). She is an author of UFI's series: *Guide to Family Issues* and directs the development and updating of the *UN Negotiating Guide*. She holds a Master's Degree from Harvard University (Kennedy School of Government). Marcia and her husband, Greg, have three children and six grandchildren.

✒ *Family Capital*

Marcia Barlow

Family capital: The fuel that drives development

Is there anyone working in the international arena that would turn down an offer of additional "capital" to secure success for the ambitious plan set forth in Agenda 2030: The Sustainable Development Goals (SDGs)? Can a person, or for that matter a country, ever have enough "capital?"

Many are familiar with the term "capital" as it refers to things related to economics, business and finance. Or, some may be familiar with the term "human capital" or in recent decades, the study of "social capital." But a less familiar term, and perhaps the most important form of capital, is that of "family capital." Why? Because all other forms of capital – human, social, cultural, economic - emanate from the wellspring we call "family."

What is family capital?

The concept of "family capital" describes the resources the family unit can bring towards accomplishing important personal and societal goals. Anat Gofen-Sarig referred to it as:

> The ensemble of means, strategies, and resources embodied in the family's way of life that positively influences the future of the children.[1]

But I offer this more robust definition:

> **Mothers, fathers, and their children engaging in the business of life supported by an extended and intergenerational family network – all working together to create a virtuous web that serves the economic, emotional, physical and spiritual well-being of all family members; and ultimately serving communities and nations.**

What allows family capital to fulfill such an important role?

Nobel Laureate Gary Becker declared:

> No discussion of human capital can omit the influence of families on the knowledge, skills, values, and habits of their children and therefore on their present and future productivity.[2]

A report of the UN Secretary-General also emphasizes the critical role of family:

> As basic and essential building blocks of societies, families have a crucial role in social development. They bear the primary responsibility for the education and socialization of children as well as instilling values of citizenship and belonging in the society. Families provide material and non-material care and support to its members, from children to older persons or those suffering from illness, sheltering them from hardship to the maximum possible extent.[3]

The unique contribution of family capital lies, in part, in this description from David Imig of Michigan State University: "Family capital is the result of the system principle that the whole is greater than the sum of its parts."[4]

The family unit is able to do more when it combines its abilities, rather than an individual, alone, endeavoring to tackle various challenges. But a family is so much more than an amalgamation of any given group of individuals working together toward a common end.

Unlike many societal entities, a family has the ability to take resources, however limited, and use them in the most efficient manner. The nature of family allows it to intimately know the people involved and allow the resources to go to their highest and best use. Being the most efficient, a family would be more likely to produce a surplus of financial, human and social resources that could flow to the society at large.

Commitment to share resources

Members of a family are bound together for more than economic interest with a commitment to share resources (talents, skills, energy, fidelity, emotional vitality, spirituality) and to invest them in the well-being of those closest to them. "Relatedness" (genetic kinship) brings about a synthesis of these important components- along with an increased commitment and fidelity to the relationship - which a conglomerate of disparate individuals can rarely provide. Self-interest is tempered by "relatedness."

Social scientist W. Bradford Wilcox has hypothesized:

> There is a connection between strong families and state prosperity, because
> 1) marriage and family life deepen men's connection to the labor force,
> 2) they boost income and assets, and
> 3) they improve the accumulation of both social capital and human capital.[5]

All forms of capital take time to accumulate and accumulation is much less likely to occur in an unstable, short-term environment. Investment of resources is less likely to occur if a relationship is viewed as unstable and unreliable with participants uncommitted. The intact family decreases the odds that those unhelpful traits would emerge. Divorce, cohabitation and other alternative family structures typify those less stable relationships.

Family capital is greatly <u>diminished</u> when families disintegrate or fail to form and it is <u>maximized</u> when adults marry and create a stable unit and environment for all members, especially children, to flourish.

How can family capital contribute to the success of the Sustainable Development Goals (SDGs)?

Perhaps we can get a glimpse of family capital's power by considering questions such as these:

- How do you solve the problem of **poverty and hunger** without considering the role of the family in meeting temporal needs and providing sustenance to its members?

- How do you achieve **education** of all the world's children without considering the day-to-day involvement and efforts of parents?

- How do you reduce **maternal and child mortality** without recognizing the role of mothers, fathers and families and what is occurring in the home?

- How do you combat **HIV/AIDS and other diseases** without the day to day involvement, teaching and caring of committed parents and family members?

When we speak of "Sustainable Development Goals" attention must be given to what actually is sustainable. By definition, a system that is sustainable involves methods that do not completely use up or destroy available resources, enabling them to last or continue for extended periods. *There are few things more organic, natural and sustainable than a mother, father and their children.*

The family unit provides a wonderful combination of the following characteristics: 1) productivity, 2) efficiency, and 3) continuity – all of which contribute to increased sustainability.

Within a stable, intact family there is less poverty and hunger, better outcomes for children, greater economic achievement, more wealth, and less crime and violence. This type of family has increased capacity to produce a net positive economically, higher education attainment, consume fewer natural resources, allow for efficient specialization, and contains the critical intergenerational component. It has the added advantage of decentralizing power and reduces the risk of government overreach.

Following are several examples:

Environment

> Divorced households in the U.S. could have saved more than 38 million rooms, 73 billion kilowatt-hours of electricity, and 627 billion gallons of water in 2005 alone if their resource-use efficiency had been comparable to married households… The [study] results suggest that mitigating the impacts of resource-inefficient lifestyles such as divorce helps to achieve global environmental sustainability and saves money for households.[6]

Poverty and hunger

Scholars at United Nations University acknowledge the power of family capital:

> Children thriving in poor communities were statistically most likely to live in families characterized by traditional fireside family values; devoted mothers and fathers, happy marriages, and warm cooperative bonds with siblings, grandparents, other relatives and the broader community.[7]

"[F]amily structure is a better predictor of outcomes like economic mobility, child poverty, and median family income than are race or education."[8] In the U.S. 70 percent of never-married mothers would be able to escape poverty if they were married to the father of their children.[9]

Education

Parental involvement in their child's education is a more significant factor in a child's academic performance than the qualities of the school itself.[10]

We know that kids who come from married families tend to graduate from high school and graduate from college at higher rates. They are more likely to be gainfully employed as adults and to work more hours. This is true for both young men and young women; if you are concerned about women's [empowerment and] professional opportunities you should be concerned about their family structure growing up.[11]

Economic growth and full and productive employment

Married men with kids are 13 percentage points more likely to be in the labor force than their comparable single peers....Married families have more money to manage, and they tend to manage it more prudently than families headed by single parents and cohabiting couples. They draw on economies of scale. They pool income. They have higher rates of saving. They get more financial support from their kin. And they are more likely to stay together, which also reinforces their economic position.[12]

Among couples who married and stay married, the per person net worth increased on average by 16 percent with each year of marriage. Compared to those who remained single, getting married increased one's wealth, on average, by 93 percent.[13]

What factors will increase family capital?

- Encourage marriage and children – in that order.

- Recognize that divorce, cohabitation, single parenthood, and other family forms, however well-intentioned, do not make the same contribution to sustainable development.

- Launch civic efforts to strengthen marriage and family.

- Increase the understanding that human beings are not a hindrance to sustainable development, but a necessary and critical component.

- View public policies and programs through a family-impact lens.

The authors of the influential "Family Impact Report," emphasize that "...families do better in a supportive policy environment—one in which, for example, schools actively seek parental engagement; employers recognize that workers are also family members; agencies and organizations are family-centered in their philosophy and operation; and laws support family members' roles as caregivers, parents, partners, and workers."[14]

Conclusion

Empowering the family and enhancing family stability are crucial inputs in the sustainable development process. High levels of family capital are essential for a country as it will have a direct impact on human, moral, and social capital, and upon efficient resources use, economic activity and economic structures. The family unit is best suited for producing caring, competent, and productive citizens who can meet the demands and challenges of an ever-changing world.

A resolution adopted by the UN General Assembly reminds us:

> The SDG targets, especially those relating to the reduction or poverty, education of children, and gender equality, are difficult to attain unless the strategies to achieve them focus on the family....[15]

As we work together as a world body to solve problems and create a better world, we would do well to examine the contributions of the family and the capital the family produces. **We should view the family not as a receiver, a consumer or even a "taker" of goods and government largesse, but as a potential powerhouse that will aid in growth and development.**

It is time to recommit ourselves to empowering the family, for without it, the essential goals of the international community cannot be met.

_____

Endnotes

1. Gofen-Sarig, Anat, "Family Capital: How First-Generation Students Break the Intergenerational Cycle", (IRP Discussion Paper #1371-08), University of Wisconsin-Madison, Institute for Research on Poverty (2007).
2. Becker, Gary, A Treatise on the Family. Cambridge: Harvard University Press (1991).
3. Reports of the Secretary-General, Follow-up to the tenth anniversary of the International Year of the Family and beyond, A/66/62-E (November 2010).
4. Imig, David R., "Family Capital versus Family Social Capital: Different Boundaries, Different Processes," Michigan State University, https://msu.edu/~imig/abstract.htm.
5. Wilcox, Bradford W., Lerman, Robert I. and Price, Joseph, "Strong Families, Prosperous States: Do Healthy Families Affect the Wealth of States?" American Enterprise Institute and the Institute for Family Studies (2015).
6. Yu, Eunice and Liu, Jianguo, "Environmental Impacts of Divorce," Center for Systems Integration and Sustainability, Michigan State University, MI 48823-5243 (2007).
7. United Nations University (1995), http://archive.unu.edu/unupress/unupbooks/uu13se/uu13se01.htm
8. Wilcox, Bradford W., Lerman, Robert I. and Price, Joseph, "Strong Families, Prosperous States: Do Healthy Families Affect the Wealth of States?" American Enterprise Institute and the Institute for Family Studies (2015).
9. Rector, Robert, Johnson, Kirk, Fagan, Patrick and Noyes, Lauren, "Increasing Marriage Will Dramatically Reduce Child Poverty," Heritage Foundation Center for Data Analysis Report No. CDA03-06 (2003).
10. Dufur, Mikaela J., et. al., "Does capital at home matter more than capital at school? Social capital effects on academic achievement," Research in Social Stratification and Mobility Vol. 31 (March 2013) pp. 1-21.
11. Wilcox, Bradford W., Lerman, Robert I. and Price, Joseph, "Strong Families, Prosperous States: Do Healthy Families Affect the Wealth of States?" American Enterprise Institute and the Institute for Family Studies (2015).
12. Ibid.
13. Zagorsky, Jay, "Marriage and Divorce's Impact on Wealth," *Journal of Sociology* 41, 4 (2005): pp. 406-424.
14. Bogenschneider, Karen, et al., "The Family Impact Rationale: An Evidence Base for the Family Impact Lens," The Family Impact Institute (2012) p. 14.
15. Resolution adopted by the [UN] General Assembly on 20 December 2012, Preparations for and observance of the twentieth anniversary of the International Year of the Family, A/RES/67/142

Articles for SDG 1

Some 1 billion people in developing countries live in extreme poverty, with two thirds of them living in rural areas. Millions of people are chronically undernourished owing to land degradation, declining soil fertility, unsustainable water use, drought and loss of biodiversity. The poorest and hungriest people worldwide are most vulnerable to external factors and shocks, including excessive commodity price volatility, climate change and a shift in trade policies and flows (paragraph 9).

Economic and Social Council, HLPF, 22 June 2016
E/HLPF/2016/5

Timothy M. Rarick, PhD, is a professor of Marriage, Family & Child Development at BYU-Idaho. He specializes in Parenting and Family Advocacy & Policy and currently serves on the Advisory Board for United Families International. Dr. Rarick earned graduate degrees in Marriage, Family, & Human Development from Kansas State University. Tim and his wife, Jodi, have four children.

1 - End Poverty

Fatherhood: The Antibiotic to the Poverty Problem

Timothy M. Rarick, PhD

According to the World Bank, in the year 2015 the extreme poverty rate (less than $2/day) around the world allegedly dropped below 10% for the first time.[1] Although this is good progress, extreme poverty, for 702 million people, remains an international crisis. We know that women and children are deeply impacted socially and academically by living in poverty.

Politicians, economists and other organizations have many ideas for solving this crisis. United Nations officials, for example, have set a noble goal "to end poverty in all its forms everywhere by 2030"—also known as Sustainable Development Goal #1.[2] Is this goal well intentioned? Indeed. Is it attainable? That depends on how one makes sense of the problem. Misdiagnosing the source of this poverty problem can lead to the wrong prescribed solution—no matter how well-intentioned.

Symptoms vs. infections

When a person is suffering from cold or flu-like symptoms it can be very difficult to discern the cause of these debilitating effects. Bacterial and viral infections can manifest very similar symptoms such as: coughing, sneezing, fever, inflammation, etc.[3] However, the method for treating these symptoms largely depends on whether this is a bacterial or viral infection. Whereas cold or flu medicine can only treat symptoms, thankfully, antibiotics can rid your body of the bacterial infection, taking care of both symptoms and the problem.

In a similar way, we can approach the plague of poverty by setting goals and prescribing ideas that primarily treat symptoms . . . or we can see the bigger picture and find ways to root out the source of the problem. Some ideas may include simply raising the minimum wage and creating more stable, well-paid jobs—but they can only go so far in treating the symptoms of poverty. Besides, we need competent, educated individuals who can qualify for such jobs. The deeper poverty problem (or infection) may be rooted in the state of the family.

The family: The cause and the solution

Renowned Russian developmental psychologist Urie Bronfenbrenner summarized his research, stating: "The family is the most powerful, the most humane, and by far the most economical system known for building competence and character."[4]

Consider this powerful, evidence-based statement! Now consider how the current trends in out-of-wedlock childbearing, divorce and cohabitation are threatening the power of the family unit. Furthermore, each of these threats produces a common result: fatherlessness. These infections, along with many others, have decimated stable homes and families for millions of children worldwide. Until we address the breakdown of the family—particularly the absentee father problem—there will never be a sustainable alternative to eradicating poverty.

Fatherlessness

Current social science research powerfully asserts: ". . . there is a Father-Factor in our [world's] worst social problems. In other words, for many of our most intractable social ills affecting children, father absence is to blame."[5] In the United States over 24 million children are growing up without their biological father; in the year 2014 nearly a quarter of children lived in father-absent homes.[6] Dr. Pat Fagan writes: "The Index of Family Belonging for the United States is now just above 45%, which means that 45% of U.S. children on the cusp of adulthood have grown up in an intact married family."[7]

This is, in large measure, due to the rise of divorce rates and out-of-wedlock births over the past 50 years. In 1960 only 6% of babies were born to unwed mothers in the United States.[8] Thanks to the sexual revolution of the 1960's and the passing of no-fault-divorce laws in many countries, that number has risen to over 40% today and continues to increase. Similar trends can be seen in countries around the world. Creating a worldwide culture that teaches sex is a deserved commodity and marriage is based in adult desires and emotions has done more damage to the family structure than almost anything else.

In the overwhelming majority of divorce cases in many countries, custody of the children is given to the mother.[9] Although children who are victims of divorce still have a father, the severing of their parents' marriage often severs the consistent influence from the father. This has had devastating effects—especially in the economic realm, as we will see in the next section.

If one does not have a good grasp on economics and social science one might assume that poverty is driving the family breakdown rather than the other way around.

The vicious cycle of fatherlessness and poverty

The positive impact that committed fathers have on women, children and society is staggering. For example:[10]

- Infant mortality rates are nearly two times higher for infants of unmarried mothers than for married mothers.

- Boys in households with a father present had significantly lower odds of incarceration than those in single-mother families.

- Fathers raise their daughters' chances of success in academics, earning potential and relationships when they are present and involved.[11]

- Father involvement in schools is associated with greater academic success and achievement for both boys and girls.

- Children in father-absent homes are almost four times more likely to be poor. In 2011, 12% of children in married-couple families were living in poverty, compared to 44% of children in fatherless families.

Are we seeing the connection between fathers and poverty? Dads have the power to decrease the odds of poverty by over 30% and increase the earning potential for his children. One of the crippling effects of poverty is the cycle that is perpetuated throughout the generations. This runs in parallel with the fatherless cycle. Just as children raised in poverty are likely to raise their own children in the same poor economic conditions, so it is with girls born to unwed mothers. Daughters born out-of-wedlock are much more likely to give birth to fatherless children.

Figure 1.1 helps illustrate the connection between fatherlessness and poverty. Keep in mind, even though this cycle and its connections are based in research, it is important to note that none of these factors cause the others to happen. For example, a child who is born out of wedlock is not guaranteed to be

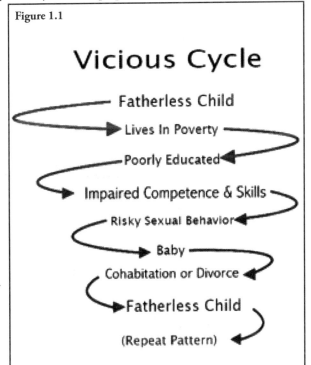

Figure 1.1

Vicious Cycle

Fatherless Child
Lives In Poverty
Poorly Educated
Impaired Competence & Skills
Risky Sexual Behavior
Baby
Cohabitation or Divorce
Fatherless Child
(Repeat Pattern)

poorly educated or live in poverty. Each preceding item simply makes the following factor much more likely to occur.

Education, skills and competence are keys to economic freedom and success. They are the antidote to poverty. A family headed by a married father and mother provides the best setting to not only succeed economically, but to raise confident, competent, well-educated children who can increase their earning potential and "promote inclusive and sustainable economic growth, . . . employment and decent work for all" (SDG #8). Social scientists claim:

> An abundant social-science literature, as well as common sense, supports the claim that children are more likely to flourish, and to become productive adults, when they are raised in stable, married-couple households. We know, for example, that children in the United States who are raised outside of an intact, married home are two to three times more likely to suffer from social and psychological problems, such as delinquency, depression, and dropping out of high school. They are also markedly less likely to attend college and be stably employed as young adults.[12]

Stable families will create a society and worldwide economy that is sustainable, because the intact family is the fundamental unit of society. As the families of the world thrive, so do the economies (see Figure 1.3).

Rethinking our approach to poverty

The first Sustainable Development Goal calls for governments to "help create an enabling environment to generate productive employment and job opportunities for the poor and the marginalized. They can formulate strategies and fiscal policies that stimulate pro-poor growth and reduce poverty."[13]

This approach to government policy is necessary, to be sure. Job creation and government subsidies can help alleviate the symptoms associated with poverty, yet they cannot revive and sustain the socioeconomic status of an individual family—let alone a nation's economy. Furthermore, girls—and by extension women—are much more empowered by having involved fathers than by any government policy or sexual rights agenda attempting to free them from the home.

In addition to the SDG#1 proposal, we need governments

Father, mother and children   *Photo: United Families International*

to view everything through a "family-impact" lens in order to be effective over time.

In her book, *Family Policy Matters*, Professor Karen Bogenshneider put it this way:

> Most policymakers would not think of passing a law or enacting a rule without considering its economic or environmental impact, yet family considerations are seldom taken into account in the normal routine of policymaking…Policymakers explain that they do not have the staff or time to gather all the relevant data on the complex issues that confront them. As a result, they rely on information from lobbyists and special interest groups that is often fragmented, parochial, biased, and less focused on family issues.[14]

Including creating an enabling environment for families to thrive, here are several ways to bring back fatherhood and promote sustainable economic growth for all:

- Teach community programs to promote involved, responsible fathering. Research has shown if these programs are taught well and are evidence-based, they increase a father's (both married and divorced) involvement substantially.[15]

- Create educational and skill-based opportunities for fathers (and mothers) to get the training to lift themselves out of the poverty cycle.

- Improve services and education related to: sexuality, caregiving, violence and parenting for boys and men.

- Generate a true shift in policy (more than lip service) to focus on teaching all children from a young age about the value of, and their opportunity to be, both caregivers and professionals.

- Utilize mass and social media outlets to produce and share positive messages about dads, rather than as the incompetent fools many television shows and commercials show them to be.

- Inform the public about research on the harmful effects of pornography addiction. Porn has the power to destroy our most cherished relationships, thus removing fathers emotionally, physically and financially from the family.

Figure 1.2

The marriage advantage in Europe

Source: Marriage Foundation

"The Marriage Gap"
Percent of married parents throughout Europe, by region

Scandinavia   N. Europe   E. Europe   Med.

■ Highest income quintile   ■ Lowest income quintile

- Perhaps the most important of all: **Reestablish marriage!**

The institution of marriage acts as culture's chief vehicle to bind men to their children. The marriage gap between rich and poor exists in all 20 of the European countries. As Figure 1.2 indicates, 84% of parents who are in the top fifth of household income are married, as opposed to 42% of parents in the bottom fifth of household income.

Marriage matters for men, women, children, and economies. But how do we reestablish marriage in the various cultures of the world?

> **Employers:** Create policies and work environments that respect and favor the marital commitment.
>
> **Social work:** Within the limits of good practice, promote a culture of family formation.
>
> **Marriage counselors:** Begin with a bias in favor of marriage. Avoid being "value-free."
>
> **Teachers & education administrators:** Minimize the implicit and frequently explicit anti-marriage bias prevalent in many schools' curricula.[16]

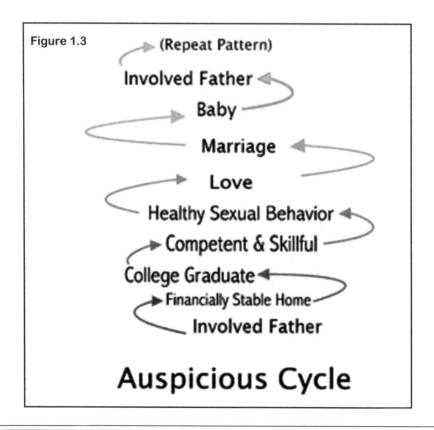

Figure 1.3

Auspicious Cycle

| Thai Family in Ubon, Thailand | *Photo: Timothy S. Evans* |

Strong fathers, strong economies: An auspicious cycle

Whereas fatherless children and poverty create a vicious cycle that perpetuates downward (see figure 1.1), the married, intact family with a hard-working, involved father creates an auspicious cycle that moves upward (figure 1.3).

Along with his wife, a father has the power to promote or increase the financial, academic, professional, and relational competence in a child. Being a responsible person is a matter of character, which is best built in the home. At a young age, boys can and should be taught by both parents—and the predominant culture—to be responsible with: their money, their education, their work, their sex drive and their future children. Boys and men need to learn there is more to life than self-centered, pleasurable pursuits. The values of hard work, integrity and responsibility will be perpetuated throughout generations and society.

Will this take time? Absolutely! Just as cold medicine gives immediate, temporary relief to symptoms, an antibiotic brings gradual yet permanent healing. Only with this kind of approach can the economies—and families—of the world be truly sustainable.

Let us bring back fatherhood and heal the plague of poverty.

Endnotes

1. Kottasova, Ivana. "World Poverty Rate to Fall below 10% for the First Time." CNNMoney. October 5, 2015. Accessed July 10, 2016. http://money.cnn.com/2015/10/05/news/economy/poverty-world-bank/.
2. "Poverty - United Nations Sustainable Development." UN News Center. Accessed July 13, 2016. http://www.un.org/sustainabledevelopment/poverty/.
3. Ratini, Melinda. "Bacterial vs. Viral Infections: Causes and Treatments." WebMD. April 10, 2015. Accessed July 13, 2016. http://www.webmd.com/a-to-z-guides/bacterial-and-viral-infections.
4. Bogenschneider, Karen. *Family Policy Matters: How Policymaking Affects Families and What Professionals Can Do*. 2nd ed. Mahwah, NJ: Lawrence Erlbaum Associates, 2006. page 52.
5. Mclanahan, Sara, Laura Tach, and Daniel Schneider, "The Causal Effects of Father Absence." Annu. Rev. Sociol. Annual Review of Sociology 39, no. 1 (2013): 399-427. doi:10.1146/annurev-soc-071312-145704.
6. Sanders, Ryan. "The Father Absence Crisis in America [Infographic]." The Father Absence Crisis in America. November 12, 2013. Accessed July 14, 2016. http://www.fatherhood.org/The-Father-Absence-Crisis-in-America.
7. Fagan, Patrick. "The Third Annual Index of Family Belonging & Rejection." Marriage & Religion Research Institute. Accessed July 14, 2016. http://marri.us/index-2013.
8. U.S. Census Bureau, National Center for Health Statistics, 2011.
9. Grall, Timothy. "Custodial Mothers and Fathers and Their Child Support: 2011." United States Census Bureau. October 2013. Accessed July 10, 2016. https://www.census.gov/prod/2013pubs/p60-246.pdf.
10. "Statistics on the Father Absence Crisis in America." Father Facts. Accessed July 14, 2016. http://www.fatherhood.org/father-absence-statistics.
11. Nielsen, Linda. *Between Fathers & Daughters: Enriching and Rebuilding Your Adult Relationship*. Nashville, TN: Cumberland House, 2008.
12. Longman, Phillip and Paul Corcuera, Laurie Derose, Marga Gonzalvo Cirac, Andres Salazar, Claudia Tarud Aravena and Antonio Torralby, "The Empty Cradle—How Contemporary Family Trends Undermine the Global Economy," *The Sustainable Demographic Dividend*, Social Trends Institute, 2010. http://sustaindemographicdividend.org/wp-content/uploads/2012/07/SDD-2011-Final.pdf
13. "Poverty - United Nations Sustainable Development." UN News Center. Accessed July 13, 2016. http://www.un.org/sustainabledevelopment/poverty/.
14. Bogenschneider, Karen. *Family Policy Matters: How Policymaking Affects Families and What Professionals Can Do*. 2nd ed. Mahwah, NJ: Lawrence Erlbaum Associates, 2006. page 4.
15. Cowan, Philip A., Carolyn Pape Cowan, Marsha Kline Pruett, Kyle Pruett, and Jessie J. Wong. "Promoting Fathers' Engagement With Children: Preventive Interventions for Low-Income Families." *Journal of Marriage and Family* 71, no. 3 (2009): 663-79. doi:10.1111/j.1741-3737.2009.00625.x.
16. Popenoe, David. *Life without Father: Compelling New Evidence That Fatherhood and Marriage Are Indispensable for the Good of Children and Society*. New York: Martin Kessler Books, 1996.

Family-focused Poverty Strategies

Jastus Suchi Obadiah

Family-focused strategies aiming at poverty reduction often include income support policies, such as universal child allowances or child-focused earnings supplements. There is also a growing interest in specific policies in support of single-parent families through: cash allowances, tax incentives, tougher child-support enforcement or discouraging marriage dissolution. Benefits for family members caring for older persons and persons with disabilities have also been considered to help families cope with caring responsibilities and promote intergenerational support.

The importance of family-oriented strategies for poverty eradication has been increasingly gaining ground in development efforts around the world. In particular, gender and child-sensitive social protection policies addressing family poverty and reducing the vulnerability of younger and older generations have been a focus of attention in an increasing number of countries in the developed and developing world alike.

A variety of income transfer programs have also been enacted to help the poorest families. The main goals have been to address child poverty and break the intergenerational transfer of poverty and inequality. Social transfer programs in developing countries provide cash transfers to families living in poverty or at risk of poverty.

Conditional and unconditional cash transfers target families living in poverty but differ in scope and context. Initially introduced in Latin America, they are increasingly being implemented in Africa and Asia. The level of the benefit varies from 20% of mean household consumption in Mexico, 4% in Honduras, and lower amounts for similar programmes in other countries (UN, 2011).

Family-friendly public policies are crucial to the survival of the family unit. As an effective structure of development, the importance of sound, family-oriented policies cannot be overstressed (UN, 2011).

Projects that identify family as the entry point seem to have more success than those that target other social units. The photos and captions within this chapter detail many of the projects achieved with the family as the functional unit.

Jastus Suchi Obadiah, is a Luyia native of Kenya. He is currently employed as the East African Supervisor for Reach the Children and is a consultant with other NGOs on development related issues. He obtained a Bachelor of Arts degree in Community Development from Daystar University in Nairobi and specialized in Rural Development. This chapter is written from the perspective of a native African, who has worked as a director of community development projects in Africa for eight years.

Family: The basic unit of society

According to International Cooperative Administration (ICA), community development is a social process in which: (1) People in a community organize themselves for planning and action, (2) People define their common and individual needs, and (3) People execute their plans with maximum reliance on their own community resources (SC Mayo, 1958).

Families are in and of themselves small communities. They follow all of the steps listed by the ICA. In a family children learn values and work ethics. They learn how to help others. Sons and daughters learn to honor their parents and each other in their unique roles. Families should be a safe place, with a one-of-a-kind opportunity for fathers and mothers to work hand-in-hand solving family-related problems. Family is important in poverty eradication because it is the basic unit of society, the first school of life. It may be the only school where no one graduates. It is life-long. Whether an individual is a parent, grandparent, aunt, uncle or child, all are contributors in a well-functioning family unit.

Communicate with families in poverty

One common African saying in Kenya goes: "To understand women, talk to them." Men will go to their fellow men to ask what women are thinking and feeling. To know what a woman is thinking, a man must ask a woman. The same principle applies when helping the poor. If you want to know what the poor think, you must ask the poor. Many developers focus on information given by others rather than information from the poor themselves.

In a self-assessment project in Makueni County, Kenya, communities were asked to evaluate ways to alleviate their own poverty. The community proposed the following: (1) improved infrastructure such as roads, electricity and provision of water; (2) free education, especially for primary and secondary schools (until 2003, education was not free in primary schools in Kenya – now primary education is free and secondary schools have been subsidized); (3) land policy changes so both men and women may own land and use it for agriculture. They also proposed: irrigation, machinery, subsidized inputs (fertilizer, seeds, etc.) and land to be used for public projects such as construction of a market place, etc.

In another village, people suggested food storage facilities so they could store their food longer. They also suggested credit facilities to allow local-access-capital for their businesses (AMREF, 1998).

However, in a few situations, the target group may propose things that they really do not need. Thus a comprehensive analysis needs to take place. For example, some community members proposed construction of better houses. To use an easily-understood analogy: If you help a chick break out of an egg, the chick is weakened by your help. This should not be the role of developers. It is important to only assist people to help themselves. Using another common analogy: If they need a hook for fishing, so be it. We help them get the hook, but we do not continuously give them the fish.

In a village at Luwero, Uganda, the Reach the Children (RTC) organization targeted older grannies with numerous grandchildren, the majority of whom were HIV/AIDS orphans. When asked what they wanted, these grannies said that they had enough food, but did not have money. They wanted commercialized agriculture so they could earn an income. Originally, RTC thought that food insecurity would be their greatest concern. However, the children looked healthy, but had no clothes. This was evidence that money was their problem – they wanted a means of earning it. It is important to identify real, actual needs, and the locals are the best source for that information.

Most of the time developers think that they already know what the people need. But when it comes to survival, the poor are very creative. They are instinctively working toward their own development. They engage in a wide range of income-generating activities which earn them something. A household survey done in 1997 in Kenya illustrated this point: It was found over 50% of the rural population in Kenya is engaged in subsistence-farming activities. In this case, small-scale businesses and petty-trade are important (AMREF, 1997).

Evaluate previous activities

An evaluation of previous events and activities could be one approach to finding solutions for today's challenges. It is surprising to find some communities in developing countries facing food insecurity whereas a few centuries ago they had an abundance. Why? What happened? There are many factors to this, most of it being population growth, but could it be that something can be borrowed from those ancient people?

This is a question a rural developer posed to a group of villagers in Western Kenya: Why do you have food insecurity today? This question allowed the villagers to go back to some traditional approaches that enabled them to produce and store enough food for their community. For example, they were able to reflect on how their ancestors preserved food: grains through drying and protecting them with cow dung ash; meat immersed in honey after being boiled; fish and meat with smoke-cures; other foods by salting or boiling. Grainaries were built to stockpile enough grain for supplies throughout the year – crops such as millet, sorghum, beans, ground nuts and cowpeas were grown.

Cultural impact on development

Some cultural practices have not favored development. Gender-biased traditions prevented women from controlling resources, which inhibited their ability to make their voices heard in family decisions. Women are an important resource in realizing development in families and society as a whole. Some family members have been cursed – chased from home due to perceived disobedience.

There are numerous anti-development practices that affect individuals, families and communities. Some farmers in western Kenya let their fields spoil while attending an extended funeral of a neighbor or relative, and thus fail to harvest their crops to sell.

The traditional role as nurturers and care-givers is critical in this process. According to Kwawu and Murray, women's work is generally low-paid, low-status, hazardous and only produces products for home (subsistence) consumption. Therefore it is not considered as important as paid work. Yet the woman's role in the home, with her children, is vital for the very existence of society and the socializing process of children. If we are to change society to appreciate both men and women, home is the place to make this happen. Parents should take the lead in teaching their children these important principles (Murray et al., 1993).

The dairy cow project initiated by Reach the Children is more than empowering families directly. Soon the owners of the cows discovered that they could not supply all the grass needed, so other families recognized the need and planted grass to sell to the dairy cow owners. This enabled them to earn a living, too. With over 40 cows donated in that area, locally-trained veterinary officers now have work to do, and the vet shops have a market for their products as they sell dairy medicines and animal feeds to supplement what the farmers can produce.

Another example is the SHIEBU Dairy Goat Network, a community-based organization that reaches out to both men and women. Before an animal is given to either spouse, the other spouse must agree. Both men and women are targeted for membership, but their policies are aimed at eliminating family conflict that may arise due to resource control. Nepher, one of the SHIEBU group leaders, said:

> I believe our focus is on family and reaching out on individuals. Family gives them the support they require to grow and develop. We encourage self-help groups because of such support too, but nothing can replace the family's role in developing individuals.

Gender inequality continues to be a major impediment to poverty eradication. Research in developing countries indicates that the more women contribute to household needs rather than men, the more money is spent on food, childcare and overall family well-being. This finding has resulted in more emphasis on women and not men. The question must be asked, when will men learn and change? It is important to take measures to encourage men to take up a bigger share of household and childcare responsibilities within families. This can only be accomplished if developers will recognize the importance of the family as an important social institution, recognizing that anything that threatens the family unit's survival also contributes to social and economical challenges – such as poverty.

The root causes of the practices and attitudes on gender issues must be sought in order to work out solutions that will affect change. As the issues differ, so must the strategies for dealing with them. Among most African nations, the need to understand the logic of the undesired is critical for two reasons. First, the societies are undergoing very rapid change in the name of development. In many ways, African countries are in transition and "at a crossroads." Identifying and understanding gender issues at the roots, and in the appropriate context, is crucial to influence which direction that development will effect the society. Second, these societies are largely multilingual in a very complex manner, with different traditional practices. Consequently, there are multiple operating norms, concepts, or values at the take-off point (Mbeo et al., 1989).

Both men and women play an important role in the labor force. A 1977/78 survey in Kenya urban areas showed that 68% of the men were engaged in the labor force, compared to 39% for women. However, in rural Kenya, it showed that 68% of the women were engaged in the labor force. This is an important difference to consider, since 80% of the population in Kenya lives in the rural areas.

Include men and women in development plans

The issues affecting women are mostly cultural and thus any methodology that will ensure gender equality must recognize the cultural aspect. The focus must be on the policies and family structures in the respective cultures. In most African countries women work the most, yet they control very little when it comes to resources. Although the focus has been on women, there is a great need to empower men and focus on gender (men and women) and development, rather than women and development.

According to Omondi, one of the greatest dilemmas hindering gender equality and development is the African male's attitude – which tends to view the gender debate as diversionary and unimportant. Omondi used linguistic illustrations to show close interaction between language and culture, demonstrating how the former is often a subtle vehicle for cultural and attitudinal values. From this premise, she argues that because "gender and related issues are learned with language, each language becomes a source of information on the people's thinking and their norms" (Mbeo et al., 1989).

Some women argue that the *family unit* is the only social institution where attitudes and the world view of most African men can be changed. They say that if this happens in the home, then real development will take place: a woman will have a say at home, allowed to be in control of resources and steer development to another level. Although much progress has been made in the years since the International Decade for Women in 1975, growth has been slow.

A partial list of achievements since 1975 includes: women can now control the export of their crops; policies have changed to allow women to inherit; and women can even claim properties from their parents or husbands. Another promising development is the participation of women in agricultural organizations and workers unions. This is now happening in sectors where men have dominated for years. Parents are encouraged to socialize their children at home so they grow with an appreciation for both genders. This will continue to have a positive impact on each family, and children will achieve greater self-reliance in their future family.

Infrastructure is key for reducing rural poverty

A good infrastructure is a key – for several reasons, including: (1) the need to transport farm produce to the market, and (2) the need for electricity to develop rural industries. Good health facilities (doctors' offices, clinics, hospitals) are also part of the infrastructure needed – providing easy access to health facilities. When people are healthy, they become more productive.
(*See SDG 9 on Infrastucture, page 179.*) .

The threat of rural-to-urban migration

Most urban-related challenges originate in rural areas. There are usually few industries in rural areas and thus there are limited opportunities for jobs and education. Urban areas attract a rural people – as they move to "greener pastures." This has a very negative effect on traditional African families. Although kinship in Africa is still very strong, it is being threatened by rural-to-urban migration. This separation (of mostly men from their families) has contributed not only to the spread of the HIV virus, but also to economic instability and food insecurity.

Julius Kasue, a rural villager from Eastern Kenya near the Chyulu hills, complained about how villagers use their resources to educate their young ones, only to lose them when they grow up – as they all move to towns to settle there permanently. Any project that can provide job opportunities, schools, hospitals and electricity in the rural areas can reduce rural-to-urban migration. Rural industrialization offers many solutions that could help create self-reliance for rural families and prevent the brain-drain that is being experienced in rural communities, as the educated move to the cities.

These rural industries could also act as markets for the agro-products produced by rural people. Many families could benefit from them as they access credit to further increase their productivity. Industries in rural areas can act as important foreign exchange earners and this may lead to subsidized funds for obtaining machinery needed to sustain other sectors, such as agriculture, etc. Rural industries act as liberating agents, as vulnerable members of the community receive opportunities to earn a living, access education and other related opportunities. Industries in rural areas also enhance urbanization because they attract development: infrastructures, schools, hospitals, roads, electricity and water. This brings towns closer to the people in a well-planned manner. Indeed, rural industrialization can be said to bridge the gap between rich and poor, allowing more people to access income and improve their living standard. The Kenyan government began a rural electricity program three years ago. Through this initiative, many families are improving their economic status.

Sustainable projects begin with families

In response to world challenges, developers use the term "sustainable development." This has gained considerable prominence in development debates since 1987, when the concept was broadly popularized through the efforts of the World Commission on Environment and Development. The term was coined by representatives from industrial and socialist nations. It means: development that meets the needs of today without compromising the ability of future generations to meet their own needs. In simple terms, sustainable development means continuity of things, including the human species and all the ecological factors of the planet Earth.

This goal for sustainable development demands the united front of all nations in the world, as we share the same planet. Thus, sustainable community or village development encompasses a holistic perspective in considering life (Akatch et al., 1998). In 1998 Dorset's Rural Community Council published an attractive eight-page pamphlet written by Graham Duncan, portraying a hypothetical "sustainable village" (Dorset Community Action, 1998). The main aim was to empower villagers to adopt sustainable development in their villages. Two big ideas for sustainability were to live on the earth's income, not its capital, and to reduce inputs and re-use outputs. These were targeted at individuals, families and community. They emphasized: (1) Consume local produce; (2) Share resources and build communities; (3) Reduce, re-use and recycle; and (4) Build the local economy. In discussing recycling they also proposed recycling ideas, too (Moseley, 2003).

Among the social agents used to facilitate sustainable development, the family remains the basic unit where these principles can be acquired through the process of socialization. Two others are churches and schools. The Johnson family from Texas visited Kenya in December 2005. While they were visiting Nairobi National Park, their daughter Merian asked a local tour-guide, "Where should I throw this plastic paper?" "Just throw it over there," the guide responded. "No," replied the 13-year-old girl. "I was taught that I shouldn't pollute the environment." The local guide was amazed to see the power of this young girl. This is the power of a family in action and how a family can install sustainable principles in the society.

Technology development

Promoting appropriate technology is another key in eradicating poverty. "Appropriate technology" is a friendly term to describe when local people utilize their own resources. If technology is appropriate, it should be both affordable and sustainable. Appropriate technology is known and used by locals – using local resources. For example, use of oxen in farming could make a difference in the lives of many rural people, instead of relying on tractors, which may be very expensive to buy or maintain. Appropriate technology not only uses local resources but promotes innovations and creativity. For example, using oxen to plow, not just as beasts of burden, is more appropriate to some rural areas.

Extension education is key

Extension education is key to improving the lives of people because people are the greatest resource available in development (Dhama, 1965). Dhama looked at the process of development holistically. To understand how extension education helps rural farmers, the process must be understood.

According to Mildred Horton, extension education has four main points: 1) The individual is a supreme democracy; 2) The home is the fundamental unit in civilization; 3) The family is the first training group of the human race; 4) The foundation of any permanent civilization must rest on the partnership of the man and land (Van den Ban and Hawkins, 2002). Extension services are provided in many forms. Service centers are sometimes provided, but extension services can also be more informal. The informal type of extension is one that has no syllabus and the farmer's problems and needs are the main considerations. It has no classroom; – advice is provided in the farmer's home or farm, or any convenient place. The formal type of extension is planned, has written objectives and training content. This type of extension is carried out through short courses, field visits or short-duration tours at community centers, research stations or for a longer duration of time at designated farmer-training centers (Nambiro, 2006).

In Kenya, extension services were primarily provided by the government until the 1990s. In a paper about how extension services are provided and the reasons behind these services, Nambiro, Omiti and Mugunieri say:

> Through the 1990s, the established modes of delivery of extension services began to shift in favour of those that involved farmers in the design or prioritization of these services. This re-orientation of extension towards participatory processes was catalyzed by the increasing realization that effective and sustainable extension programs could only be achieved with the more active participation of the various end-users, especially farmers.

Extension services are critical in improving the lives of many Africans. Centers are used for education and also as a resource for farmers' concerns. Many people aren't able to afford to go to a college or university for the answers they need to make things work better on their rural farms. They can get the education and information they need at their local extension service – through mentoring with extension leaders.

Extension services: Mentoring rural families

Mentorship happens when someone skilled (whether older or younger is immaterial) guides a person with less experience or knowledge to acquire new knowledge. This new knowledge helps transfer skills and experience, shortening the learning.

A practical example of this technique is a farm-input program called One Acre Fund in western Kenya. Farmers are grouped into units and each unit has a group leader. Group leaders are trained by, and attached to, the main mentor, who monitors each group closely as they apply the knowledge learned in workshops. These workshops are all practical workshops. Each farmer is then taken through the same process from A to Z.

Mentoring: Crop planning

Farm mentors train group leaders on (1) varieties good for the area, (2) correct spacing between plants, (3) appropriate fertilizer needs, and (4) farm loan applications. Once each farmer/group leader has gone through this process, they are able to stand on their own and do the same to help other farmers.

First, each family is taught how to budget and the mentor does follow-up, monthly or quarterly. Once the heads of each family understand budgeting, they then are introduced into groups where they are taught micro-savings. They are required to save at least a dollar monthly (this money earns interest monthly).

At a group level, a mentor is sent (monthly or quarterly) to mentor families on record keeping and basic accounting. They are taught the importance of savings accounts. As each family saves, the village savings and loan capabilities increase. Eventually, the individual farm families can access basic credit to get money for: farm inputs, school uniforms, school fees or to start other micro-enterprises.

A good example of this technique is applied by Rafiki Wa Maendeleo Trust (RWMT) in partnership with Chalice Program and Aphia Plus in western Kenya. More than 90% of families don't have medical insurance, yet Kenyan government has established an affordable medical insurance plan called the National Health Insurance Fund (NHIF). Each household is required to pay about five dollars each month in order to benefit. Luckily, this rate can be reduced to two dollars per month when the household's status is confirmed to be highly vulnerable. RWMT mobilizes families to enroll. They invite NHIF officials to come on the site and register families. Many families don't see the need or benefits at first, but once a medical need arises in the family and the card is able to help them, others learn from them and willing go into it and spread the word.

Another example is education. Originally many rural families did not value education very much, but through extended family relationships, one capable member takes upon him/herself the need to educate another member from the extended family. When this member is educated and successful, other members within the family realize the same need and get motivated to educate their children, too. Through this approach, many families in rural areas of East Africa are encouraged to send their children to school and see them through college. Seeing is believing.

Emergency mentoring

In some situations there is no time to wait in order to bring about desirable change. Examples would be outbreaks of a disease or food security situations. In these situations change is urgently needed. The mentor must act promptly in order to save lives. In such situations, community members are mobilized and mentors are called to serve them. The Kenyan Ministry of Health has an effective structure using Community Health Workers (CHWs) or Community Health Volunteers (CHVs).

Mentoring: Health

Health mentors are critical in mentoring families at the community level. They mentor people in the use of latrines, ensuring that each family has a latrine, dish stand, and in other cases, a tip tap for hand washing, or teach families basic-hygiene lessons. This system works effectively because mentors work hand-in-hand with local administrative leaders, such as village elders. They are also attached to local health facilities, where they do referrals.

Through this structure and process, rural households that do not understand basic health principles or knowledge are able to access information and be referred to health facilities where necessary. Generally, health issues are able to be tackled at the family or community level. It is important for CHVs to be role models at the community level. The process of selecting them is very important and involves both local leaders and members of the community.

Farm family to farm family

Farmers' groups are also a good, powerful way of using the "show" method – they learn from each other (one farmer is good at this and the other one at that . . .) and they mentor each other. This is more powerful than what they gain from extension workers, because they can relate to each other.

Conclusion

Mentoring, as demonstrated in the examples and explanations above, is a very effective way to transfer skills from someone with more experience and knowledge to another. Within the family, mentoring fosters positive relationships and helps family members create and focus on goals for growth in all personal levels to increase the family's and the individual's education and economic progress. The more mentoring is done, the more quickly learning will be facilitated.

References

"A Family for Every Child," Mentor Program, http://www.afamilyforeverychild.org/Activities/Oregon/Mentor/

AMREF (African Medical and Research Foundation) (1998), Participatory Poverty Assessment Report, DFID, Nairobi, Kenya.

AMREF (African Medical and Research Foundation) (1997), Participatory Poverty Assessment Report, DFID, Nairobi, Kenya.

Akatch, et al. (1998), Department of Urban and Regional Planning University of Nairobi, Center for Urban Research, Nairobi:Kenya.

Carger, C.L. (1996). "The two Bills: Reflecting on the gift of mentorship". Peabody Journal of Education 71 (1): 22–29. doi:10.1207/s15327930pje7101_4.

Chambers, R. (1983), *Rural Development: Putting the Last First*, Essex: England, Longmans Scientific and Technical Publishers.

Daloz, L. A. (1999). Mentor: Guiding the journey of adult learners. San Francisco: Jossey-Bass.

Family Platform. *Social Inequality and Diversity of Families*, http://www.familyplatform.eu/en/1-major-trends/reports/7-social-inequality-and-diversity-of-families.

Huang, Chungliang and Jerry Lynch (1995), Mentoring - The TAO of Giving and Receiving Wisdom, Harper, San Francisco.

Human Development Report 1993, http://hdr.undp.org/en/reports/global/hdr1993/

International Poverty Center (2008), *Cash Transfers, Lessons from Africa and Latin America, Poverty in Focus*. http://www.ipc-undp.org/pub/IPCPovertyInFocus15.pdf.

Kahn, Ajaz Ahmed and Helen Mould (2008), Islamic Relief Worldwide, http://www.islamic-relief.com/indepth/downloads/islamanddebt.pdf.

Opportunity NYC website, http://www.nyc.gov/html/ceo/html/programs/opportunity_nyc.shtml.

Lord, J. and McAllister P. (2009), *What Kind of World do you want?* http://www.whatkindofworld.com/wp-hw/wp-content/uploads/2010/01/what_kind_of_world_do_you_want.pdf.

Jakonda, Z. Sulaiman (2001), *Your kingdom come: a book on wholistic Christian development*. Jos, Nigeria, RURCON.

Kelsey, L.D. and C.D. Hearne (1963), *Cooperative Extension Work*, Cornell University Press, New York.

Mbeo, et al (1989), Women and Law in Kenya-Perspectives and Emerging Issues: Public Law Institute, Initiative Ltd., Nairobi:Kenya.

Moseley, M. J, (2003), Rural Development-Principles and Practice: SAGE Publications, London. Thousand Oaks.

Murray, et al (1993), Reorienting Home Economics in Africa, Home Economics Association for Africa (HEAA).

Nambiro, Elizabeth, John Omiti and Lawrence Mugunieri (2006),Decentralization and Access to Agricultural Extension Services in Kenya. International, Association of Agricultural Economists Conference, Gold Coast:Australia, August 12-18, 2006.

Child and Family Services, "Parent Mentor Program," https://child-familyservices.org/parent-mentor-program/

Singh, Katar (1999), Rural Development: Principles, Policies and Management. New Delhi: India, Sage Publications.

United Nations (2009), Rethinking Poverty. Report on the World Social Situation, New York.

United Nations (2010), Report of the Secretary-General on the Follow-up to the tenth anniversary of the International Year of the Family and beyond, New York.

Waldfogel, J. The role of family policies in antipoverty policy. Focus, vol. 26, No. 2, Fall 2009.

Van den Ban, A.W. and Hawkins, H.S. (2002), Agricultural Extension, CBS, Publishers and Distributors, New Delhi (Refer for further details on Extension Education).

Waldfogel, J. (2009), The role of family policies in antipoverty policy. Focus, vol. 26, No. 2.

World Bank $1.25/day poverty measure http://econ.worldbank.org/WBSITE/EXTERNAL/EXTDEC/EXTRESEARCH/0, content-MDK:22510787~pagePK:64165401~piPK:64165026~theSitePK:469382,00.html

Family Preservation Program

www.careforlife.org

The Family Preservation Program (FPP) is a family-centered approach giving disadvantaged families and individuals new skills, attitudes and motivation to live healthier and more independent lives. The FPP methods motivate families to adopt healthy behaviors, good sanitation and nutrition habits, as well as to become financially, economically and emotionally self-reliant. Within the 28 months of the program, families form new habits, acquire vital skills and grow in crucial knowledge. With newly found self-esteem, family members develop a positive attitude and a sense of ownership of their living conditions, their lives and their communities.

The FPP program encourages community members to work together for the benefit of all. Local leaders work side-by-side with their community members to assess, then use local supplies and solutions. Using their own resources and helping each other to work and to seek solutions, fathers and mothers see themselves achieving results. Their increased confidence gives families the courage to become independent, taking charge of their own lives and providing for themselves.

Families improve through working on combined areas of need

Many organizations focus on just one aspect or area of involvement, such as agriculture, literacy or education. But just as a builder constructs not only one room but creates the entire house, the Family Preservation Program focuses on a specific range of needs to help impoverished families transform into thriving, self-reliant units. Implementing simple practices, activities and instruction in the following eight areas of emphasis produces real and permanent change:

1. **Education opportunities**
2. **Psycho-social well-being**
3. **Income generation**
4. **Home improvement/construction**
5. **Community participation**
6. **Health and hygiene**
7. **Food security and nutrition**
8. **Sanitation**

BEST PRACTICES

Families decide on their own path to development

The Family Preservation Program encourages development of native leadership in the community, thus expanding the ability of local leaders and families to make decisions regarding their own development. Nothing is done for people that they can do for themselves. For example, for each of the eight divisions or associations of a community (consisting of 20 to 25 families), its members elect a full slate of officers. In addition, within its ranks, people are chosen for their natural abilities and given training to be promoters in the areas of: health, education, income generation, house improvement and childhood well-being.

Families gain control of their lives and their future

I. Families set goals

With assistance from a trained Care for Life mentor, families determine ten goals in areas such as: health, sanitation, education, income generation and house improvement. The assigned mentor or field officer, teamed with a native community leader, visits every other week over a six-month period to instruct and encourage the families toward their goals.

Families participate in four six-month periods of setting goals, working toward goals and receiving joint follow-up visits of FPP and community leaders. Each family that achieves 80 percent of its goals receives the planned benefits for each of the periods:

- Agriculture kit (tools, seeds, watering cans)
- Small business start-up supplies
- House improvement materials
- Tuition for technical short-term courses, such as vehicle repair, electronics, construction.

II. Families save and borrow from their own credit/savings associations

Participating families are encouraged to take part in the self-reliance associations, whose purpose is to provide a means to save for families that do not have access to regular financial services. When the amount of money saved by the membership is sufficient, any participant can borrow from this source and then repay the loan with interest.

Families experience behavioral changes

Unlike crisis-driven short-term interventions, the FPP pursues consistent, long-term behavioral change. Families gradually acquire new habits, which are solidified during the 28-month program as they take increasing ownership of their lives. As the Family Preservation Program guides families through the inspired process, long-term changes result with the persistent and sustained efforts of the families.

BEST PRACTICES

Marta and Amim Antonion family, Naraze, Sofala Province, Mozambique

Marta and Amim Antonio, live in the village of Naraze in the Sofala province of Mozambique. Their village is in the second year of Care for Life's two-year Family Preservation Program.

Marta is a Care for Life's Children's Club promoter in her village. In her zone of 25 families, she is responsible for bringing the children (ages nine to fourteen) to the village machessa, or community center, for a weekly lesson. Amim is a fisherman and works for 30 days on the boat before coming home for a day or two of rest. "This is Marta's business," Amim says, indicating the structure behind him. The counter has neat piles of tomatoes, fish, and cookies and small bags of nuts and crackers hang from the walls. Larger bags of rice and beans sit side-by-side with water cans out front.

Marta opened the store last year as a result of a loan she received from her village's credit association, set up by Care for Life. Her loan has been paid off and business is thriving. As Amim talks, a child comes over to buy some beans and Marta makes change and sends the child on his way, bag swinging at his side.

Life is different for them now, they tell us. "Before, we didn't know very much about business but now it is changing. Right now I have funds and they go to savings. When I have a situation, I go to savings and I take out some money. Before we would look for someone who we could borrow money from and we would pay them back with some tax. It wasn't good. You would work for 30 days and all month you would save, and then you just pay debt. With saving, it is good. As an example, in our business, if we see our business is low, we go to savings. We take some and we can put it into our business."

Alleviating Agricultural Poverty
Robert C. Roylance

The economic stability of developing countries is an essential part of meeting the Sustainable Development Goals, due to the following:

1. **Financial security improves the ability of families to provide a higher level of education so they can understand the importance of resource preservation and the actions that can be taken to improve the environment,**

2. **Farmers will then be able to afford to take measures that will improve the long-term productivity of the soil, and**

3. **The resulting higher crop yields will reduce the need to develop more land for food production, thereby reducing deforestation while maintaining or improving biodiversity.**

Agriculture growth is especially effective in reducing poverty

WORLD BANK:

- **Seventy-five percent of the world's poor live in rural areas.**

- The evidence that growth in agriculture is, on average, at least twice as effective in reducing poverty as growth outside of agriculture, is thus no surprise.

- **Agricultural growth reduces poverty directly by raising farm incomes, and indirectly through generating employment and reducing food prices.**

- Pro-poor agricultural growth is centered on small-holder farmers who are made more competitive and sustainable through institutional and technological innovations and empowered through producer organizations.

These interventions must be complemented by massive investments in rural education to transition into more skill-intensive employment and successful migration.

http://web.worldbank.org/WBSITE/EXTERNAL/EXTDEC/EXTRESEARCH/EXTWDRS/0,,content-MDK:21501332~pagePK:478093~piPK:477627~theSitePK:477624,00.html

---

Without financial stability, farm families will continue to focus their time and attention on surviving, while the environment will continue to deteriorate. The key to financial stability in the agriculture sector is to adhere to the principles and programs that are an integral part of GAP (Good Agricultural Practices). GAP addresses important issues such as environmental, economic and sanitary sustainability. This would include such agriculture cultural practices as crop rotations, Integrated Pest Management, Integrated Soil Fertility Management, water management systems, tillage systems and crop residue management systems.

From the standpoint of environmental sustainability, these practices can also (1) improve long-term soil productivity, (2) increase crop production, thereby reducing the need for more farmland, and (3) improve the financial stability of families so they will be more inclined to participate in preserving recourses and educating their children (World Bank, 2009).

The following elements are necessary in order to bring impoverished countries to financial stability:

1. Extension agents to introduce new technologies

There is a lack of credible extension agents trained in the use of the latest technologies. It is essential that the up-to-date technology is available to farm families. This can only happen when major international agricultural universities are utilized in a cooperative arrangement with the local colleges and universities.

Extension Agents instructing farmers on specific cultural practices – Photo by FAO

2. The formation of community associations

Small family-farmers cannot succeed by themselves. As they join with other families in community associations, they can collectively take advantage of: agriculture extension and training, group marketing, low-cost supplies and administration services. These associations are usually in the form of cooperatives or community development centers.

These are members of the Mutituni Community Development Center that are engaged in collective marketing, orphan care, GLOBALGAP compliance, microfinance, etc.

3. The adoption of Best Agricultural Practices (BAP)

With the adoption of Best Agricultural Practices (BAP), several agriculture management systems can assist peasant-farmer families in the adoption of effective cropping programs. These include Integrated Pest Management (IPM), Integrated Soil Fertility Management (ISFM), irrigation systems, mechanization and others. Taken as a whole, these programs would be overwhelming to the common family farm; however, with the assistance of farmers' associations and agriculture extension agents, these concepts can be gradually integrated into their operations. In addition to providing financial security, these programs also have strong environmental protection provisions, including: soil improvement, elimination of the need to destroy forests for additional farmland, improvement of water aquifers, maintaining or improving bio-diversity, etc.

Rows of drip tape and a French Bean field – The production of crops utilizing the BAP procedures

4. The development of farmer-friendly GLOBALGAP programs

Developing GLOBALGAP programs will assist farmers to become certified for safe food production. GLOBALGAP requirements are very extensive and challenging to most farmers – especially the small peasant farmers and their families. However, it has been proven that by using the appropriate programs and approaches, the small peasant farmer can comply. The GLOBALGAP program requires the farmer and his family to conform to the following basic requirements:

- Follow Good Agricultural Practices (GAP)
- Provide traceability for agricultural produce marketed
- Insure strict sanitary and hygiene compliance
- Eliminate animal access to all fields
- Insure strict storage and inventory control procedures for pesticides and fertilizers.

This will require the cooperation of commercial agencies currently assisting corporate farmers in this process, plus a funding agency to subsidize the development of these programs. It may also be necessary to assist in funding the initial stages of ongoing operations.

When farmers and their families participate in the sanitation and hygiene portion of these programs, they will also modify their everyday lives by changing their hygiene habits.

Sorting beans on a stainless steel table
Packing French Beans under GAP regulations

Weighing beans
Packaging without GAP certification

5. Eliminate agriculture subsidies in developed countries

Most of the developed countries of the world are currently subsidizing their farmers. This allows them to sell crops below their costs of production and has a negative impact on the world market. In some cases it prevents farmers from growing certain crops, such as: cotton, corn, soybeans, small grains and sugar. It is very hard to understand why developed countries of the world knowingly establish subsidies that will further destroy the livelihoods of poor peasant families. The following personal stories illustrate this point:

1. In Kenya, a government agriculture extension agent was all excited about the truckload of cotton seed he had just received and was anxious to show me seed stored in a nearby shed. My heart sunk because I knew the low world-price of cotton would eliminate any possibility of a positive return; in fact, growing cotton would result in a very significant loss. I sat down with him and asked him to identify the costs that would go into raising the cotton crops. He would not have to consider the seed costs because it was given to them. When he was finished, I asked him what the price of cotton was and it suddenly hit him that the seed in the shed was of no value. The previous year the U.S. had provided a major cotton subsidy to their farmers and they had planted fence row to fence row, driving down the world market.

2. In Pakistan, I had the opportunity of meeting with a group of farmers who hoped that I could help them with some of their agriculture issues. However, before the meeting got started, the one thing they had on their mind was how the U.S. cotton subsidies had ruined their markets. The only thing that happened that day was they were able to get their frustrations out. They said they were given no choice but to raise poppy seeds or join a terrorist camp.

3. In Uganda, we were doing a feasibility study on establishing soybean farming operations. It looked like the farming conditions would be ideal; however, while visiting local grocery outlets we found rows of soybean oil containers with the label of USAID. Prices were well below the anticipated cost of production for the Uganda farmers. Evidently these containers of soybean oil were heavily subsidized by the US government. My experience in Kenya was similar regarding the price of corn.

Examples of irrigation systems used in developing countries (drip tape and siphon tubes)

6. Encourage the development of irrigation projects and efficient irrigation systems

There is a great need for water in many of the communities of developing countries. By improving existing irrigations systems and developing existing water resources, a great deal of this need could be satisfied. Additional water would be beneficial toward creating financial stability and improving soils.

7. Help farmers develop good credit

Developing good credit to obtain funding for farming operations – small peasant farmers have a difficult time saving enough money so they can buy the seeds and supplies to plant the next crop. Community associations and microfinance organizations can be helpful in helping farmers plan ahead. In addition, they help the families set up savings accounts in local banks.

8. Help farmers embrace modern technology

Encourage countries to conform with agriculture production systems that allow them to be competitive in the world markets. Current restrictions and customs are making it very difficult for farmers to compete in the world markets. Restrictions such as fertilizer and pesticide usage, restricted crop varieties, etc., are putting the farmers at a real global disadvantage.

9. Reduce unreasonable import fees

Due to graft and corruption, unreasonable import and export fees are quite common. This puts farmers at a serious disadvantage when it comes to buying the necessary imported farm equipment, farm supplies and other agriculture items. There are also additional fees connected to the exporting of agricultural commodities.

Target 2.3
By 2030, double the agricultural productivity and incomes of small-scale food producers, in particular women, indigenous peoples, family farmers, pastoralists and fishers, including through secure and equal access to land, other productive resources and inputs, knowledge, financial services, markets and opportunities for value addition and non-farm employment.

Target 2.4
By 2030, ensure sustainable food production systems and implement resilient agricultural practices that increase productivity and production, that help maintain ecosystems, that strengthen capacity for adaptation to climate change, extreme weather, drought, flooding and other disasters and that progressively improve land and soil quality

---

Family Capital for Sustainable Agriculture

Using family capital – the combined talent, resources and physical capability of the farming family – can help solve the problems of hunger and increase agricultural productivity. Several articles in this book should be helpful.

Articles related to sustainable agriculture: Page

Best Practices:

Robert C. Roylance: As General Manager for Farm Management Company, Robert managed numerous corporate farms in theU.S., UK, Mexico and Canada. After retirement he and his wife, Susan, spent eight months of the year, for four years, in Kenya and Uganda, targeting poverty alleviation, orphan care and HIV/AIDS prevention. These targets included: the organization of community associations, export and local marketing, drilling boreholes (deep wells), laying pipelines, hand digging shallow wells, advising farmers on crop production, micro-credit, building schools, establishing a home-based community orphan program and the development of the Stay Alive HIV/AIDS prevention education program for children. He also provided agriculture consultations for farms in Egypt, Paraguay, Guatemala and Haiti.

2.3 – Double Agricultural Productivity

Robert C. Roylance

Food shortage in Africa

Professor Gordon Conway, Imperial College of London, told BBC News:

> Africa already imports US $40bn worth of food each year, it is an enormous amount. If we do not produce more food in Africa, that will get worse and worse, and the continent will suffer as a result. . . . Secondly, if we do not pay attention to land degradation in Africa then the land itself will continue to degrade and that will further reduce the yields we are getting at the moment (BBC News, 214).

Doubling maize yields in Africa

To avoid massive hunger and extensive damage to natural resources, it is imperative that systems be put in place to at least double the maize yields in Africa. This goal does not seem unreasonable when the maize yields in Africa are compared to other growing regions of the world (see "Maize Yields by Region").

    In order to meet the goal of doubling the yields of crops in Africa, some very aggressive steps must be taken. This goal requires a whole new mindset and some agricultural procedures of the past will

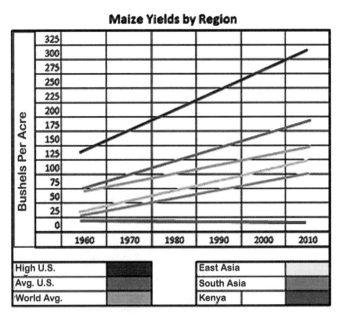

Maize Yields by Region

have to be abandoned. If we expect the African farmers to advance on the world stage, we need to empower them to pursue actions proven not only in developed countries, but actions being adopted by countries pulling themselves out poverty. If this approach can be embraced, it is possible to create highly-productive land that can continue to improve indefinitely.

Two examples of achieving highly-productive soils

Example #1: *(See photo at right.)* Some of the most productive land in the world is located in England and it continues to get better every year. This is accomplished by growing exceptional yields, which in turn produces high volumes of crop residue that is incorporated back into the soils. Additional amounts of nitrogen fertilizer are applied directly to crop residues in order to assist in the breakdown of fibrous materials and overcome the nitrogen tie-up associated with soils tilled and interspersed with crop materials. As these larger amounts of material break down each year, the fertility continues to escalate. The positive long-term effects of higher organic levels continue to release increased amounts of nitrogen. This can amount to as much 60 units of nitrogen for every percent of organic matter in the soil. This will go a long way to reduce the need for commercial fertilizers.

Example #2: New irrigated fields were developed out of sagebrush land in Washington State during the 1970s (*similar to photo at right*). These fields had high levels of sand content and were classified as non-arable by the government. However, after several decades of a strong maize/corn rotation and a good tillage program, where all of the corn fodder was returned to the soil, these fields are now some of the highest producing corn fields in the U.S.

An example is the corn field on the right, which has consistently produced exceptionally high yields. The fertility of the soil has been improved following the production of high tonnages of crop residues, a byproduct of the high-producing corn crop. These high producing fields have evolved from waste land (see sagebrush picture on preceeding page), but are now highly productive.

This is a result of incorporating the plant residue back into the soil after the harvesting of each crop, over a period of several years. Notice the high quantity of crop residues left in the field after the corn has been harvested.

The following table compares some of the higher corn-yields grown in Washington State to the yields in Kenya for 2014. (The information from the first three farms in Washington State comes from the National Corn Growers Association.) The average yield for the first three farms, converted to hectares, is 18.9 T/HA. Even though these yields seem high, there are other areas in the U.S. where corn production is even higher. The purpose for showing these exceptionally high yields is to point out what is possible and show the comparison with current maize yields in Africa.

Comparative Analysis of Maize Yields – U.S. vs. Kenya			
Farmer	**Location**	**Bu Per Acre**	**Tons Per Hector**
Stokrose Farms	**Warden, Washington**	295	20.40
Zecchio Farms	**Granger, Washington**	275	19.00
Cox Farms	**Warden, Washington**	250	17.29
U.S. average	**U.S. Farms**	180	12.50
Peasant farmers	**Kenya 2011**	25	1.73
Peasant farmers	**Kenya 2012**	21	1.45
Peasant farmers	**Kenya 2013**	20	1.39

It's important to point out that the Kenyan yields are country averages, whereas the U.S. yield in the chart above is representative of some very good farms. The average corn yields in the U.S. are around 180 bushels per acre, or about 12.50 tons per hectare.

Another significant aspect is the steady climb in yields in the U.S., whereas the yields in Kenya are on the decline.

This chart represents the cumulative efforts of soil scientists at university experiment stations, working with proactive farmers. The farmers' constant push for more effective production practices has resulted in these amazing crop yields.

These statistics point out: (1) there is an incredible opportunity to assist Kenya and other African countries to substantially increase yields, and (2) the declining corn yields in Kenya are symptomatic of failed policies from the past that need a radical change. As yields decline, and farmers make less money, social ills also increase. Try as we might, we cannot change social ills until we get the soil degradation under control. Declining yields and increasing populations are a recipe for disaster.

The following list outlines some action items critical to restoring the productivity of the land.

1. Implement a soil-fertility management program

Many fields in Africa have been depleted of soil nutrients as well as soil humus and organic matter. This leaves fields with little or no ability to produce crops that are sustainable.

Therefore, it is essential for soil-fertility management programs to be implemented. ISFM (Integrated Soil Fertility Management) is a program that could be of great benefit to farmers and should be considered by governments to help in poverty-stricken regions dependent on agriculture. It includes a comprehensive evaluation of the soil through prescribed testing procedures. This program is currently being used by progressive farmers in Africa and could be utilized to a greater extent by common farmers, if they had the proper assistance. One of the problems with soil testing in Africa is the ability to get accurate and timely information – because of the limited number of soil laboratories. Normally, the only soils labs available are run by the universities. ISFM principles include a real concern for the environment, encourage the judicious use of chemical fertilizers and promote the use of organic fertilizers (Sanginga, 2009).

A difficult aspect of ISFM is the ability to determine the nutrient levels in the existing fields. This is due to the high cost of lab testing. It is prohibitive for small farmers to incur this expense on their own; therefore, the communities need to have general soil-testing programs so the small farmers will have an idea of where they stand. Community associations, such as community development centers (CDCs), could provide the needed support. (See article in SDG 1 on "Overcoming Agricultural Poverty.")

Families can provide the extra labor needed to insure a successful organic fertilizer program that includes the management and application of livestock manures. They can also make it possible to utilize labor-intensive, crop-residue management systems.

2. Implement a pest-management program

Families can be a great resource in pulling weeds, scaring off destructive birds, picking off insects and trapping rodents (and scaring away elephants – which they do). However, there are times when diseases and certain insects require a more sophisticated approach. Then the careful use of Integrated Pest Management (IPM) can be used and farmers would still be able to meet most environmental standards.

IPM evaluates the basic threat of a specific pest and then considers the most prudent way forward. When evaluating insects, it is important to also consider the number of beneficial insects that are present. They may provide a more effective control than other alternatives (Neuenschwander, 2003).

3. Implement an effective residue-management system

The application of crop residues and other organic materials to the soils will greatly enhance the soils' ability to accept and retain water, provide good aeration to the root systems, encourage the development of beneficial microorganisms and improve the availability of soil nutrients. These translate into higher crop-production levels and lower unit-production costs. (*See "Halt and Reverse Land Degradation," in SDG 15 – page 217.*)

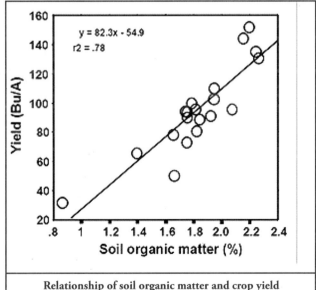

$$y = 82.3x - 54.9$$
$$r2 = .78$$

Relationship of soil organic matter and crop yield at end of long-term cropping experiment

4. Improve water resources

Water is a very scarce resource in many parts of Africa; however, there are many opportunities to enhance the availability of water. These opportunities include: the development of deep boreholes, hand-dug wells, pipelines, reservoir systems and pumping systems from lakes and rivers. It is not unusual to see family members taking turns running simple treadle pumps to transfer water from shallow, hand-dug wells to their fields. These pumps can also be used to transfer water from nearby waterways. This is a first step in using simple irrigation equipment. It could lead to more advanced irrigation systems that could bring increased crop production.

5. Improve irrigation systems

Crops raised under efficient irrigation systems are not only more likely to be profitable, but will also generate additional amounts of crop residues that can be used to build the soils. In many parts of Africa water is in short supply, so it is essential to use efficient irrigation systems, such as surface drip, sub-surface drip or effective level-basin systems. Traditional hand-watering systems are usually family projects and are a reasonably efficient watering system. The following pictures compare different types of irrigation systems, beginning with the most efficient, that also contribute to high levels of production.

Level Basin

Level-basin irrigation systems are very efficient with water, power and labor. The infiltration rate of the water has a positive impact on deep rooted crops. Level-basin irrigation requires level topography and soils that will hold a flood and high volumes of water.

Subsurface Drip

The subsurface drip line is seven to ten inches below the surface. It is one of the most water-efficient irrigation systems; however, it is only suited to a specific crop rotation plan. It is sometimes difficult for the planting and cultivating operations -- to position the rows directly over the pipe. GPS positioning has helped in this regard. This system is more expensive, but it can last up to twenty years.

Modified Surface Drip

The drip tape is essentially laid down at the same time the seed is planted – depending on the crop. This very popular option is used for many crops. However, the pipe is destroyed when the crops are harvested so the expenses are quite high. It does an excellent job of distributing water efficiently.

Surface Drip

Surface drip is similar to the modified drip system; however, it is difficult to manage during the growing season and its efficiencies are not as high. There is a definite advantage to keeping the soils surface dry, which reduces the weed and evaporation problems. This is a less expensive way for the small family-farmer to get highly efficient use of water for their crops.

Center Pivot

The center pivot can cover large areas of land with a high degree of water uniformity. Labor operational costs are low; however, capital requirements are high. In addition, these systems require high levels of electrical power. These systems work better on sandy soils

Hand Lines

Uniformity of water distribution for hand lines is very low and labor costs are very high. The power requirements are quite high. Capital costs are reasonable. If family members provide the labor it reduces the operating cost of this system.

Furrow Irrigation

Furrow irrigation requires more water, and under some conditions has a negative impact on crop quality and yields. This system is usually very labor intensive, but is often used when family labor is available.

Wheel Lines

Wheel lines are similar to hand lines as far is uniformity of water distribution is concerned. They have lower labor costs; however, the capital costs are higher. The wheel lines usually have lower crop yields when compared to some of the other irrigation systems.

The picture to the right shows a farm with multiple center-pivot irrigation systems. This system is widely used in new farm-land development in the U.S. The corn field on page 41 is irrigated with a center-pivot system, such as on the right. This system can be used for high technology farming practices (inputs applied through the water). While the initial investment is high, the labor costs are low, and yields are generally high.

Borlaug and Dowswell (1994) state that agriculture in sub-Saharan Africa, more than in any other part of the world, is in crisis. The low-input low-output systems of agriculture which maintained Africa at subsistence levels is no longer able to feed the people. In addition, there are the associated problems of land degradation accelerated by low-input systems, which in some instances has exceeded the resilience threshold of soils. Naturally and human-induced low-quality soils now characterize much of the African landscape; however, there are areas where high levels of productivity are still possible (Eswaran et al., 1997).

Conclusion

A reformation is required to increase crop production, enhance income-making capabilities and stop land degradation. With these issues in mind, it is proposed that a new movement be initiated to motivate farm families in Africa to make the necessary changes in their traditional farming practices. This undertaking would encompass the following objectives:

1. Seriously evaluate the traditional ways of soil tillage.
2. Make bold moves toward proven mechanization systems.
3. Use a scientific approach toward the use of farm inputs.
4. Improve marketing opportunities and outcomes.
5. Enhance the utilization of family labor.

There is extensive farmland degradation happening in many parts of Africa, with the resulting continual decrease in crop yields. Unfortunately, most of the farmers are totally oblivious to this fact. This problem impacts almost every aspect of African society, as the economy also declines. With programs to provide the proper education and support, this degradation can be halted and turned around to make the land sustainable for families and communities.

With increased education on soil fertility principles, the family farmer can contribute toward increased productivity, and help double crop yields. Education is the key to ensure positive changes.

References

BBC News, "African soil crisis threatens food security," Mark Kinver, 4 December 2014 http://www.bbc.com/news/science-environment-30277514

Eswaran, H., Almaraz, R., Reich, P. & Zdruli, P. (1997), "Soil quality and soil productivity in Africa," Journal of Sustainable Agriculture, 10, 75–94. http://soils.usda.gov/use/worldsoils/papers/africa3.html

Sanginga, N. and Woomer, P.L. (2009), Integrated Soil Fertility Management in Africa: Principles, Practices, and Developmental Process, Tropical Soil Biology and Fertility Institute of the International Centre for Tropical Agriculture (TSBF-CIAT), Nairobi, Kenya

National Corn Growers Association (2015), "World of Corn Offers Online Facts and Figures," Chesterfield, Missouri.

http://www.ncga.com/news-and-resources/news-stories/article/2015/03/2014-world-of-corn-offers-online-facts-and-figures

Neuenschwander, P. et all, (2003) Biological Control in IPM Systems in Africa, CABI Pub. in association with the ACP-EU Technical Centre for Agricultural and Rural Co-operation and Swiss Agency for Development and Cooperation, Wallingford, Oxon, UK.

Sanginga N, Woomer PL (2009) Integrated soil fertility management in Africa: principles, practices and developmental process. Tropical Soil Biology and Fertility Institute of the International Centre for Tropical Agriculture, Nairobi, Kenya.

A New Soya Entrepreneur
As recorded by Edward Kaweesa

Back: Edward Kaweesa (from FARM STEW),
Mathus and Emmanuel (my sons)
Front: Henry, my husband, myself, Helen and Isakel
(five of my children are not in the photo)

My name is Florence Byogero. I am married and have nine children. My husband is a builder and our family has tried to survive on his income. I tried to look for a job so that I could contribute to the family income, but nowhere could I find a job. It was very hard for my husband to support the family alone on the little income he was earning. Life started getting to be very difficult. My children couldn't get enough to eat and we could not pay their school fees.

In November 2015, the FARM STEW team came to our village (Kasokwe, Kaliro District, Uganda). Their soya nutrition training was conducted at our home and we invited all the village to attend. We were taught how to make milk, eggs and mandazi from soybeans.

We were also taught the principles of NEW START:

Nutrition,
Exercise,
Water,

Sunshine/Safety,
Temperance,
Air,
Rest and
Trust in God.

These eight simple health principles can help us live a full, abundant life.

This training opened my eyes – I was looking for a job in the wrong place. I already had work to do, it was a matter of implementing. Following the soya nutrition training I started to make milk, eggs and mandazis [like a small donut], with the help of my children. We sold them at the nearby local market. I started with 5,000/= Uganda shillings ($1.5 US) and earned 10,000/= Uganda shillings in one day! The business has grown little-by-little. I am so happy that I now have my own business. In addition, my family is looking healthy as we use soya products and eat fruits and vegetables that are grown at home or in our village.

My dream is to produce soya products on a large scale so that I can supply supermarkets with these great products. Our challenge is that we lack the machinery that can grind larger quantities of the soya. So for now, we are using what we have at home – our mortar and pestle and hardworking members of our family. It is a good place to start!

BEST PRACTICES

The team of local Ugandans returned a few months later to teach us more about farming and health.

I really thank the FARM STEW team for coming to train us. We have been growing soya on our small farm for a long time, planting and using it, but having little knowledge about how nutritious and important it is – especially for our children.

But most of all, I thank Joy Kauffman, the founder of FARM STEW, for enabling many underprivileged people to improve their health and living standards.

Florence Byogero

Right: Making soya milk
Below: Betty Mwesigwa (left side) conducting FARM STEW training

FARM STEW seeks to elevate the living standard of rural and small farm families throughout the world by partnering with local leaders to "end hunger, achieve food security, improve nutrition, and promote sustainable agriculture." For further information: www.farmstew.org

Progress towards the Sustainable Development Goals
Report of the Secretary-General, 3 June 2016
E/2016/75

21. Between 2000 and 2015, the global maternal mortality ratio, or number of **maternal deaths** per 100,000 live births, declined by 37 per cent, to an estimated ratio of 216 per 100,000 live births in 2015. Almost all maternal deaths occur in low-resource settings and can be prevented. Globally, 3 out of 4 births were assisted by skilled health-care personnel in 2015. Under-five mortality rates fell rapidly from 2000 to 2015, declining by 44 per cent globally. Nevertheless, an estimated 5.9 million **children under the age of 5** died in 2015, with a global under-five mortality rate of 43 per 1,000 live births. The neonatal mortality rate, that is, the likelihood of dying in the first 28 days of life, declined from 31 deaths per 1,000 live births in 2000 to 19 deaths per 1,000 live births in 2015. Over that period, progress in the rate of child survival among children aged 1 to 59 months outpaced advances in reducing neonatal mortality; as a result, neonatal deaths now represent a larger share (45 per cent) of all under-five deaths.

26. **Substance use and substance-use** disorders have also created a significant public health burden. Worldwide, average alcohol consumption in 2015 was estimated at 6.3l of pure alcohol per person among those aged 15 or older, with wide variations across countries. Alcohol consumption was highest in the developed regions (10.4l per person) and lowest in Northern Africa (0.5l per person). In 2013, only about 1 in 6 people worldwide suffering from drug-use disorders received treatment. Approximately 1 in 18 people with drug-use disorders received treatment in Africa that year, compared with 1 in 5 in Western and Central Europe.

28. Around 1.25 million people died from **road traffic injuries** in 2013. Halving the number of global deaths and injuries from road traffic accidents by 2020 is an ambitious goal given the dramatic increase in the number of vehicles, which nearly doubled between 2000 and 2013.

Raymond R. Price, MD, FACS
1. University of Utah
   - Director Center for Global Surgery
   - Clinical Professor Department of Surgery
   - Adjunct Associate Professor, Department of Family and Preventive Medicine, Division of Public Health
2. Intermountain Healthcare
   - Director of Graduate Surgical Education, Intermountain Medical Center

3 – Health
Prevent Death from Injury
Raymond R. Price, MD, FACS

3.2 – By 2030, end preventable deaths of newborns and children under 5 years of age, with all countries aiming to reduce neonatal mortality to at least as low as 12 per 1,000 live births and under-5 mortality to at least as low as 25 per 1,000 live births

3.4 – By 2030, reduce by one-third premature mortality from non-communicable diseases

3.6 – By 2030, halve the number of global deaths and injuries from road traffic accidents

Empowering Families Prevents Injury and Saves Lives

After an exhilarating trip to the top of the Kelimutu volcano on the island of Flores, Indonesia, to see the three striking summit crater lakes of varying colors— Tiwu Ata Bupu (blue), Tiwu Ko'o Fai Nuwa Muri (green), and Tiwu Ata Polo (red)—our team of volunteers working in a nearby village began our descent along the winding road, partially washed out by the tropical rainstorms the previous few days. My wife and I, along with a few others, tried walking, or slipping along the muddy narrow road, watching the others comfortably ride inside, and on top, of a truck nearly too large for adequate passage along the road. I watched three of my

children, ages 9-14, in and on the truck, enjoying this exciting adventure.

The truck's passenger side wheels slowly, almost eerily, began to rise off the dirt road. Even when everyone realized the truck was beginning to roll over, very few were able to jump off or out of the truck. Panic embraced those of us trying to pull the truck's wheels back down, as some worked feverishly trying to help others escape from the truck. Disaster seemed imminent as the truck continued its slow roll, despite all attempts otherwise.

Then suddenly, the truck stopped halfway up–in midair. Luckily, a portion of the rocky slope of the volcano provided a buttress, preventing the truck from rolling over entirely – allowing everyone to exit the truck safely. No one was injured, and after righting the truck back down on all wheels with everyone's help, the truck and our team made it safely off the mountainside.

Lack of services in a remote location

As a trauma surgeon for many years, I contemplated the precarious situation we had avoided—multiple trauma victims on a remote island, eight hours by bus to the nearest hospital, where the hospital did not have any emergency-care capabilities. The nearest air medical transport would be from Australia, but the airfield on the island

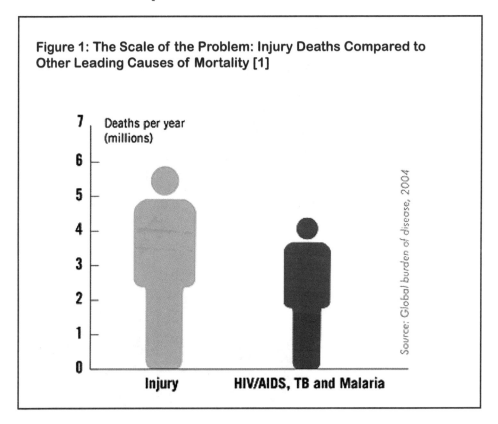

Figure 1: The Scale of the Problem: Injury Deaths Compared to Other Leading Causes of Mortality [1]

Deaths per year (millions)

Source: Global burden of disease, 2004

Injury   HIV/AIDS, TB and Malaria

Figure 2: Projected Changing Causes of Death 2004-2030[1]

Total 2004	Total 2030
1 Ischaemic heart disease	1 Ischaemic heart disease
2 Cerebrovascular disease	2 Cerebrovascular disease
3 Lower respiratory infections	3 Chronic obstructive pulmonary disease
4 Chronic obstructive pulmonary disease	4 Lower respiratory infections
5 Diarrhoeal diseases	5 Road traffic crashes
6 HIV/AIDS	6 Trachea, bronchus, lung cancers
7 Tuberculosis	7 Diabetes mellitus
8 Trachea, bronchus, lung cancers	8 Hypertensive heart disease
9 Road traffic crashes	9 Stomach cancer
10 Prematurity and low birth weight	HIV/AIDS
11 Neonatal infections and other	Nephritis and nephrosis
12 Diabetes mellitus	Suicide
13 Malaria	Liver cancer
14 Hypertensive heart disease	Colon and rectum cancer
15 Birth asphyxia and birth trauma	Oesuphagus cancer
16 Suicide	Homicide
17 Stomach cancer	Alzheimer and other dementias
18 Cirrhosis of the liver	Cirrhosis of the liver
19 Nephritis and nephrosis	Breast cancer
20 Colon and rectum cancers	Tuberculosis
22 Homicide	

lacked any form of landing lights, so could only be accessed during the day and only with good weather. Lack of resources, inadequate medical personnel, remote location in a very tropical environment without an emergency medical response system and lack of modern medical care in general (the reality for more than half the world's population) seemed insurmountable obstacles for life-saving-care had the truck rolled over, injuring many people.

I wondered what the local villagers had done a few years earlier for medical care when an earthquake destroyed their village (which we were helping to rebuild). Who responded to the injured patients? Who transported them to any type of medical outpost?

Figure 3: The Five Leading Causes and Number of Child Deaths, by Age Group, United States, 2009[6]

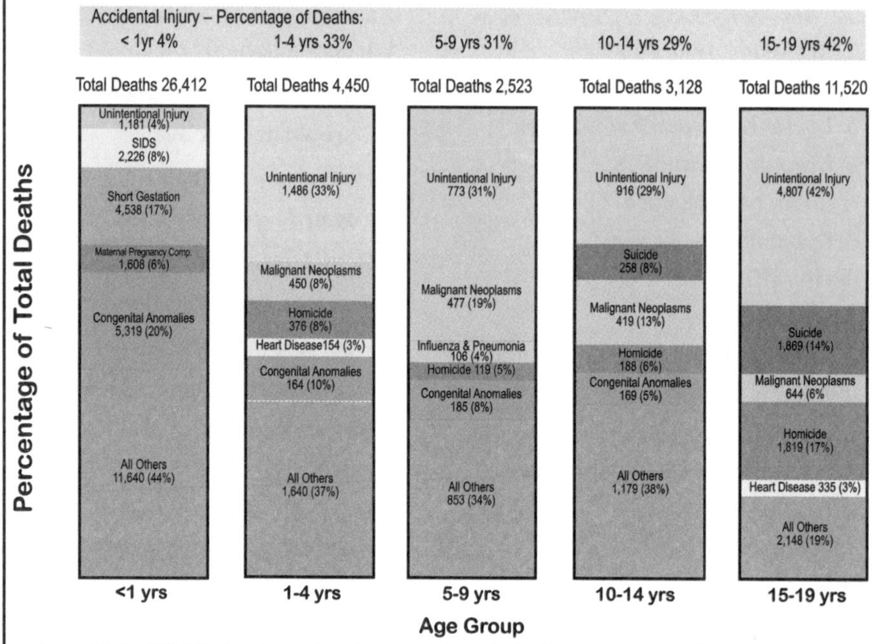

Source: National Vital Statistics System from the national Center for Health Statistics, Centers for Disease Control and Preventiion; accessed through WIXQARS.
National Action Plan for Child Injury Prevention
(http://www.cdc.gov/safechild/pdf/National_Action_Plan_for_Child_Injury_Prevention.pdf)

Who provided the care for those recovering from their injuries? The only resources they really had were each other—their families—their immediate families and extended families.

More people dying from injuries

Over 100 million people worldwide suffer traumatic injuries, leading to 5.8 million deaths each year. Few recognize that this global pandemic represents more people dying from injury than from HIV/AIDS, malaria and tuberculosis combined![1,2] (Figure 1: Injury – The Scale of the Problem)

Over 95% of deaths from injury occur in low- and middle-income countries (LMICs), representing one of the most serious manifestations of inequity in healthcare. While the leading causes of unintentional injuries vary by age (drowning, poisoning, suffocation, fires, burns, falls, and motor vehicle, bicycle, and pedestrian-related crashes), road-traffic accidents alone are projected to be the fifth-leading cause of death by 2030 in LMICs![1,3] (Figure 2: Changing Causes of Death 2004-2030) In many countries the leading cause of death for ages 5-44 results from unintentional injures, with road-traffic accidents representing the majority of causes.

For children under five-years-old, in countries with substantial progress in eliminating or decreasing deaths from infectious diseases and other etiologies, injury emerges as a significant cause of death and disability. (Figure 3: In high-income countries (HICs), unintentional injuries account for nearly 40% of all childhood deaths.)[4] Even in countries where child mortality continues to be determined mainly by prenatal causes and infectious diseases, injury still represents a substantial proportion of child deaths (<5 year old).[4]

The nations of the world recognized that to "ensure healthy lives and promote well-being for all at all ages" (Sustainable Development Goal #3), society must find ways to decrease deaths from injury by half by 2030.[5] Commonly, policy makers intimate that governmental organizations bear the main responsibility for the health and safety of their constituents.[6] Other stakeholders included in the debates searching for solutions often include: businesses, schools, media, health care providers, insurers and medical institutions.[6]

The family: The most influential stakeholder

The family, potentially one of the most influential stakeholders to significantly prevent death and disability from injury, is absent from much of the discussions about solutions. A complex interplay of multiple interpersonal and environmental factors necessitates a broad array of potential solutions. In a HIC like the United States, the more than 20 million non-fatal, unintentional child injuries cost the US $347 billion every year.[7] Decreasing case fatality rates in LMICs from trauma to equal that currently in HICs would save two million lives and $450 billion dollars per year.[8] Recognizing and mobilizing the influence of fathers and mothers to protect their children has not only social, but serious economic, impact for society as well as the family.[7]

Parent-focused strategies

Parent-focused strategies are effective in preventing injuries to young children in the home. Mothers and fathers each provide significant influence in protecting their children and preventing injuries. Consistently, studies show nurturing mothers protect their children as they monitor and provide adequate supervision for their young children.[7] Mothers, both physically and verbally, tend to prevent their children from engaging in dangerous activities; children tend to use greater caution in the presence of their mothers.[9,10]

While governments may pass child-safety restraint laws, parents become the primary educators and enforcers when they buckle their children into their car seats. Counseling parents about the reduction of injury rates can actually influence car seat use.[11,12] By wearing seatbelts all the time and patiently waiting until everyone in the car has a seat belt on before starting the car, parents set an example that tends to create life-long protection strategies for their children – strategies needed to decrease deaths from trauma by 50% by 2030.

In middle childhood, individual child traits and peer relations play an increasingly important role in child safety. However, a positive father-child relationship, and especially a positive father-son relationship, continues to provide a protective component important to protect children from injury during middle childhood.[13] Targeted training toward fathers building stronger interpersonal relationships with their sons reduces injury risk among children in middle childhood.[13]

Drowning

Drowning is one of the most common causes of death among primary school children in rural Thailand (and many other countries).[14] Most injuries, especially drowning, are preventable. Families play a central role in preventing drowning, including modification of the child's environment (closer supervision around bodies of water) and engaging in safe practices.[7] Less than one-fifth of children in Thailand know how to swim. Strategies that encourage parents to teach children to swim at a young age and improve infrastructure to facilitate swimming skills for school children reduce drowning risk in rural Thailand (Laosee 2014).[14]

Boys in the Amazon Basin, Ecuador   Photo by Dr. Ray Price

Burn injuries

Burn injuries are among the most devastating of all injures. While more than 265,000 people die from fire-related burn injures yearly, millions more suffer life- long disabilities and disfigurement, which have dramatic psychological, social, and economic effects on the survivors and their families.[8] Burn injuries predominantly fall on the world's poor, as 95% of fire-related deaths occur in LMICs where children, especially those under age five, constitute the highest risk.[15]

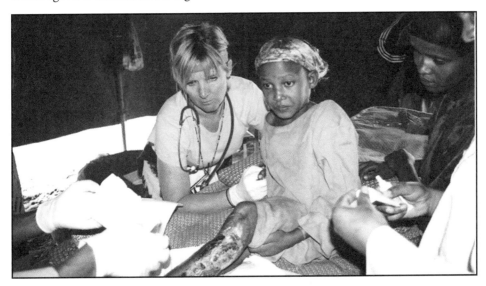

Burn prevention programs for children in developing countries require urgent attention.[16,17] Successful strategies in South Africa provided culturally-appropriate education in different formats (written, pictorial and verbal) in areas frequented by parents and children to encourage more closely monitoring children in hazardous areas (kitchens, especially with open fire stoves) and better planning of homes to reduce hazards.[17]

Open-fire cooking in the home.

Families provide long-term care

Families not only provide a significant resource to prevent injury from many etiologies (road-traffic accidents, drowning, burn, violent crime, falls, etc), families also form the foundations that support long-term care following disabling injuries and throughout recovery.

When government and medical facilities were crippled from the devastating earthquake in Haiti, families provided the immediate life-saving care and ongoing long-term strengthening support throughout recovery to their injured loved ones.

Conclusion

To decrease deaths from injury by 50% by 2030 and to end preventable deaths of children under 5 years old, strategies must recognize and support the untapped potential of families to save lives and decrease disability from injury.

The economic impact and public-health benefits from family engagement will be realized with worldwide efforts that target the family as an integral solution to some of the greatest challenges facing the world today.

Sources for Charts:

Figure 1:
http://www.who.int/violence_injury_prevention/key_facts/VIP_key_facts.pdf
http://apps.who.int/iris/bitstream/10665/44288/1/9789241599375_eng.pdf

Figure 2: Changing Causes of Death 2004-2030 [1]
http://www.who.int/violence_injury_prevention/key_facts/VIP_key_facts.pdf

Figure 3: The Five Leading Causes and Number of Child Deaths, by Age Group, United States, 2009 [6]

See also: National Action Plan for Child Injury Prevention
http://www.cdc.gov/safechild/pdf/National_Action_Plan_for_Child_Injury_Prevention.pdf

Bibliography

1. *Injuries and Violence: The Facts-The Scale of the Problem.* 2015 [cited 2016 June 11]; Available from: http://www.who.int/violence_injury_prevention/key_facts/VIP_key_facts.pdf.

2. deVries, C. and R.R. Price, *Global Sugery and Public Health: A New Paradigm.* 1st ed. 2012, Sudbury Jones and Bartlett Learning, LLC. 300.

3. Wesson, H.K., et al., *The cost of injury and trauma care in low- and middle-income countries: a review of economic evidence.* Health Policy Plan, 2014. 29(6): p. 795-808.

4. Alison Harvey, E.T., Margie Peden, Hamid Soori, Kidist Bartolomeos. *Injury prevention and the attainment of child and adolescent health.* Bulletin of the World Health Organization 2009 [cited 2016 June 11]; 87:390-394:[Available from: http://www.who.int/bulletin/volumes/87/5/08-059808/en/.

5. *Sustainable Development Goals: 17 Goals to Transform our World – Goal 3: Ensure Health Lives and Promote Well-being for All at All Ages.* United Nations 2015 [cited 2016 June 11]; Available from: http://www.un.org/sustainabledevelopment/health/.

6. Thomas R. Frieden, M., MPH, D. Linda C. Degutis, MSN, and P. Grant T. Baldwin, MPH. *National Action Plan for Child Injury Prevention: An Agenda to Prevent Injuries and Promote the Safety of Children and Adolescents in the United States.* 2012 [cited 2016 June 11]; Available from: http://www.cdc.gov/safechild/pdf/National_Action_Plan_for_Child_Injury_Prevention.pdf.

7. Schnitzer, P.G., *Prevention of unintentional childhood injuries.* Am Fam Physician, 2006. 74(11): p. 1864-9.

8. Gosselin, R., et al., Surgery and Trauma Care, in *Disease Control Priorities 3rd ed: Essential Surgery*, W. Bank, Editor. 2015, World Bank: New York City.

9. Schwebel, D.C. and C.M. Brezausek, *The role of fathers in toddlers' unintentional injury risk.* J Pediatr Psychol, 2004. 29(1): p. 19-28.

10. Morrongiello, B.A. and T. Dawber, *Mothers' responses to sons and daughters engaging in injury-risk behaviors on a playground: implications for sex differences in injury rates.* J Exp Child Psychol, 2000. 76(2): p. 89-103.

11. DC, G. and G. CC, *Effectiveness of health promotion programs to increase motor vehicle occupant restraint use among young children.* Am J Prev Med, 1999. 16(1 suppl): p. 12-22.

12. C, D. and R. IG, *Individual-level injury prevention strategies in the clinical setting.* Future Child, 2000. 10: p. 53-82.

13. Schwebel, D.C. and B. MS, *How Do Mothers and Fathers Influence Pediatric Injury Risk in Middle Childhood?* J Pediatric Psychology, 2010. 35(8): p. 806-813.

14. Laosee, O., J. Kiewyoo, and R. Somronthong, *Drowning risk perceptions among rural guardians of Thailand: A community-based household survey.* J Child Health Care, 2014. 18(2): p. 168-177.

15. Ahuja, R.B. and S. Bhattacharya, *An analysis of 11,196 burn admissions and evaluation of conservative management techniques.* Burns, 2002. 28(6): p. 555-61.

16. Parbhoo, A., Q.A. Louw, and K. Grimmer-Somers, *A profile of hospital-admitted paediatric burns patients in South Africa.* BMC Res Notes, 2010. 3: p. 165.

17. Parbhoo, A., Q.A. Louw, and K. Grimmer-Somers, *Burn prevention programs for children in developing countries require urgent attention: a targeted literature review.* Burns, 2010. 36(2): p. 164-75.

Reduce Maternal and Infant Mortality
Renae Morgan Bowen

Impact of the family

This chapter is designed to explore the power that the *family* can have in decreasing the percentage of maternal mortality in an impactful way. From becoming better informed about maternal health in general, to literal assistance to a woman who is hemorrhaging after giving birth, there is a human resource that this chapter asserts is not being adequately utilized, that can dramatically change the life or death outcomes of a childbearing woman: the family. This is an invitation for political figures, donors and others who are invested in the cause of saving women's lives, to come together and promote programs that educate and empower the family to make a difference in reducing both maternal mortality and infant mortality rates.

Building upon a strong foundation

Let's look at some examples of programs that are currently making a difference while also including the family in their efforts to achieve improved care for childbearing women.

The American Academy of Pediatrics has developed a simplified Neonatal Resuscitation Program called Helping Babies Breathe™ (HBB). The materials used are primarily pictorial, with limited verbiage, designed to adequately instruct even limitedly-literate midwives and skilled-birthing attendants to resuscitate an infant born with breathing difficulties. Participants in this training review the following in the training manual's "Prepare for birth" instructions: "Identify a helper and review the emergency plan.... Prepare the birth companion or another skilled helper to assist if the baby does not breathe.... A birth companion can help the mother and call for another helper."[1]

Oft times, a midwife does not have an assistant present at the birth of a child.

Renae Morgan Bowen is the Quality Director for a federally-qualified Health Center, assisting underserved populations to get access to comprehensive healthcare and tracking clinical performance measures to improve health outcomes. She is an advocate of "family capital," married and the mother of one.

If there is any type of complication, this becomes extremely taxing for one pair of hands to handle. Simply the presence of a family member as a "birthing companion" can make a large enough difference that the AAP has determined to state it in a curriculum with limited written instruction. This concept of preparing and utilizing an untrained family member in a complicated birthing situation is taught in each HBB course.

An extensive, collaborative report led by WHO, UNICEF, UNFPA and The World Bank, titled *Trends in Maternal Mortality: 1990 to 2008*, defines pregnancy-related death as, "any death during pregnancy, childbirth, or the postpartum period even if it is due to accidental or incidental causes" (p.4).

Healthy mother and baby in Ethiopia
Photo by Timothy S. Evans

With this definition in place, they set about tracking maternal mortality rates. They utilized various evaluation techniques to acquire the most accurate maternal mortality rate for 2008 and then compared it to previous years to determine how effective different efforts have been in reducing maternal mortality.

Two of the evaluative tools, reproductive-age mortality studies (RAMOS) and verbal autopsy surveys, included family members to achieve their results. The RAMOS approach involves "identifying and investigating the causes of all deaths of women of reproductive age in a defined area/population by using multiple sources of data (e.g. interviews of family members, vital registrations, health facility records, burial records, traditional birth attendants)."

Interviews with family members helped in classifying whether the deaths were maternal in nature, or not. The verbal autopsy approach relies on interviews with *family members* and the community to identify the maternal and/or pregnancy status of the deceased woman (p.8). Though results vary depending on the extent of family member's knowledge of the events leading to the death, these surveys recognize the family as a human resource that can help deduce the cause of death and its maternal nature.[2]

Recognizing family culture

Culture of various different countries, not to mention individual communities, often seems to become a large obstacle in development. It is daunting at first and takes time to truly understand the foundations behind why people in a community or country do things a particular way. Because it takes this extra time, consideration of cultural barriers tends to be swept under the rug while programs blaze ahead, hoping a difference can still be made despite this underlying difficulty. Yet, once the time is invested in better understanding the culture of those you are working with, it changes from being a hindrance to a help.

When people know that you are suggesting health improvements with their culture in mind, they are much more open to helping achieve the improvements necessary. They frequently come up with solutions that are more productive and sustainable than anything the developing organization would suggest.

In San José de Secce, Peru, it was noticed that there was a very high maternal-mortality rate, due to 94 per cent of women choosing to give birth at home instead of in a health center. Upon further investigation, it was discovered that there was doubt among residents about the capability of the local medical professionals. They considered giving birth in the clinic just as dangerous as de-

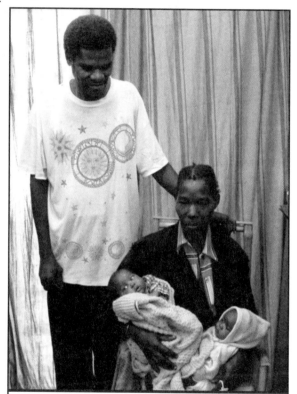

Healthy twin babies   *Photo by Care for Life – Mozam-*

livering at home. This perception alone was the leading cause for the high mortality rate of women in this community. In response, a culturally sensitive project was developed to break down the barriers and in the end, reduce the maternal death rates. Paul Hunt and Judith Bueno De Mesquita from the Human Rights Centre at the University of Essex published:

> The project promoted communication between health professionals and the community, user participation, and a closer relationship between traditional midwives and health personnel. In health centers, the environment of the delivery room and care given during

prenatal checkups, delivery and the postnatal period were adapted to make them culturally sensitive. These measures included creating a private environment, with curtains to keep out drafts and anyone not associated with the birth, as well as the provision of a bed and a sturdy rope, so that women could give birth in an upright position, or squatting and gripping the rope, as they wished. The protocol for care also stipulated, among others, that the person attending the birth should speak Quechua and preferably be female. *In addition, in accordance with the beliefs of the communities, the protocol included the requirement to deliver the placenta to the family member present so that it could be buried, and the opportunity for the user to remain in the health facility for up to eight days.* According to an assessment, after the project was implemented, there was a great increase of deliveries at health centers.[3]

Health center delivery incentives:

The Mayange Health Center in Rwanda has seen an increase of mothers giving birth at the clinic with a reduction of maternal mortality by 25 per cent. This is a result of many improvements: First, the number of trained nurses has gone from 3 to 18 (six times the orginal amount!); Second, women are being educated about the importance of staying in the health center for an extended amount of time after giving birth.

Theophile Ndabereye, who works at the clinic states, "Even if mothers are in a hurry to go back to their home after they give birth, we show and explain to them why it is very important that they stay with us for three days, and they understand and they stay, for the sake of their new babies."

Third, improvements to the available health insurance have motivated more people to deliver in the health center.

> The women and their families in Mayange can trace many of these changes to the government's health insurance programme, Mutuelles de santé, which is run by community representatives and local health providers. Access to the programme increased from 7 per cent to 85 per cent of the population between 2002 and 2008. Those enrolled pay an annual premium equivalent to US$2. Women who attend four appointments during a pregnancy deliver at no cost.[4]

A combination of these different incentives has led to a large reduction percentage in maternal deaths. It must be noted that in order to achieve such dramatic results, these incentives must be extended to the poorest of the poor, for therein lies the largest number of women perishing from pregnancy and childbirth-related complications. Failing to fully incorporate the poorest demographic of women neglects to use available resources to improve maternal mortality rates in the areas where they will make the most impact. Like efforts have been made in other countries, but in failing to focus on the poorest areas, did not end with as favorable an improvement as was seen in this effort in Rwanda.

Main problems of maternal mortality

The four predominantly preventable complications in pregnancy and childbirth are hemorrhaging, infection, high blood pressure and obstructed labor. Each of these conditions presents symptoms that can be recognized by family members. With instruction, there are simple practices that family members can do to help prevent an unnecessary death from these ailments.

1. Hemorrhaging is a sudden issue of heavy bleeding. This can occur any time from directly after birth to days after, when the patient is no longer under supervision of a hospital, health clinic or midwife. Midwife Kerrianne Gifford has written some basic instructions for what a hemorrhaging woman, as well as a birthing companion, can do to reduce the amount of bleeding. She said:

> . . . mother tries, if conscious, to massage her uterus herself to the point that it feels very firm and rounded, bleeding will sometimes stop instantly. If she has help, then there is a technique called bi-manual compression. In the absence of immediate midwifery help it would be worth anyone trying it if the woman is bleeding catastrophically with a postpartum hemorrhage. It means someone having to continually compress the uterus externally and internally until help arrives.[5]

The helper can also ensure that the mother has urinated, which enhances the chances for the compression on the uterus to be successful.

In the American Academy of Pediatrics' Helping Babies Breathe™ program the text encourages early breastfeeding after delivery (p. 12).[6] This not only benefits the infant, but according to some research, is also a method to help reduce/prevent hemorrhaging. If a woman begins hemorrhaging when no medical assistance is readily available, the family member can encourage the child to suckle. Breastfeeding prompts a woman's body to release natural oxytocin, which redirects the blood flow from the uterus to the woman's nursing breast. This oxytocin release also causes the uterus walls to contract and helps stop hemorrhaging.

Oxytocin has been the favored solution to hemorrhaging, but it requires refrigeration, which is not available at all, in many locations where it could be beneficial. In January 2010, *The Lancet* published the findings of a trial comparing the outcomes of administering oxytocin, versus a sublingual misoprostol which does not require intravenous injection, nor refrigeration. Misoprostol proved to be clinically equivalent to the oxytocin, and thus is a very good alternative option for health centers without refrigeration amenities. This creates a better storage option for this medication, which then reduces the shortages in this treatment that often occur in such rural clinics.[7]

Another contributor to fatal hemorrhaging is anemia, which is common in pregnant women, but even more prevalent and life-threatening in those living in developing countries due to nutritional deficiencies. Women and other members of the family can be educated about the importance of giving a woman proper nutrition, as well as added nutrients such as folic acid, to help reduce the number of anemic women and anemia-related hemorrhaging.

In situations where the bleeding cannot be stopped or reduced with an at-home remedy, a plan for how to transport the mother to a medical clinic could be created as part of the birthing plan. Mothers- and fathers-to-be can work together to figure out how they would get proper medical assistance should hemorrhaging occur after the skilled birthing attendant has left. Couples may ask family members to assist in transporting the vulnerable woman, a neighbor may be asked to go retrieve a medical professional, a clinical vehicle may be alerted to come pick up the hemorrhaging woman and transport her back to the health center or hospital.

2. **Infections** can be contracted during pregnancy and/or childbirth and may manifest themselves immediately upon labour or not until days or even weeks after the mother has returned home. Symptoms can range from a fever and chills to redness, swelling and intense pain. Family members who are in regular contact with the newly delivered woman should be educated to identify signs of infection so they can get the individual to a medical professional who can prescribe an oral antibiotic to fight the infection. Family members can also be included to insure the patient takes the entire prescription of the antibiotics. Oftentimes, the medication makes the symptoms go away and the individual starts feeling better so they will stop taking the medicine prematurely. With support from relatives, the individual will take the entire prescription, thereby preventing the likelihood of the infection returning.

Relatives also need to understand the importance of rest and proper hydration for the woman's health. This requires a mental and cultural shift in some communities, as a lot of expectations are placed on the woman to run the household and gather water. Engaging and educating the family about the importance of allowing a woman to heal after delivery is crucial to her being able to return to these responsibilities in full health.

The cultural practice of female genital mutilation/cutting (FGM/C) is still a common practice in parts of Africa, as well as some Asian and Middle Eastern countries. Cultural beliefs promote this practice, but inhabitants of these areas do not realize that FGM/C "poses serious physical and mental health risks for young girls and women, especially for those who undergo extreme forms of the procedure. It is linked to increased complications in childbirth and even maternal deaths [due to blood loss and infections]."[8]

3. **High blood pressure** is a common malady amongst pregnant women. It is hard to detect high blood pressure unless tested by a healthcare professional. With the blood pressure cuff and a trained professional, high blood pressure can be quickly identified and treated. When high blood pressure is life threatening, symptoms appear of: headache, dizziness, blurred vision, chest pain and shortness of breath, and/or nausea/vomiting. In the developed world, medications are easily accessible to help

minimize high blood pressure and reduce risk. These medications are not as readily available in the developing world.

However there are still strategies that can be employed by the pregnant woman and her family to reduce this threat. Her family must first try to ensure that the pregnant woman gets to the health clinic several times in her pregnancy to be checked for high blood pressure. In order to help motivate them to take the time and effort to do this, they must first be properly educated on how dangerous high blood pressure can be for both the mother and child. Bed rest is essential to lower a high-risk mother's blood pressure down to a non-threatening level. Family members can assume household responsibilities to allow the woman to stay reclined as much as possible prior to the delivery.

Supporters can make certain she is positioned on her left side (left lateral recumbent) which will allow her body to relax and the blood to circulate in the most effective manner. Women with high blood pressure during pregnancy are considered high risk pregnancies and need constant observation.

Eclampsia is known to be related to high blood pressure. Eclampsia is the term given to the severe effects of hypertension, such as seizure or going into a coma. It has been noted that the largest percentage of mortality due to this is found amongst women either in their teen years or above the age of 35 who are delivering their first child or multiples. "While many different drug regimens historically have been used to treat this serious maternal condition – eclampsia in most countries remains one of the 5 most common causes of maternal death – the drug of choice today is magnesium sulfate, MgSO4." Magnesium sulfate is the safest, most efficient, and lowest-cost treatment available to treat eclampsia.[9] Like the related problem of high blood pressure, eclampsia can occur without any indicative symptoms. Families need to be better informed of the importance of a woman having her blood pressure checked at regular intervals within her pregnancy. They should also look for the following symptoms that can forewarn of pre eclampsia and eclampsia. (Again, these may not be present in all women, but are signs that can be watched for.)

- Severe or persistent headache
- Double vision or seeing spots
- Unusual bleeding or bruising
- Excessive weight gain
- Extreme swelling
- Powerful pain in the middle or right side of belly
- The baby has slowed its movement
- Reduced or no output of urine
- Nausea and/or vomiting

4. Obstructed labour is primarily caused by a woman's body being underdeveloped and incapable of properly delivering a newborn. This can be due to age of the mother, malnutrition or infections. Justin C Konje and Oladapo A Ladipo wrote in the *American Journal of Clinical Nutrition*:

Obstructed labor can also occur in subsequent pregnancies in which maternal nutrient deprivation may result in a distorted pelvis, or in women prone to pelvic fractures and other acquired pelvic deformities. Nutrient deficiencies such as calcium, vitamin D, folic acid, iron, and zinc deficiencies interact in combination with various biological and biosocial factors to determine the prevalence of obstructed labor . . . . Efforts must be made to increase the awareness of the importance of good health, especially during the adolescent period, including the need for a balanced diet and the elimination of infections in early childhood that commonly exist in malnourished children. Such infections potentiate the effects of nutrient deprivation on growth.[10]

There are cultures where it is believed that as soon as a girl begins menstruating, she is suitable for marriage. Child marriages are common in these communities and as a result, many girls become pregnant in their young teen years. This causes substantial problems, as the child's body has not yet achieved its full stature, again resulting in obstructed labour due to an insufficiently sized pelvis. Konje and Ladipo suggested:

> Policies that encourage formal education of young women, delay the age of marriage, and promote family planning and contraceptive use may result in the age of first pregnancy being delayed and, therefore, increase the chance of girls completing adolescent growth.[11]

Hemorrhaging, infections, high blood pressure and obstructed labour are the four biggest contributors to maternal mortality, all of which are preventable. With better educational programs, plans for transportation and getting the family involved, the likelihood of a woman getting regular check ups during pregnancy improves. Family members can help detect symptoms of possible problems and get the woman proper treatment before losing her, and possibly the baby.

According to UNICEF, it is also important to remember that "for every woman who dies from these complications, approximately 30 more suffer from injuries, infections and disabilities which are usually untreated, and are often humiliating and painful, debilitating and lifelong."[13] Stephanie Urdang adds:

> For many, this brings an end to their mothering and caring roles, and can lead to removal from their families in disgrace. For example, fistula, a condition unknown in the industrialized world that can result from prolonged and obstructed labour and leaves survivors incontinent, frequently isolates women from their families and communities.[13]

A UNICEF brochure states:

> To improve maternal health, UNICEF supports women-friendly health care programs to increase the number of births attended by skilled medical staff; expand access and upgrade services for prenatal and obstetrical care; strengthen midwifery practice through training of traditional birth attendants; and improve access to prenatal and postnatal care and counseling for pregnant women, their families and communities so they are able to recognize warning signs that require immediate assistance.[14]

Notice that "women, their families and communities" are all involved in UNICEFs efforts to improve maternal health. How can we better involve all three of these units in our efforts to reduce maternal mortality? It is possible for us, our friends and family to be better aware of medical assistance available to vulnerable women? Endowed with such knowledge, we can overcome the feelings of helplessness when we encounter those who are suffering from pains incurred during pregnancy or childbirth.

The United Nations outcome document of the five-year review of the Copenhagen Social Summit encouraged us to:

> Recognize that the family is the basic unit of society and that it plays a key role in social development and is a strong force of social cohesion and integration. In different cultural, political and social systems, various forms of the family exist. Further recognize that equality and equity between women and men and respect for the rights of all family members are essential for family well-being and for society at large, and promote appropriate actions to meet the needs of families and their individual members, particularly in the areas of economic support and provision of social services. Greater attention should be paid to helping the family in its supporting, educating and nurturing roles, to the causes and consequences of family disintegration, and to the adoption of measures to reconcile work and family life for women and men.[15]

Education has a powerful pull in creating better understanding between men and women, thus promoting parity. Education is not an unfamiliar strategy for rising above poverty. Results have already shown that in educating a woman, it has only positive repercussions on her entire sphere of influence. We assert that maximizing the education of young boys as well as grown men can also have positive repercussions for the health of his family and community. UNICEF published:

> The lives of girls and boys are deeply entwined, and so must be the solutions to their problems. For the rights of girls and women to be fulfilled, boys and men must be educated – in schools, health clinics, youth clubs, religious institutions, businesses, the military and police – to 'unlearn' negative patterns of behavior and learn positive new behaviors based on tolerance and equality.[16]

Educating fathers and extended family membes

In May 2011, the *Maternal and Child Health Journal* published an article focusing upon the importance of paternal involvement in reducing infant mortality rates, which directly relates to his interactions with the mother during her pregnancy. The article notes the deficiency in incorporating men in the family planning, prenatal support and after birth details:

> Maternal and child health (MCH) programs aim to address some of the more important social determinants of infant mortality at the family and community level, but a

significant gap has been the lack of incorporation of the father. Research suggests that paternal involvement, which has been recognized as contributing to child development and health for many decades, is likely to affect infant mortality through the mother's well-being, primarily her access to resources and support. In spite of that, more systemic social barriers faced by fathers and the influence on their involvement in the pregnancy have received little attention.

This article continues to outline significant benefits of paternal involvement in pregnancy. Fathers can provide emotional and financial support, so the mother is less stressed. With the presence of a paternal partner, women are more likely to make it to prenatal appointments and maintain other healthy lifestyle practices, which benefit the baby in utero.[17]

In addition, a Swedish study showed that "fathers who were not supportive of women during early pregnancy were still uninvolved and unsupportive a year after the infant was born. The

Healthy baby & parents   *Photo by Care for Life – Mozambique*

findings indicate that fathers' early involvement during pregnancy might prevent a lack of support to mother and baby after birth."[18] The research results show that there is a positive reaction by women when the paternal guardian of the unborn child remains engaged and involved. Using this data to strengthen the focus of education courses about healthy pregnancy for boys, as well as girls, can truly make a difference.

Educating the family

There are situations however, where a paternal figure cannot be as involved in supporting the pregnant woman as is the ideal. He may have died due to other causes, be physically distant or disinterested in involvement with the mother and child. The pregnant girl still need not be left to try to maintain a healthy pregnancy on her own. Extended family can step in and lend the physical, emotional and financial support required to improve the chances that their relative will have a safe delivery. The problem once again is educating the family members on how a woman needs to be cared for during and after her pregnancy. Many family members are willing, but are not able to help due to lack of knowledge.

It is the obligation of family members to become educated as to how to support a pregnancy-aged woman, but they cannot live up to this assignment when they do not know it is theirs to begin with. We know that there is a lack of familiarity within the general populace on issues of gender equality, proper medical care and reproductive health education, but there are not yet tools for overcoming these things. The ignorant are powerless to act and find local mechanisms for bringing about innovative solutions to the maternal health dilemma. Educate and empower women to know what they can do to heighten their chances of a safe delivery. Educate and empower the family with the resources for supporting their pregnant wives and daughters. This is a powerful way to help bring about the needed change for reaching the SDG Targets 3.1 and 3.2.

Continued and increased success in reducing maternal mortality required

Dr. Jemilah Mahmood, Chief of UNFPA's Humanitarian Response Branch, declared the following:

> We are observing a shift in pattern in emergencies from the acute and sudden onset to a more complex situation of recurrent and protracted crises. Humanitarian response that follows also needs to shift its focus increasingly on achieving longer-term objectives that allow for more sustainable action....[19]

Conclusion

The family is the key to achieving the longer-term objectives that Dr. Mahmood speaks of. For so long we have seen the family, or individual members of it, as victims of sudden crises. We proclaim that they need not remain victims who are powerless to help themselves. Rather, they are a powerful solution in assisting those trying to help, as they work together to rise above the crises, to rise above poverty and to continue raising the standard of care for women. Let us find ways to empower and incorporate the family into the current efforts we are making. Then we will see even more improved statistics in the battle to reduce maternal mortality worldwide.

Endnotes

1. Errol R. Alden, et al. Helping Babies BreatheSM: Learner Workbook. 2010. p.6
2. Estimates developed by WHO, UNICEF, UNFPA and The World Bank. Trends in Maternal Mortality: 1990 to 2008. http://whqlibdoc.who.int/publications/2010/9789241500265_eng.pdf. p.4, 8.
3. Paul Hunt, Judith Bueno de Mesquita. Reducing Maternal Mortality – The contribution of the right to the highest attainable standard of health. Human Rights Centre. University of Essex. p.7
4. Stephanie Urdang, New drive to save the lives of mothers, infants: Commitment, money and innovation can reduce high mortality rates, AfricaRenewal, January 2010, p.6
5. Angela Horn, What if you have a post-partum haemorrhage after a home birth? What if the midwife isn't there? http://www.homebirth.org.uk/pph.htm
6. Errol R. Alden, et al. Helping Babies BreatheSM: Learner Workbook. 2010. p.12
7. Jennifer Blum, et al. Treatment of post-partum haemorrhage with sublingual misoprostol versus oxytocin in women receiving prophylactic oxytocin: a double-blind, randomised, non-inferiority trial, The Lancet, Volume 375, Issue 9710, Pages 217-223, 16 January 2010
8. Nafissatou Diop, Abandoning Female Genital Mutilation/Cutting: Key steps to bring the practice to a quicker end, Monday Developments Magazine. July, 2011. p.19
9. Liljestrand J, Rathavy T, Moore J, Savy B. Critical components of birthing care in Cambodian health facilities: the quality of Active management of third stage of labor (AMTSL) and of eclampsia management. ACCESS, Phnom Penh, p.11
10. Justin C Konje and Oladapo A Ladipo. Nutrition and obstructed labor. American Journal of Clinical Nutrition, Vol. 72, No. 1, 291S-297S, July 2000. © 2000. American Society for Clinical Nutrition
11. Justin C Konje and Oladapo A Ladipo. Nutrition and obstructed labor. American Journal of Clinical Nutrition, Vol. 72, No. 1, 291S-297S, July 2000. © 2000. American Society for Clinical Nutrition
12. UNICEF. Equality, development and peace; May, 2000. p. 19
13. Stephanie Urdang, New drive to save the lives of mothers, infants: Commitment, money and innovation can reduce high mortality rates, AfricaRenewal, January 2010, p.6
14. UNICEF. Equality, development and peace; May, 2000. p.23
15. (Social Summit +5: 56)
16. UNICEF. Equality, development and peace; May, 2000. p. 5
17. Amina P. Alio, et al. Addressing Policy Barriers to Paternal Involvement During Pregnancy, Maternal and Child Health Journal.
18. Kerstin Erlandsson and Elisabet Häggström-Nordin. Prenatal Parental Education From the Perspective of Fathers With Experience as Primary Caregiver Immediately Following Birth: A Phenomenographic Study. The Journal of Perinatal Education. Winter 2010, Volume 19, Number 1. pp.19-20
19. UN forum on reproductive health in protracted crises kicks off in Spain. 28 September 2009. http://www.un.org/apps/news/story.asp?NewsID=32306&Cr=reproductive+health&Cr1=.

Beyond Zero – Kenya

Reported by Susan Roylance

The *Beyond Zero* program in Kenya is a wonderful example of a new program that focuses on maternal, newborn and child health – as well as HIV control. The First Lady, Margaret Kenyatta, has provided the leadership to promote health interventions to:

1. Improve access to HIV care and treatment,
2. Reduce maternal and newborn deaths,
3. Increase child survival and development, and
4. Promote leadership and accountability at the family, community, county and national levels for full implementation of HIV, maternal and child health commitments.[1]

The following chart shows the goals of the program:[2]

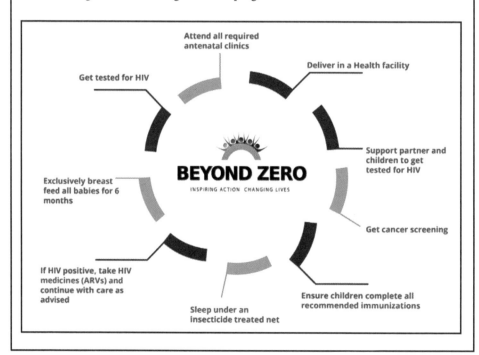

BEST PRACTICES

To achieve these goals, the First Lady provided amazing leadership to gather the resources needed to purchase mobile health clinics for the 47 counties of Kenya.

James W. Macharia, former Cabinet Secretary for Health, explained: "Through these mobile clinics, women will no longer need to travel long distances to health centers, and will also eliminate the transport cost barrier which are major contributors for women giving birth at home with unskilled delivery."[3]

In 2013, when the program began, only 44% of Kenyan women delivered under the supervision of a skilled birth attendant, and women in rural areas were more than twice as likely to deliver at home. The maternal mortality rate was 488 deaths per 100,000 live births.

"No woman should die while giving life"

"No woman should die while giving life," said First Lady Margaret Kenyatta. "Child birth should be a joyous moment for families and communities . . . . It is our collective responsibility to ensure that this does not happen.[4]

She began the focus by running in marathons "to raise money to eradicate maternal and infant mortality." Kenya is well known for their champion marathon runners, and she ran alongside marathon greats Douglas Wakiihuri, Tegla Loroupe and Catherine Ndereba. This effort garnered considerable national and international attention to her Beyond Zero program. She said: "We run to keep mothers and newborns alive, we run because every mother should be able to hold her baby and take her baby home and that baby should live to be strong and have many more birthdays."[5]

As the first lady trained and participated in marathons, her Beyond Zero program gained greater attention, and many partnerships developed – to provide the funds for mobile clinics in the remote areas of Kenya.

Mobile health clinics

On the 24th of May 2016, the 40th mobile clinic was delivered in Lamu county. The clinic was donated by Britam, a British-American investments company, with offices in Nairobi, Kenya. (*Update*: On August 17th the 46th clinic was delivered in Muranga county.) This is a premier example of public/private partnerships to achieve the SDG goals.

Each mobile clinic has four partitions:

1. Common area at the entrance,
2. Maternal consultation/procedure room,
3. Pediatric consultation/procedure room, and
4. Laboratory/pharmacy area.[6]

BEST PRACTICES

Full participation and involvement of men

In addition to providing important medical services, each clinic has become a focal point for teaching good family medical practices. Beyond Zero also includes "highlighting the importance of a holistic focus at families ensuring the full participation and involvement of men."[7] The following picture shows a outreach campaign for male participation in Garbatulla, Isiolo county, in February of 2015.

Maternal health training for men

[R]esearch and experience reveal that men play a key role in determining women's access to critical health services. This includes their role in antenatal and postpartum care through mechanisms such as determining the availability of transport for women to reach a clinic, decision on referral to a higher-level facility, prevention of mother-to-child transmission of HIV, ensuring good nutrition and reducing workload during pregnancy, assistance with birth preparations and emotional support, encouragement and support for good infant nutrition, including early and exclusive breastfeeding and childhood immunization.[7]

This is a wonderful example of using "family capital" to achieve an important Sustainable Development Goal (Targets 3.1 and 3.2 of SDG 3).

Healthy children build a better future

In a special celebration at the delivery of the 40th mobile clinic in Lamu County,

BEST PRACTICES

Her Excellency Margaret Kenyatta commented:

> I truly believe that health is the bedrock of everything good we want to see in this county, and in our country's economic growth, peace, unity and security. Healthy people are more innovative, and more productive people. Healthy citizens can start and sustain a profitable business. Strong, healthy women can serve their families better, invest more in raising moral children, and engage in economic activities more effectively. Healthy children can read, study, learn, dream and hope, and they are more likely to build a better future for us.[8]

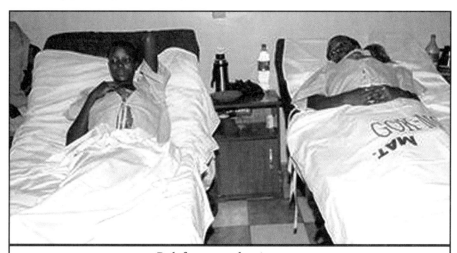

Beds for maternal patient care.

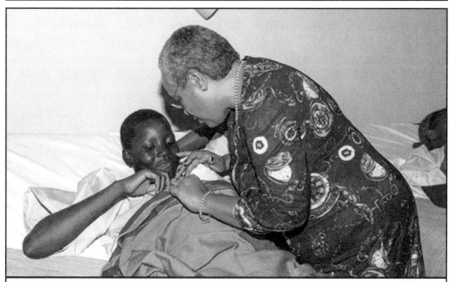

Her Excellency Margaret Kenyatta visiting with a new mother and discussing the kangaroo principle.

BEST PRACTICES

Photos provided by the Office of the First Lady, Kenya, and from the official Facebook website.

Endnotes

1. "Beyond Zero Campaign, Technical Report: 2014-2015," Office of the First Lady, Republic of Kenya, page 36.
2. Ibid, page 21.
3. Macharia, James W., Beyond Zero, Republic of Kenya, page 12.
4. Ibid, page 9.
5. "Unique resource mobilization efforts," Beyond Zero Campaign, Technical Report: 2014-2015, page 22, Office of the First Lady, Republic of Kenya.
6. "Appropriate design and specification of mobile clinics," Beyond Zero Campaign, Technical Report: 2014-2015, page 24, Office of the First Lady, Republic of Kenya.
7. "Critical role of male involvement as a driver to sustaining health outcomes," Beyond Zero Campaign, Technical Report: 2014-2015, page 13, Office of the First Lady, Republic of Kenya.
8. "Speech by Her Excellency Margaret Kenyatta," Facebook, Office of the First Lady, 24 May, 2016. https://m.facebook.com/OfficeoftheFirstLadyofKenya/posts/1128936547163721

The Role of Attachment in the Family for Achieving the Sustainable Development Goals

Chelsey A. Vincent, LMSW

The research and application of attachment theory has continued to develop and is relevant to achieving the Sustainable Development Goals, particularly in relation to the following objectives:

Goal 3: Ensuring healthy lives and promote the well-being for all at all ages

Target 4.2: By 2030, ensure that all girls and boys have access to quality early childhood development, care and pre-primary education so that they are ready for primary education

Paragraph 25 (2030 Agenda): We will strive to provide children and youth with a nurturing environment for the full realization of their rights and capabilities, helping our countries to reap the demographic dividend, including through safe schools, and cohesive communities and families.

Paragraph 26 (2030 Agenda): To promote physical and mental health and well-being, and to extend life expectancy for all. . . .We are committed to the prevention and treatment of non-communicable diseases, including behavioral, developmental and neurological disorders, which constitute a major challenge for sustainable development.

Attachment impacts the achievement of these goals in four main ways:

1. Every person has attachment patterns that impact their overall well-being throughout their lifespan.
2. Attachment patterns contribute to the strength or weakness of individuals, families and communities, and their ability to face challenges and meet goals.
3. Parents are the primary teachers in their children's lives and the attachments they create with their children will impact their brain development and readiness for learning and development now and in the future.
4. Secure attachment can reduce and prevent many non-organic mental and physical diseases and disorders, as well as mitigate the impact of diseases and disorders when they occur.

When preparing and implementing policy regarding the nurturing and protection of children, we must view each through an attachment lens to completely understand why the most important nurturing happens within the family, what happens when it goes awry, and how to support this vital function in society.

What is attachment?

Attachment is a biological process that is wired into our brains for survival and social-ization (Bowlby, 1958, 1988; Perry, 1999). This survival mechanism means we re-spond to threats and disruptions to attachment as a matter of life or death (Panksepp, 1998). This fundamental need motivates individuals to create emotional connections, known as bonds or attachments, with important people in their lives. In multiple ex-periments, researchers found that emotional nurturance was just as important as phys-ical nurturance and that the impact of emotional starvation was as devastating as physical starvation (Bowlby, 1988).

Attachment patterns fall into two distinct categories: secure and insecure. It is im-portant to note that all of these attachment patterns exist on a continuum with secure or insecure patterns manifesting in varying degrees. Attachment patterns are influ-enced over the lifespan, but are most impressionable in the first year. They are prima-rily based on interactions with caregivers, e.g. mother and father, and how they respond to emotional and physical needs. Every child sends out attachment cues to their par-ents and the parents' attunement (ability to understand and appropriately respond) to these cues determines the security or insecurity of the bond. These patterns become the framework for interaction with others and often become intergenerational.

What is secure attachment?

Secure attachment is the optimal pattern for the overall well-being of an individual. It is most effectively achieved within the context of a stable family unit. Secure attachment is a feeling of safety in relationships with others. During early development children begin to formulate ideas about themselves and those around them. This means knowing that they are loved, valued and that they can depend on family members to respond in ways that recognize their emotional needs as human beings – and that close relationships are safe and rewarding. This happens through a variety of positive experiences and inter-actions such as: touching, kissing, eye contact, talking, playing, singing and rocking.

Securely attached children begin to develop resilience and emotional regulation, meaning the ability to understand and navigate emotions with healthy coping mech-anisms. These skills contribute to increased functioning and well-being over the lifes-pan. Securely attached families provide a protective factor for the nurturing of children and the health of communities. When a child develops a secure attachment with his or her parent, they have a safe base from which they can begin to explore their world and focus on important developmental milestones (Bowlby, 1988).

The development of secure attachment can be undermined in many ways that will be discussed later. One specific policy concern regarding attachment is how children are affected when they grow up in chaotic systems both inside and outside of the family. However, it is important to note that some of the challenges faced by a child growing up in an externally chaotic system can be mitigated by a securely attached family.

What is insecure attachment?

Insecure attachment falls into the subcategories of: avoidant, ambivalent/resistant and disorganized attachment (Ainsworth, et al, 1978). The manifestation of insecure attachment patterns is the result of inconsistent or negligent caregiving, particularly a lack of emotional attunement. Extreme cases of insecure attachment can be found in orphanages or other institutions. Instances of failure to thrive can be a result of insecure attachment (Altimer, et al., 1985; Benoit, et al., 1989; Ward, et al., 2000).

Other examples of insecure attachment manifesting are instances when children have been removed from the parent because of neglect or abuse. However, there are many less extreme conditions under which insecure patterns may arise, such as: parents that are not emotionally attuned to their children; families that have suffered divorce, separation, incarceration or death of a loved one, families where one or both parent's attachment patterns are insecure; or where there is substance abuse and addiction in the home. These can produce negative interactions and experiences that undermine the emotional bonds between children and parents. These experiences may result in attachment traumas, which undermine the development of the child. Under these circumstances, negative relational and behavioral patterns can emerge that can benefit from interventions, such as: neurobiological and attachment informed therapy, community outreach and child welfare involvement.

Like secure attachment, insecure patterns impact the development of individuals in significant ways in terms of how they view themselves and the world, e.g: I am not important; I am unlovable; I cannot trust others; interpersonal relationships are scary or hurtful; I do not know what to expect from those around me. Emotional regulation in children and adults with insecure attachment patterns is hampered and coping mechanisms may be ineffective or harmful, including: addiction, promiscuity, avoidance of intimacy, abuse and aggressive behaviors (Perry, 1999). Furthermore, those with insecure attachment patterns resulting from adverse childhood experiences are at an increased risk of developing mental and physical health conditions and disorders (Anda, et al., 2006).

Why is it important?

Many issues associated with the decay of communities, particularly urban communities, are symptoms of decaying families. Society is a series of social connections which reflects the attachment patterns individuals develop within the family.

Photo: "La nueva de la familia" by Andrés Nieto Porras from Palma de Mallorca, España

Healthy attachments lead to: the secure bond between parents, the rearing of competent children and the desire to perpetuate the welfare of humanity. From prenatal gestation to death, experiences in the family become the model for how to navigate the world.

Furthermore, when children go through traumatic experiences, one of the most important predictors of how they will overcome that experience is the response of their caregiver(s) (Perry & Dobson, 2010). Children with the most resilience are those with secure attachments to their parents or other caregivers. Overall, individuals and families with more secure attachments have greater resilience and are more confident in their ability to overcome adversity.

Moreover, a child's early attachment experiences with parents and caregivers impacts the neurological development of the brain (Perry, et al., 1995; Perry, 1999). These interactions create neural pathways in the brainstem and limbic systems (emotional center of the brain) which impact the organization of other brain lobes, including the prefrontal lobe, which is responsible for vital functions such as: judgment, personality, impulse control and decision making (Perry, 2009). In short, secure attachment creates a stronger neural basis for overall brain development resulting in higher measurements in other aspects of functioning and well-being as previously outlined, while brain development in children and adults with insecure attachments puts them at a higher risk for negative outcomes (Gaskill & Perry, 2012). Thus the crucial need to support secure attachments is clear in regard to sustainable development and the nurturing of the child.

How do we promote healthy, secure attachment in families, particularly in vulnerable families and communities?

The basis of secure attachment is an attuned parent-child relationship, meaning a parent recognizes, validates and lovingly responds to a child's emotions and needs rather than ignoring, criticizing, diminishing or overreacting. It also requires respect for the child's growth and age-appropriate autonomy. These ideas work best when implemented with this in mind.

Promote the development of enriching environments

Creating developmentally stimulating activities coupled with nurturing relationships allows children to develop a sense of security and predictability. This secure base allows children to focus on achieving their developmental milestones.

1. Regularly eating meals as a family.

2. Weekly family gatherings without electronics so that important attachment behaviors can occur such as eye contact and being mentally and emotionally present with each other. These gatherings can include playing games, reading aloud, singing songs, cooking together, making a craft. Encourage each family member to plan the weekly activities.

3. Encouraging parents to enter into the child's world through non-electronic interactive play. It can be as simple as getting down on the floor to be at the same level as the child. This makes the child feel like they have more access to the parent, thus encouraging engagement.

4. Parental involvement in children's academics, parent-school organizations and extracurricular activities.

5. As children grow and gain more independence, the parents and child can hold monthly councils to discuss the needs, goals, challenges and dreams of the child. These collaborative discussions can help parents stay involved with their child and help the child feel supported by the parent.

6. Use mistakes to teach, opposed to responding in a punitive manner.

Encourage families to share personal stories with their children

Children that know their story of their family stories have a greater sense of self (Bohanek, et al., 2006). Ideas to create a family narrative include:

1. Talk to children about how their parents met, what parents' childhoods were like, what their grandparents or great-grandparents were like, where their family originates from, and the story of how they made it to where they are.

2. Help children process their emotions while finding strength and meaning behind their personal stories and family histories. Even difficult stories can help children develop resilience by knowing that their ancestors were able to overcome adversity.

3. Carry on family traditions or begin new traditions. Traditions create a sense of stability and continuity for children by linking the past and the future.

Photo by Robert Whitehead

4. Reflect on past events and situations to help children navigate their current challenges.

Work with families in hospitals and other community settings

Settings such as hospitals, school, church, and community centers can help provide psychological and developmental education about attachment needs and cues.

1. Promote measures that increase the time mother and father spend with their child just after birth and throughout the critical development period for attachment (birth to one year) and beyond.

2. Parent-child attachment groups help parents understand the key components of developing secure attachments with their children under the guidance of clinicians and other trained professionals.

3. Encourage parents' investment in their children's social and emotional development with socio-emotional groups for children and families to begin to understand how emotions work and how to navigate emotional conflicts within the family by teaching the Connection-Break-Repair model.

   a. Education on how socio-emotional development can enhance parents' ability to engage with their children to promote secure attachments.

   b. Help families set healthy boundaries to support the child's autonomy, while providing parameters to keep children safe, both physically and emotionally.

Promote policy that strives to keep families intact

Protect the integrity of stable families and support struggling families. To protect vulnerable children we must support and strengthen their current family arrangements or move them into stable family units when attachment security is not attainable..

1. Use of rituals and traditions to create a sense of unity and continuity.

2. Support family-centered time and activities.

Provide therapy and support for at-risk families and children

This requires attachment-based, neurologically-informed clinical interventions to confront attachment issues and trauma. For highly vulnerable families, in-home services provide more continuity of services.

Support and advocate for stable marriages

1. The security of the parents' relationship will influence the child's attachment security and create the model for the child's future intimate relationships.

2. Use an attachment framework to understand and treat intimate partner violence in the family.

Conclusion

When constructing and implementing policy affecting children and families it is crucial to be aware of attachment, particularly in communities where the family is at risk. The best resource for the nurturing and development of children is healthy families. Whether or not one is informed about attachment, it is continually at play in families and communities. That attachment, which holds power to do good, can have equally devastating power when it is not supported, as evident in many communities where families are disintegrating. If the Sustainable Development Goals are to be achieved, secure attachment in the natural and fundamental institution of the family must be supported.

References

Ainsworth, M. D. S., Blehar, M. C., Waters, E., & Wall, S. (1978). *Patterns of attachment: A psychological study of the strange situation.* Hillsdale, NJ: Erlbaum.

Allen, J. P., Marsh, P., McFarland, C., McElhaney, K. B., Land, D. J.; Jodl, K. M., & Peck, S. (2002). Attachment and autonomy as predictors of the development of social skills and delinquency during mid-adolescence. *Journal of Consulting and Clinical Psychology*, Vol 70(1), 56-66. doi.org/10.1037/0022-006X.70.1.56

Altemeier, W., O'Connor, S. M., Sherrod, K. B., & Vietze, P. M. (1985). Prospective study of antecedents for nonorganic failure to thrive. *Journal of Pediatrics*, 106, 360–365.

Anda, R.F., Felitti, R.F., Walker, J., Whitfield, C., Bremner, D.J., Perry, B.D., Dube, S.R., Giles, W.G. (2006). The enduring effects of childhood abuse and related experiences: a convergence of evidence from neurobiology and epidemiology. *European Archives of Psychiatric and Clinical Neuroscience*, 256 (3) 174 – 186.

Benoit, D., Zeanah, C. H., & Barton, M. (1989). Maternal attachment disturbances and failure to thrive. *Infant Mental Health Journal*, 10, 185–202.

Bohanek J.G. , Marin K.A., Fivush R, Duke M. P. (2006). Family narrative interaction and children's sense of self. Family Process, 45(1) pp 39-54

Bowlby, J. (1958). The nature of the child's tie to his mother. *International Journal of Psycho-Analysis*, 23, 19-52, 107-127

Bowlby, J. (1988). *A secure base: Parent child attachment and healthy human development.* London, England: Basic Books.

Gaskill. R. L., & Perry, B.D. (2012). "Child sexual abuse, traumatic experiences and their effect on the developing brain." In Goodyear-Brown, P. (Ed.), *Handbook of child sexual abuse: Identification, assessment and treatment.* (pp. 29-49). New York: Wiley.

Panksepp, J.. (1998). *Affective neuroscience: The foundations of animal and human emotions.* New York: Oxford University Press.

Perry, B. D., Pollard, R. A., & Blakley, T. L., et al. (1995). "Childhood trauma, the neurobiology of adaptation and use-dependent development of the brain: How states become traits." *Infant Mental Health Journal*, 16, 271-291.

Perry, B.D. (1999). *Bonding and attachment in maltreated children: Consequences of emotional neglect in childhood.* CTA Parent and Caregiver Education Series 1(3). Child Trauma Academy Press.

Perry, B.D. (2005). *Maltreatment and the developing child: How early childhood experience shapes child and culture.* The Inaugural Margaret McCain lecture (abstracted); McCain Lecture series, The Centre for Children and Families in the Justice System, London, ON.

Perry, B. D. (2009). Examining child maltreatment through a neurodevelopmental lens: Clinical applications of the neurosequential model of therapeutics. *Journal of Loss and Trauma*, 14, 240–255. DOI:10.1080/15325020903004350

Perry, B.D., & Dobson, C. (2010). The role of healthy relational interactions in buffering the impact of childhood trauma. In Gil, E. (Ed), *Working with Children to Heal Interpersonal Trauma: The Power of Play.* Guilford Press, New York.

Perry, B.D. (2014). *How trauma affects child brain development* [Radio broadcast]. KUNM, NPR Affiliate Retrieved from http://kunm.org/post/how-trauma-affects-child-brain-development

Rankin, J. H., & Kern, R. (1994), Parental attachments and delinquency. *Criminology*, 32, 495–515. doi: 10.1111/j.1745-9125.1994.tb01163.x

Ward, M. J., Lee, S. S., & Lipper, E. G. (2000). Failure to thrive is associated with disorganized infant-mother attachment and unresolved maternal attachment. *Infant Mental Health Journal*, 21(6), 438-442.

Uchino, Bert. (2009). "Social Support and Physical Health: Understanding the health consequences of relationships." *Perspectives on Psychological Science* 4(3), 236-255.

Parents as First Educators of Health

Christine de Marcellus Vollmer

The situation today

Generations that constantly renew themselves are produced in families. This book is dedicated to the science of maximizing the synergies found in the family unit which make family the best producer of Human Capital.

The family unit today is more integrated and interdependent with society as a whole than in former times, which brings great advantages and also difficulties, as media, authoritarian governments and ideologies tend to interfere – weakening family structure.

What is needed, then, is to empower parents in their vital role as first educators of the new generation of citizens by bringing them the latest knowledge of anthropology, psychology, brain development and associated science in a way that is practical and effective for raising their children in a manner that will result in their sexual and reproductive responsibility and health. So much is known today about the development of children and adolescents and the risks to them of incomplete or incorrect information that this matter is of extreme urgency.

A method for our time

The mission of the foundation that I preside over is 1) to examine: data, research and studies of the great minds of the last century in this area, and 2) to develop a method of character formation and sex education that can be used effectively by parents, families and schools.

The International Conference on Population and Development in Cairo recognized in paragraph 7.3 of the Programme of Action, that:

> . . . full attention should be given to the promotion of mutually respectful and equitable gender relations and particularly to meeting the educational and service needs of adolescents to enable them to deal in a positive and responsible way with their sexuality.

At Cairo+5 (73-c) the Development Goals were further developed to demand programs which:

. . . should include support mechanisms for the education and counselling of adolescents in the areas of gender relations and equality, violence against adolescents, responsible sexual behaviour, responsible family planning practices, family life, reproductive health, sexually transmitted diseases, HIV infection and AIDS prevention (Programme of Action, para. 7.47).

In the Platform for Action of the Fourth World Conference on Women (para 267), the firm recommendation was made to parents and those responsible for children that the:

. . . rights and duties of parents and legal guardians to provide, in a manner consistent with the evolving capacities of the child, appropriate direction and guidance in the exercise by the child of the rights recognized in the Convention on the Rights of the Child, and in conformity with the Convention on the Elimination of All Forms of Discrimination against Women. In all actions concerning children, the best interests of the child shall be a primary consideration. Support should be given to integral sexual education for young people with parental support and guidance that stresses the responsibility of males for their own sexuality and fertility and that help them exercise their responsibilities.

Although our research and development of a suitable program for families and schools was already well under way, this urging by the United Nations gave us added impetus. The essence of our program is to provide a way to guide boys, girls and adolescents in the formation of their individual character, affectivity and sexuality in order to become persons of integrity and success in their private, educational and community lives. A key phrase in the Beijing document cited above is "rights and duties of parents and legal guardians to provide, in a manner consistent with the evolving capacities of the child." This, of course, precludes exposure to explicit sexual information during the latency period so well described in the psychiatric literature and obliges us to base our pedagogy firmly upon the natural stages of development of children and adolescents, and requires a firm grounding in the knowledge of brain and hormonal development and their psychological manifestations.

The international and interdisciplinary group developing this program launched it in the year 2000 and has since offered this to families and schools in countries all over the world to fulfil the exhortation from Cairo+5 which says (para 73-d):

Acknowledge and promote the central role of families, parents and other legal guardians in educating their children and shaping their attitudes, and ensure that parents and persons with legal responsibilities are educated about and involved in providing sexual and reproductive health information, in a manner consistent with the evolving capacities of adolescents, so that they can fulfil their rights and responsibilities towards adolescents.

Basic structure for a new and effective pedagogy

This comprehensive program, *Alive to the World*, has now completed 15 years of successful use in 15 countries of Latin America and is spreading quickly. *Alive to the*

World is now distributed by publishers in Argentina, Chile, Peru, Ecuador, Mexico, El Salvador, the United Kingdom (in English), Poland (in Polish) and the Republic of South Korea (in Korean). Editions are in preparation in France, Hungary, Romania, Germany and Croatia.

The success and great demand for this program is due to the fact that it is faithful to the development of the children and adolescents it was designed to serve. The vehicle for the material is a continuous story of a group of children as they grow and develop in their school, sports, family and community. It is the faithfulness to the stages of human development and the universality of the situations treated in the story that makes the students love these books so much.

The 13 books, K-12, require only 45 minutes per week, during 30 weeks of the school year, but accompany the reader continually by stimulating his or her logic and reasoning about situations or conflicts that every person comes across as they grow up. From learning to enjoy fair play and team spirit, through respect for the property of others, to comprehending the confusing emotions of puberty with its changing attitudes and relationships, values are identified and understood. The story as a pedagogical device is wonderful for several important reasons:

- Many character-types can be displayed, so avoiding stereotyping and encouraging the appreciation of variety in personalities and talents.
- The situations faced by the real-life persons can be observed and learned in third person through the book characters, thus avoiding invasive attention.
- Many models can be observed and conclusions drawn. The varied adult masculine models scattered through the books are particularly interesting to the readers who are boys.
- Leadership and perseverance can be observed in action, rather than as a difficult list of qualities.
- Romances of very different types can be observed with no value judgements pronounced, but realities understood about sincerity, real friendship and dependency problems.

"Flourishing" and the keys to success in life

Humility, or the realistic acceptance of who we are and what our talents and our weaknesses are, is a cornerstone of the pedagogy in *Alive to the World*. The Virtuous Circle of Humility is demonstrated early on by the simple example of accepting advice in learning a sport. This Virtuous Circle and its corollary, the Vicious Circle of Arrogance, leading to low self-worth and more boasting, are useful when applied at several stages of development, as is the Golden Rule of "doing to others as one would like them to do to one." These are transversal themes that all children and adolescents understand and can apply with no sense of shame or blame.

Perseverance, resilience, teamwork, fair play, reciprocity, justice and understanding the situation of others, and how these qualities are attained, are demonstrated subtly but constantly in the idioms of each age group in such a way that all students feel that to live these virtues is possible, in fact their right and goal.

Various research groups have confirmed the need to learn these virtues, such as University of Pennsylvania researchers Martin Seligman and Angela Duckworth, through their in-depth longitudinal study of success.[1] Their study was conducted at all socio-economic levels and identified the values leading to success at all levels. These were neither intelligence nor meticulousness, but were mainly skills which can and should be learned. The most important of these were grit and gratitude. Grit, or that winning combination of resilience and perseverance, is sometimes inborn, but is mainly learned. Grit is often learned through sports and other competitive activities, if properly guided. Gratitude is learned mainly by example and helped by explanation. Hope is another of Seligman and Duckworth's key values, along with social skills. These and others are easily and naturally taught through a continuous story like *Alive to the World*.

For those interested, there are many other researchers who have determined the need for an effective new pedagogy for values and character education.[2]

Significance and happiness

Much has been written about raising self-esteem, but the definitive word on this is from Viktor Frankl in *Man's Search for Meaning*, one of the world's ten most-published books according to the Library of Congress. According to this neurologist, psychiatrist, concentration-camp survivor, great teacher and therapist, the greatest underlying desire of the human heart is to have a sense of significance: to feel that his or her life has meaning and worth.

Frankl's deep and rich experience, not only in the concentration camps but in his long career helping patients, proved to him that it is altruism, or the reaching out towards others or working for a cause or goal bigger than oneself, that creates that sense of worth that all men and women need and want. Frankl described happiness as "the by-product of worthwhile actions." The selfish search for happiness only brings a desire for more and ultimately brings frustration, while the sense of self-worth escapes because the subconscious understands the non-transcendence of self-serving.

Without weighing down students with academic considerations such as these, the story does show the practice and benefits of altruistic behavior, lifting the reader to a plane where the natural ambition to be someone of worth, a useful member of the team or group, an individual who contributes, can be visualized and understood. The characters in the story are none of them perfect, but each strives to overcome shortcomings which are very human.

Sexual and family responsibility

Once the values and skills of generosity, reciprocity, consideration and integrity have been lived and understood through the story in the lower grades, and the students are conversant and familiar with the workings of these and other virtues, increasingly appreciating them in others and in themselves, they can apply them to their new feelings and relationships as they enter adolescence.

The new attitudes to parents and to authority, and new feelings about girls and boys, are easily understood in the light of what has been learned before. Of course, as all parents know, difficulties and a new "deafness" often appear. These cases appear also in the story, which helps these teenagers to see themselves as others see them when being rebellious, difficult or rude. More importantly, attraction with all its complications, which starts to appear in the story, gives the reader a varied mirror in which to see many of the things he or she is feeling.

Teachers and parents

One of the key tools of the *Alive to the World* program is, of course, the series of 13 textbooks. These were designed originally for use in schools and have 13 teacher guides. There is one teacher guide for each level, containing the objectives, pedagogical indications, activities and points for discussion for each chapter of the student text. It is a flexible tool that teachers appreciate as it saves them the time of preparing the class.

Naturally this applies to parents giving this course at home. For those children who are receiving it at school there is some simple material for the parents to keep them abreast of the values being learnt at school.

The good news

The wonderful news that *Alive to the World* is producing is that no matter the circumstances that surround a child, that child wants to be a worthwhile person and respected as such. This is a fundamental characteristic with which humans are born. What occurs is that too frequently the environment urges anti-social behavior. This can be due to family breakdown, an overly materialistic milieu, neighborhood violence or simply too much violent and sex-filled TV viewing. These circumstances tend to overlay the underlying desire to be positive, and an effort to achieve significance is sought in the wrong place.

Giving children and adolescents real knowledge about how to be strong, worthwhile people liberates them to be themselves. It gives them the freedom to refuse the lures of sex and drugs. The skills of negotiation and decision-making which are needed for this are the application of some of the values learnt and are indispensable to acquire at this age as well, affording the students great enjoyment at the same time.

The three levels of the person

In order to be effective in attaining the desired goal of helping children and adolescents to be their best selves and fulfill their potential, we must target the whole person. In this way we lead them to integrate the three levels of the person. These are, of course, the spiritual (the intelligence and the will), the emotional and the physical (or corporal) level. Specialists of character education, such as Thomas Likona call this "teaching the Head, Heart and Hand."[3] These levels of education have also been described as stimulating Knowledge, Motivation and Skills. If these three levels are not well aligned, the decisions and goals of the intelligence are often frustrated by emotional interference.

This new method of teaching, used by *Alive to the World*, is called the "Pedagogy of Integration of the Human Person,"[4] and is based on the vision of the person as an integral whole, who in order to be happy must have an inner balance. This balance is found when the student follows a path starting with the discovery of what is best, using good reasoning in order to understand his or her reality. All lesson plans include discussion, with an emphasis on logic and critical thinking, so each student can discover for him or herself, in the clearest manner, the way to happiness.

Understanding is not enough, however, and the *Alive to the World* program helps them to energize this reality with their passion, their particular interests, their deepest feelings and motivations. We know that this emotional force, or energy, is key and if we do not help them to channel it towards positive goals, not only the goals will not be attained, but that energy will become an obstacle as it is directed toward other activities. So, rather than attempting to stifle the strong feelings of our children and adolescents, the aim is to help them apply their passion to the realistic objectives they propose for themselves.

Of course, we are also aware that understanding and having a passion for something is not enough: action is necessary. Our Pedagogy of Integration is not complete if it does not equip the student to take the steps which lead to success, each in his or her way. In fact, we are convinced that inner balance is attained when people act according to what they understand to be the best for them and to which they are fully committed.

It is important to remember that understanding and integration of the universally accepted virtues, such as: loyalty, generosity, courage, solidarity and forgiveness are indispensable in this process, in view of the undeniable human need to feel self-worth.

The Pedagogy of the Integration of the Human Person, therefore, is based upon a triple base of Understanding, Feeling and Action, reflecting the three levels of the human person, and which is open to continual feedback, correction and improvement. Each level is indispensable and their development is key.

A universal need

The phenomenal success of this program is due to the fact that all children are born with a huge desire to learn. The years of asking "Why?," of curiosity, experimentation, questions and exploration are the years when the truths about human socialization need to be taught as carefully as their letters and numbers, and they enjoy this learning even more. The succeeding years of application of these facts only need guidance so these truths can be properly applied, as the young people begin to understand their potential and plot their path. Young people want the truth, and want to rise to challenges. These challenges must be offered to them with the tools to deal with them and these tools are to be discovered in the story of Charles and Alice and their large and varied group of friends.

Difficult situations

A mention here is in order in reference to the increasing number of areas of urban violence. *Alive to the World* is recently involved in experiments in this type of situation in several countries. The results have been extraordinarily encouraging. School violence is sharply reduced, truancy and even teen pregnancy are also reduced. The reason seems to be twofold:

- The students begin to see their own potential and acquire a positive attitude about themselves,
- The boys begin to reflect the models proffered in the story.

There is no doubt that one of the problems that the young face is the constant portrayal of violence and negative models of behavior. This, added to the frequent absence of a loving father, is the main contributing factor of urban problems. What is so encouraging is to see that positive models of interaction with situations, given without judgement or stereotyping, liberates the young to choose to act in positive ways, and this brings them great satisfaction.

Conclusion

Our world clamors for a return to values. This explains the international spread of *Alive to the World*, because everywhere there is an awareness of the need to teach integrity where materialism and cultural change have eroded the values which were universally known to be basic to human coexistence. The ills which the SDGs aspire to remedy, particularly those pertaining to sex and violence, can only be remedied through understanding the human person and comprehending the importance of respect, integrity and positive behavior. Reproductive matters must be undergirded by respect for every human life, a consciousness of the dignity of every individual, and a true sense of responsibility within each person for themselves, for those near them, and for the future generations. These will only be achieved when education in values becomes generalized, combined with a spirit of solidarity. The other SDGs, not dealt with in this paper, will also be successfully addressed to the degree that the next generation is formed as integrated, altruistic and motivated women and men.

Endnotes

1. Cfr. DUCKWORTH, A. L., QUINN, P. D., & SELIGMAN, M.E.P. (2009). Positive predictors of teacher effectiveness. Journal of Positive Psychology, 19, 540-547.

2. Cfr. BERKOWITZ, M. W.; BIER, M. C., What works in character education: A report for policy makers and opinion leaders, Character Education Partnership, Washington, DC, 2005; LAPSLEY, D.K. y NARVAEZ, D., "Character Education," En W. DAMON, R.M. LERNER, K.A. REN-NINGER y I.E. SIGEL (eds.), Handbook of child psychology, Hoboken, N.J., John Wiley & Sons, 2006; LICKONA, T.; DAVIDSON, M., A Report to the Nation: Smart & Good High Schools. Integrating Excellence and Ethics for Success in School, Work, and Beyond, Center for the 4th and 5th Rs (Respect and Responsibility), State University of New York College at Cortland - Character Education Partnership, Washington, D.C., 2005; LICKONA, T., "Educating for Character in the Sexual Domain," Second International Congress on Education in Love, Sex, and Life Manila, Philippines November 20, 2007.; NARVAEZ, D., "Integrative Ethical Education," En M. KILLEN y J.G. SMETANA (eds.), Handbook of Moral Development, Mahwah, NJ, Lawrence Erlbaum Associates, 2006.; PARK, N., "Positive Development: Realizing the Potential of Youth: Character Strengths and Positive Youth Development," Social Science, The Annals of The American Academy of Political and, Social Science, vol. 591, 2004, pp. 40; SEMETSKY, I., "Towards and Ethics of Integration in Education," International research handbook on values education and student wellbeing, Springer, New York, 2010; SALLS, H. S., Character education: transforming values into virtue, University Press of America, Lanham, 2007; SOMMERS, C., "How Moral Education Is Finding Its Way Back into America's Schools," En W. DAMON (ed.), Bringing in a New Era in Character Education, Stanford, Calif., Hoover Institution Press, 2002. YEAGER, J. M.; FISHER, S. W. y SHEARON, D. N., Smart strengths: a parent-teacher-coach guide to building character, resilience and relationships in youth, Kravis, Putnam Valley, New York, 2011.

3. Cfr. LIKONA, T. Character matters: how to help our children develop good judgment, integrity, and other essential virtues, Simon & Schuster, New York, 2004.

4. Cfr. BELTRAMO, C. La Pedagogía de la Integración de la Persona Humana, Tesis doctoral. Universidad de Navarra, Pamplona, 2013.

An Holistic Approach to Sex Education – as Part of Sustainable Development

Louise Kirk

One of the curiosities of the modern approach to sex education is that its provision is regarded as a catch-all solution to many problems, but its overall sense of direction and best method of delivery is rarely discussed. It is as though just providing the subject saves the child, which is self-evidently not true. What is taught, and how it is taught, is even more important in this sensitive subject than if it is taught at all.

Parents as the first and best educators in sexual matters

In sex education, how you teach is part of what you teach. Much of a child's sexual education is already picked up within the family from example and observation. However, there are aspects to puberty, or the "becoming able to procreate," which are not self-explanatory. Children have a right to hear about a subject so intimate and potentially scary directly from their parents and guardians. They alone can communicate sensitive information individually, with love and in the right measure for each child. Speaking in private also upholds children's modesty, which is a natural component of chaste living.

There is something profoundly moving about learning for the first time how you came to be from the very persons who gave you life. Children feel it and parents feel it too, and so the trust between them grows into a more adult friendship, one which will last not only through adolescence but into full maturity and beyond. Giving practical guidance becomes a lot easier.

Trust between parents and children is especially important today when pornography, bullying and sexual predators are a click away. Internet filters may help control computer use, but they also present a challenge to beat – and children's technical knowledge is regularly superior to adults'. What is more, most social media, such as Snapchat and Instagram, have no parental oversight. Unfortunately, there is no fool-proof way to protect children. The best one can do is to educate them early to understand right from wrong, look them straight in the eye and be honest. "Tell me if you see anything weird or creepy. I'm on your side. I can't control you, but I trust you and I want you to be honest with me. Oh, and remember how to press the 'off' button, fast."

Interestingly, the UK government's official guidance to schools on delivering sex education says that working in partnership with parents "is essential to effective sex and relationship education." It further says in section 5.1: "Research shows that children and young people want to receive their initial sex and relationship education from their parents and families, with school and other adults building on this later."[2]

Providing support to parents

The UK guidance goes on to say that many parents find it hard to teach, which is why schools also have a "responsibility for the safety and welfare of pupils" in this area.

The task of teaching can appear much more difficult than it is. The biology of fertility is fascinating, and adults find themselves being intrigued to learn more and to discover how it is that fertility can be managed without recourse to contraception. They also want to know more about the sexual chemistry of the brain and how bonding happens in a physical way.

To help parents, I have written my own book, *Sexuality Explained: a Guide for Parents and Children.*[3] This is designed as a tool which banishes embarrassment by teaching through stories. A mother and daughter, or father and son, talk together, laugh and pose questions. The guide takes on as much of the teaching as the parents wish: having read the book through themselves, they can decide when to cover what – over a period of years. They can explain a topic in their own words, read a chapter with their children as it stands, or give the children a chapter to read on their own. The third option can work well for older children, or for those who have had a complicated sexual history and find it difficult to speak.

Secondary school lessons

At the secondary school level, a full program of sex education should include: the biology of fertility, the sexual chemistry of the brain and the capacity to bond, and explain the economics of marriage and family life. It should also be truthful about: contraception, how it works, its true failure rates when used by unattached young people and the risks it poses to health and future fertility. Young women have a right to know this and young men to respect their sexual partners. Both should be educated for the complementary roles that women and men play in the home, in the workplace and in wider society.[5]

Sex education as part of sustainable development

There is now evidence from many countries that children who are born into married families thrive most easily. People take less notice of the fact that married people themselves live longer, healthier and also more prosperous lives than those who are unattached. The difference becomes stark in old age. The elderlys' need for financial support and pension programs is becoming a growing burden in many countries. They also need personal help with things such as shopping or being propped up in bed, but more than anything else, they need and want to feel loved and wanted.

A married couple remains self-sufficient longer. They are also more likely to have built up a supportive network of relationships and for both father and mother to be in close contact with their children. Society is already finding it difficult to support lonely old people without interested families to look after them. We cannot know what it will be like when the promiscuous young of the present become old, many without having formed lasting relationships or having children to care for them.

One can't expect children to think like this.[6] But adults can and should. The evidence that marriage is good for individuals and good for society is so strong that every school should be helping to guide children towards marriage – in addition to a career. Those who need help most are those at the bottom of society who are currently least likely to marry or to have the future resources to look after themselves when they are old.

Conclusion

Sexual education has languished in thought patterns devised in the last century. It is out of kilter with current concerns for respecting nature and the environment. Change is always resisted by vested interests – and in the case of sex education and the contraceptive industry, there are many. It will take determination to adopt a new holistic approach but where the health and prosperity of individuals and of society are both at stake, we can afford to do nothing less.

Endnotes

1. The "Fertility Health Summit: Choice not Chance" was held at the RCOG, London NW1, on 15 April 2016. https://www.rcog.org.uk/en/departmental-catalog/Departments/other-events/1643 – -fertility-health-summit-2016-choice-not-chance/. The authorship of this conference is interesting as the RCOG were originally responsible for pressing the UK government for sex education in its current form.
2. The UK Government's official guidance on sex education calls parents key to their children's effective sex education but suggests that they need help (see Sex and Relationship Education Guidance Ref DfEE 0116/2000, chapter 5). https://www.gov.uk/government/uploads/system/uploads/attachment_data/file/283599/sex_and_relationship_education_guidance.pdf
3. Sexuality Explained: a Guide for Parents and Children (Gracewing), 2013. For details see: www.alivetotheworld.co.uk. The book is being translated into Spanish, Polish and Romanian with other editions proposed.
4. A study by the Guttmacher Institute of February 2015 found that even less confident parents could be effectively trained to support their children. https://www.guttmacher.org/about/journals/psrh/2015/02/parent-based-adolescent-sexual-health-interventions-and-effect
5. See also the work by Christine Vollmer on educating the young in the values and virtues which make for healthy living and counter the influences of an oversexualised society.
6. Brain studies also reveal that the physical ability to make mature decisions only develops at age 22-25.

Alive to the World

Christine de Marcellus Vollmer

Book 2 – Alive to the World

This series is about commitment, fair play and friendship. But it is also about love, cherishing, the beauty of courtship, of marriage and the miracle of life. Procreation is taught in detail, but without the external organs or other elements which cause such embarrassment and ultimately such callousness, in other programs. These are not necessary in order to understand the depth and fascination relative to being a man or woman.

The 13 books constitute a continuous story of Charles and his cousin Alice and their group of friends, who experience all the same things as the reader: school, sports, friendship, successes and failures, triumphs and trials, changes and challenges and who grow at the same rate as the students, which keeps it so interesting. There is a teacher's manual for each level, with background information, further reading, discussion points, activities and so on.

We have drawn upon the wisdom of people so varied as Piaget, Viktor Frankl, David Isaacs and others, to teach at each level the virtues and values which are most readily learned at that age. There are windows of opportunity, as we know, for learning friendship, confidence, tolerance, courage, leadership, decision-making and so on. As most parents have experienced and Aristotle explained so long ago, the best way to teach the young is through example and through stories. To give you an idea:

Book 1, **Getting to Know Myself**, is about the human being: what is family, emotions, a new addition to the family, stages of growth, basic hygiene.

Book 2, **Growing up Happy**, covers the fundamentals of being a good child: obedience, sharing, caring, making friends and the responsibility for helping out in the home.

Book 3, **We are a Great Team**, for 8-year-olds, is more challenging and centers on the desire all 8-year-olds have to be included and do well on a team. This offers us the perfect tool to teach those prized virtues of: fair play, justice, abiding by the rules, respecting the authority of a team leader or captain. Through the sports we can easily make them understand the importance of each person and the responsibility of each to pull his or her weight. Cheating can be easily recognized as ruining the game. Perseverance, sacrifice and generosity are obvious virtues valuable on a team, and of course humility is what makes winners. Half way through this book, when the virtues of sports are well understood, Charles and Alice discover that family is their first team and subject to all of the above. The school works by the same principles and of course so does a democracy.

In Book 4, **Mine, Yours or Ours**, the story of Charles and Alice finds them discovering about respect for property and the need for, and joy of, sharing and lending, and the responsibility of taking care of the property of others.

BEST PRACTICES

Book 5 – *Alive to the World*

Book 5, **Different and Complementary,** is a fun book where the immense diversity of human cultures and ways of life are an introduction to the fact that all humans share the same basic needs of shelter, food and affection, even in apparently very different circumstances. Family is a big factor in this book also and commitment is the underlying theme, as the complementarity of men and women is explored with emphasis on the different brain structure of boys and girls. These differences are explained in a way which also helps boys and girls understand why they are so different and sometimes so very annoying to each other and with such different ways and speeds of learning.

Book 6 is called **Friends!** and is an exhaustive look at friendship of all kinds – the virtues of friendship – with loyalty, truthfulness and respect at the fore. Using and being used, as well as peer pressure, are important topics in this book. Joining different kinds of groups is illustrated, too, as Charles joins the Boy Scouts and Alice briefly gets sucked in to a group of girls who like to shoplift.

Book 7 is called **Changes and Challenges** and deals with more responsibilities. It goes deeper into respect, generosity, and balancing school and family. This book discusses physical changes and the need for cleanliness and good grooming.

At each level some aspect of human procreation is covered: the miracle of life, genetics and inheritance, and so on. No explicit material or illustrations to cause embarrassment.

Books 8-13, for the 13-18 year olds, **Personality Plus**; **Taking Sides**; **Feelings and Ambitions**; **The Future Begins Now**; **Big Decisions** and **Ready for Takeoff**, all deal more in depth with the changeable feelings and integration during teenage years. Care is taken in this story of Charles and Alice and their friends to show the difference between attraction, the 'crush' and true love.

Alive to the World, Aprendiendo a Querer, Caminhos de Vida, Grandir Ensemble, is now spreading over the world, among concerned parents and teachers. It is being published in 13 countries and 8 languages, including Korean and Hungarian, which shows that this need to retrieve values and virtues is world-wide.

All of this is to say that as science, sociology, economics, psychology and philosophy all coincide to show conclusively that the family is the basis of a strong and successful society, it is imperative that virtues be clearly taught in order to keep our families strong.

Book 11 – *Alive to the World*

www.alafa.org in English
www.alivetotheworld.co.uk
www.alivetotheworld.org

The Stay Alive HIV/AIDS Prevention Education Program for Children in Africa
Reach the Children

The Stay Alive HIV/AIDS Prevention Education Program for Children (hereafter referred to as Stay Alive), implemented by Reach the Children in Africa, is **based on the concept that the most effective way to remain HIV and AIDS disease-free is by practicing abstinence before marriage and total fidelity within marriage.** The program revolves around the family. It focuses on the part each child and youth plays in their current family and the family they will create in the future. It helps children and youth understand that happiness can come from happy, healthy families.

The Stay Alive program targets children from 9 to 14 years of age. Children in this age group are statistically the least infected by HIV, as shown in the following chart. They represent a "window of opportunity" to control the spread of HIV infection in the population in the long term.

The original goal of the Stay Alive program was to develop an intervention that changed the cultural scripts leading to self-destructive sexual behaviors as youth mature. This goal is consistent with the philosophy of UNAIDS, which states:

> The future of the HIV epidemic lies in the hands of young people. The behaviors they adopt now and those they maintain throughout their sexual lives will determine the course of the epidemic for decades to come.[1]

Since 2001, the Stay Alive program has been taught in fifteen African countries to over two million children, teachers and their families. Within Kenya alone, over 350,000 people have been taught using the program in schools, community organizations, religious organizations and individual families.

The Stay Alive program, written by Wendy W. Sheffield, LCSW, consists of five modules (eight lessons each), which focus on developing consequential thinking skills, engendering hope and building empowerment. The primary aims of the program are to:

— **Teach consequential thinking skills,** responsible decision-making skills, and the skills needed to withstand negative influences – that will empower and enable them to remain HIV and AIDS disease-free.

— **Build and strengthen families** (especially family communication regarding values, healthy relationships and appropriate sexual behavior).

— **Help children and their families recognize and appreciate the critical role that abstinence and fidelity play in HIV and AIDS prevention.**

— **Engender hope, individual worth and empowerment** within African children.

BEST PRACTICES

The program is described as a holistic, developmental approach to HIV and AIDS prevention education. It provides training in the biological, psychological and sociological factors that contribute to HIV and AIDS infection. Training in biological factors includes the medical facts related to opportunistic viruses and infections, age-appropriate abstinence and self-empowerment-focused prevention practices and health promotion practices. When asked whether Stay Alive had a positive change in the lives of their children, all respondents said "yes" in the affirmative. Observable behaviors reported to indicate those changes include:

- Communication between parents and their children has been facilitated.
- Children have acquired some life skills. They think before they act.
- Mode of dress has drastically changed, eliminating inappropriate clothing which includes tight and translucent clothes that mostly have sexual connotations.
- Pupils are aware of basic facts about prevention and transmission of HIV and AIDS.
- Increased participation has been observed in classrooms. Children are asking questions openly and those who are too shy to do so are including their questions in a question box.
- Self-discipline levels have gone up and tremendous improvement observed.
- Increased understanding of reproductive health.
- Truancy and pregnancy rates have reduced significantly. Most reported that no pregnancies have been reported since the program began in their schools and a general respect for life has been maintained.
- Parents have had a positive change and are now more receptive of children's concerns and supportive of their children.
- Respect is observable in children and most of them have developed a desire to do correct and safe things.
- Children are also watching over one another to support each other in their moral decisions at home and at school.

The Stay Alive program is a positive, proactive program that not only educates children regarding HIV and AIDS, but also empowers them with the attitudes and skills they need to remain HIV and AIDS disease free (Panos, Panos & Cox, 2009). Family members have a great responsibility and must be an integral part of this remediation program.

If we expect to really make a difference in the fight against AIDS, we must involve the family unit. Any AIDS prevention program will only be sustainable if it becomes a part of everyday life.
UNAIDS Executive Director, Peter Piot, XIV International AIDS Conference, 2002

For further information: www.stayalive.org

In-Home Parent Coaching for Struggling Adolescents and Young Adults

Tim and Roxanne Thayne for Homeward Bound™

Target 3.5:
Strengthen the prevention and treatment of substance abuse, including narcotic drug abuse and harmful use of alcohol

Three major factors for long-term success

Homeward Bound is a private, for-profit organization founded in a bold attempt to curb – if not eliminate – the failures of young people following out-of-home placement in treatment. Soon the best practices being used in transition were also applied to early intervention cases, prior to out-of-home treatment. The *Journal of Child and Family Studies* (December 2005, Volume 14, Issue 4) published the results of a study on "Outcomes for Children and Adolescents After Residential Treatment: A Review of Research from 1993 to 2003." This study presented three key factors in predicting success levels long-term:

1. The extent to which the residents' families are involved in the treatment process before discharge;
2. The stability and structure of the place where the children or adolescents live after discharge;
3. The utilization of after-care support for the children or youth and their families.

All three of the factors cited from the research have to do with the family and identify parents as being in a most influential position. Thus in-home parent coaching became the vehicle for helping these young people.

Three best practices for substance-use prevention and treatment success

Homeward Bound's in-home coaching work implements three vital behaviors (principles or tools) available to any family, regardless of race, religion, socio-economic status or location – that are unparalleled in availability, simplicity and low cost. They are:

1. Parental unity and leadership.
2. Use of family councils.
3. Fostering of multiple natural mentors (home teams).

BEST PRACTICES

When used in combination, the results are families with a profoundly better chance at keeping their children and teens from experimentation and use of drugs and alcohol, or reengaging in their use.

Parental unity and leadership

Parents – working in concert with one another – create a strong, protective culture that serves as a shield to drug and alcohol use, as well as other behavioral and mental health issues. Although not all families consist of an ideal (mother and father), there is usually a grandparent or another trusted individual who can be enlisted to help in some of the parenting discussions and decisions. Divorce can be more difficult, but the methods work to increase cooperation between co-parents as they teach values and address challenges individuals in the family encounter. Homeward Bound coaches use four keys to strengthen parental unity:

1. Discuss openly with the co-parent the mutual vision for the young person and the co-parenting relationship.

2. Teach basic parenting principles that have applicability across a broad range of issues parents encounter with their youth.

3. Identify mutual expectations for the young person as a basis for co-parenting discussions.

4. Teach parents Solution Talk, an effective method of communication and joint problem solving.

Some examples of topics for discussion between co-parents are:

1. Setting clear behavioral expectations for the children.

2. Parental monitoring and supervision for drug use prevention.

3. Prioritizing the relationship between themselves and their children.

4. Moderate, consistent discipline that enforces defined family rules.

Use of family councils

Homeward Bound's process includes conducting council after council in a family's home. With some education, parents can effectively lead their families by facilitating councils. Parents might meet regularly together in council to address concerns and to plan and support one another directly (facilitating the first key to success, unity between parents). In addition, other configurations include councils between a parent and a child, or with all members of the family present.

BEST PRACTICES

Trained coaches facilitate and moderate one council type after another, until parents have observed, practiced and communicated their vision for their family, coming to a unified plan for how to move toward that vision.

Children, teens and young adults are involved to gather their thoughts and feelings on the topic, and then decisions and principles are implemented, based on the input received. Ef-

Photo by Slickmint Creative 2016

fective family councils contain four crucial yet simple elements not always found in day-to-day conversation:

1. Inclusion of, and listening to, all parties who are part of the council.

2. Maintenance of an atmosphere of caring and mutual respect.

3. Arrival at an actionable consensus before moving forward.

4. Follow-up on the results of actions taken.

As children listen, learn and process in a variety of ways, a parent may choose to council as they walk together, travel to school or work alongside one another in daily household chores. The more informal the better for most topics, but in a time of real concern – for example around treatment for an addiction where a specific decision needs to be made – a formal gathering may be most appropriate. Councils can and should be used in times of calm (i.e., planning for a large purchase or vacation), as well as in times of concern or distress (i.e.. drug use or failing in school).

When family councils are facilitated regularly in the manner described above, the consistent results have been that family relationships flourish, children feel valued and are more respectful, and members of the family become a greater resource to one another.

Fostering of multiple natural mentors (Home Teams)

Because young people naturally reach a point in their development where they turn to people outside the immediate family for validation and companionship, Homeward Bound encourages families to build and utilize a community of support. Having multiple people in a child's life who genuinely care for, are available to, and are willing to reach out to help when they are forming their identity and their opinions related to drug and alcohol use, is highly impactful. This identified group is called the "Home Team."

BEST PRACTICES

Homeward Bound coaches facilitate the creation of Home Teams by having parents reach out and share their concerns regarding their young people with others they trust who can play an influential role. These may include obvious options of a: doctor, teacher or therapist, but should be expanded to include other significant individuals, such as: athletic coaches, religious leaders, coworkers, extended family, parents of other teens, positive peers, neighbors, bosses, family friends or those who share an interest or hobby.

The power of cultivating a Home Team is that it can be identified and nurtured long before there is any trouble with drug or alcohol use. These individuals are in place to intervene early, with what can be termed "micro-interventions." Team members encourage small and continual course corrections in a youth's behavior or attitudes, building their identity and schooling them in the positive tenants of their cultural heritage, rather than waiting until there is a crisis requiring an abrupt, intensive or costly intervention. If there has already been involvement in drugs and alcohol, these team members are educated and positioned in every environment and at times of day that no professional or even a parent can cover, such as: on the soccer field, at the party, in the halls at school, etc. Their presence and permission to help creates a large safety net of support for the family.

Home Team members are efficient and cost effective because they are voluntary, and can be maintained even through a family's relocation. They are often available over the years spanning adolescence into adulthood, rather than an average of mere months when assigned by an agency or program.

Conclusion

Homeward Bound finds that parents who engage in these three best practices experience hope, a growing confidence in their ability, find a calm anchor and adopt realistic expectations by having a concrete plan for their family. After three to four months of implementing parental unity, family councils and Home Teams by using curriculum, coaching and technology, parents report an impressive increase in their confidence in their leadership, skills and influence at home. Educated and equipped parents ultimately create a healthier and more satisfying family life for their children.

Tim Thayne, Ph.D., LMFT, is a marriage and family therapist whose entrepreneurial ventures have led him to start both wilderness and residential treatment programs for struggling teens. Recognizing a dangerous gap following out-of-home treatment, he set out to eliminate recidivism. His pioneering work is detailed in his book *Not by Chance.*

Roxanne Thayne helped her husband launch Homeward Bound in 2005, and serves as director of marketing. A high school teacher by training – and an enthusiast for anything that strengthens the health and happiness of family – she teaches and presents regularly. Her book *Cheership: A Salute to the Spark and Sway of Everyday Leaders* is available in 2017.

The importance of the family's role in a child's education cannot be overestimated. The only way that the world will see the successful achievement of a good education for every child is when parents and families participate fully to support their children's education and when governments and educators support the family unit. There is no substitute for the participation and support of families in the education of children. No government agency, no child's advocate group and no body of educators can take the place of a supportive family environment and proactive parental and familial caregiver participation in the educational welfare of a child.   – Mary Harris

(See article by Mary Harris on page 108.)

Mark Matunga, PhD, made contributions to policy and strategy formulations in education in many African countries while at Microsoft Corporation for 10 years. Currently, Dr. Matunga leads Corporate Programs for Intel Corporation in East Africa. A devoted Christian and community organizer, he has spent his life transforming communities through Education and other Socio-Economic interventions. Dr. Matunga has built schools, roads and much more. He is patron of many organizations and schools, including the Mark Matunga High School (a public school named in his honour). He is married to Josephine, and a father to Darleene, Furaha, and Daddy (Wema).

4 – Education

Mark Matunga

Family capital, a sustainable development philosophy

The world came together and crafted amazing ideas on how to better the living standards of all global citizens – how the whole globe could refocus any and all resources available to make this world a better place for everybody. After long back-and-forth discussions the ideas were clustered into 17 buckets, christened Sustainable Development Goals.

Of the 17 goals, one of them stands out for me – and luckily it is the very first goal. Poverty can be best traced from the survival mechanism of the smallest unit of grouping and co-existence. It is a measure of how every individual, or a group of related people, share or access resources for survival. So, to end poverty is to ensure that the family unit is able to feed and clothe itself in addition to a decent shelter. These are basic elements that every individual, and every family, work countless hours to achieve.

The family spends or invests enormous amount of resources in terms of time and money to redefine approaches to achieve sustainable levels of satisfaction. From a grander perspective, poverty reduction is a common, shared goal of global magnitude, and yet it worries the individual and local family.

Families and individuals always pull together resources and any attempt to increase or improve the base income of a family or individual is, by any stretch of imagination, a boost toward the achievement of poverty eradication. I look at the family as an enterprise and whatever that family has as resources, combined or individual. It needs to be known that poverty levels have impact on the family's ability to access quality social services, including but not limited to education and health.

This chapter is dedicated to education and how family capital contributes toward the development and the sustainability of a community or a nation.

SDG 4 on Education

Goal 4. Ensure inclusive and equitable quality education and promote life-long learning opportunities for all

4.1 By 2030, ensure that **all girls and boys complete free, equitable and quality primary and secondary education** leading to relevant and effective learning outcomes

4.2 By 2030 ensure that all girls and boys have access to **quality early childhood development, care and pre-primary education** so that they are ready for primary education

4.3 By 2030 ensure equal access for all women and men to affordable quality **technical, vocational and tertiary education**, including university

4.4 By 2030, substantially increase the number of youth and adults who have relevant skills, including **technical and vocational skills**, for employment, decent jobs and entrepreneurship

4.5 By 2030 **eliminate gender disparities in education** and ensure equal access to all levels of education and vocational training for the vulnerable, including persons with disabilities, indigenous peoples, and children in vulnerable situations

4.6 By 2030 ensure that all youth and a substantial proportion of adults, both men and women, achieve **literacy and numeracy**

4.7 By 2030 ensure all learners acquire knowledge and skills needed to **promote sustainable development**, including among others through education for sustainable development and sustainable lifestyles, human rights, gender equality, promotion of a culture of peace and non-violence, global citizenship, and appreciation of cultural diversity and of cultures contribution to sustainable development

4.a Build and upgrade education facilities that are **child, disability and gender sensitive** and provide safe, non-violent, inclusive and effective learning environments for all

4.b By 2020, substantially expand globally the **number of scholarships available to developing countries,** in particular least developed countries, small island developing States and African countries, for enrollment in higher education, including vocational training and information and communications technology, technical, engineering and scientific programmes, in developed countries and other developing countries

4.c By 2030, substantially **increase the supply of qualified teachers**, including through international cooperation for teacher training in developing countries, especially least developed countries and small island developing States

Percentage of family income for education

A quick scan of education in the developing world (as well as in western countries) gives the picture that a huge percentage of family income, both at the individual level or collectively, goes toward paying for the education of family members. In Kenya, the matrix is a bit more complex, just like it is in many developing countries.

Guardians and parents' primary responsibility as described world-over is to provide food, shelter and clothing for the children they bring to this planet. But the highest cost that is not included in the traditional roles is the provision of education and health services. These services are often procured at a very high premium, much higher than the basic three of food, shelter and clothing.

Even though the cost of education and health is directly proportional to the quality of the service, that cost and quality maps onto the income levels. The lower-income people can only access a certain quality of education or healthcare services, whereas the higher-income can access high-cost education and health because the cost is equally high. Using a proportional average, families in Kenya spend around 20-25% of their income for education monthly or annually.

The cost of education

Goal 4. Ensure inclusive and equitable quality education and promote life-long learning opportunities for all

While this is a great aspiration, logic dictates that the achievement of this goal will largely depend on the capacity of individual families to realize their potential. Speaking of quality education in the 21st century really means: What is the cost of education? In other words, when a family has more cash, they can procure quality education. The rest are left to access education according to their combined family capital. That is the way things stand at the moment.

Conclusion

So, what is the point here? For SDG 4 to be realized, families have to be empowered and enabled to not only be able to procure quality education, but to make quality education affordable to many families since they are the ones investing in education by paying for the services in the form of fees and tuition.

Parental Involvement in Education
Mary M. Harris

The family unit is the center of a child's education, for good or for ill. The positive efforts of families everywhere, and especially in sub-Saharan Africa and Southern Asia, must be recognized, supported and lauded if every child in the world is going to receive a quality education.

When parents and other familial caregivers are involved in children's education in meaningful ways, there is a positive influence on academic performance.[1] Students whose families are actively involved achieve higher grades, have better attendance, complete more homework, are better motivated and are less likely to be cited for disciplinary action.[2]

Parents and families, all over the world, ARE providing the support necessary for their children to receive, at least, a primary education. Many are also making it possible for their children go to secondary classes and even a university. However, governments have an important role to play to provide the opportunities for all parents and family units to do the same for their own children.

Parents help develop values and attitudes

From the outset, parents are important in the attainment of educational goals for their children. Parents are critical in defining the identity of the child through ensuring that the child develops values and attitudes that are important for the family and the wider society. In the past, traditional societies in Sub-Saharan Africa had appropriate educational structures in place, developed to ensure youngsters grew as responsible, dynamic and productive members of the community. Cultural norms and morals were adequately addressed within the family unit, which was the primary source of socialization properly sustained. Parents taught these norms by engaging their children in historical narratives of their values as a family and society. Obviously, it is from home that a child gains a particular view of the world, the value of learning and self-identity.

The 21st century environment has introduced changes in the kind of skills that need to be acquired for one to be functional in society. These skills are mostly acquired through formal education. This is the thrust of emphasis on education as SDG 4 requires skills that are received through a formal setting. In the new environment the teacher is not necessarily a parent or a member of one's immediate community. However, the role of the parent in education of their children is still just as important as ever.

Families provide the learning environment

Families are most successful when parents engage with their children in learning, establish a family practice such as providing time and a quiet place to study, assign responsibility for household chores, are firm about bedtime and having dinner together. This is particularly important in areas where girls are expected to do most chores after school. For example, in areas where the main economic activity is pastoralist (raising of livestock), boys are expected to stay out late taking care of animals while girls carry out domestic chores. Efforts to sensitize parents to these needs have been the main thrust of adult education programs. The more educated a parent is, the more likely they are to be involved in the education of their children.[3]

In informal education, the role of families is still an extension of the traditional responsibility of ensuring that children gain skills necessary to be functional in society. Children were taught how to become farmers in the farming communities and pastoralists in pastoral communities. Although means of teaching were informal, the net result was education and acquisition of skills. However, due to cultural, economic and chronological dynamic shifts in the society, traditional family and community structures have largely been broken down; thereby leaving young people not only much more vulnerable, but also less adequately prepared to face the challenges of the 21st century.

Challenges of Sub-Saharan Africa

In the last few years, there has been an upsurge of interest in Sub-Saharan Africa from the international community, which has prompted numerous humanitarian efforts that continue to distribute billions of shillings in anticipation of the prevalent unemployment, bad politics, poor leadership, poverty, ignorance and diseases facing its population. Lots of dollars have been spent in identifying problems that continue to make Sub-Saharan Africa lag behind in its developmental goals. However, little to no notice is taken of the huge discrepancy between the myriad problems facing Africa and Africa's richness in natural resources: the existence of strong family ties and the value-laden cultural orientation. If tapped adequately, these resources will influence upcoming generations not only in achieving the Sustainable Development Goals, but also in developing local and world leaders; whose individual potential and possibilities are made possible through the existence of a support system that comes in the form of competent teachers and involved, concerned parents.

Most of Africa's challenges are potentially worsened by the lack of meaningful, value-based educational approaches designed to lift and support not only the role of schools, but also to raise the bar for parental involvement in a youngster's preparation to achieving the Sustainable Development Goals. As William J. Bennett, the author of The Book of Virtues, has rightfully stated: "Teaching values begins where it must – in the home with parents, but while inculcating values should begin at home, schools must also help".[4]

Parental involvement at a glance

In a study carried out by Kenya Institute of Education in 2008,[5] it was evident that parents supported the Free Primary Education and did send their children to school, participated in school management committees and contributed the required levies. In this study, although parents did not play a major role in financing education owing to FPE, parents supported education of their children through provision of uniforms and food as well as the expenses that are not included in the free education program as illustrated in the Table 1.[6]

Table 1: Parents role in supporting their children's education (KIE, 2008)[13]					
Role	Strongly Agree	Agree	Not Sure	Disagree	Strongly Disagree
Providing money for extra tuition	5	23	3	31	38
Money for examinations	12	50	1	12	8
Development of buildings and other structures	20	7	1	37	37
Payment of allowances for support staff	12	6	1	34	44
Paying for extra teachers	6	29	0	31	33
Providing labour for school projects	4	28	2	33	33
Purchase of supplementary curriculum materials	1	18	1	38	42
Providing school uniform and food	32	56	2	7	2
Working with the children on their homework	15	46	7	12	28

Parents, caregivers and the community work together

Lufumbo is a school in the western part of Kenya, with 704 students. Joining Hearts and Hands, in partnership with Reach the Children, provided the funds and oversight for the construction of this school.

The school has had a growing enrollment because of free and compulsory primary education initiated by the government in the early years of the current decade. This swelling population made it necessary for the school plan to have more classrooms. The school management committee, which is made up of school officials, local leaders and parents, had an idea to start a girls' secondary school and these classrooms will serve as part of that plan. The library will provide learners with extensive reading materials and a place to study. Other schools could also benefit from books in the library. Adequately equipped libraries are not commonly found in most African primary schools. Books for the school are currently stored in a congested office. Completion of the library will provide the school with a safe and spacious place to house books.

| Parents helping to build a school | *Photo by Reach the Children* |

The project has had a number of successes according to the chairperson of the school management committee, Mr. Manyasi. The work being carried out is supervised by the community. A duty roster has been put in place, making it easier to have work done by family members, other volunteers and paid community members. Positive community response toward work done on the project has made the project succeed. This project has also enabled skilled members of the community to earn income working on the project. Some of the skilled members are parents of students at the school. This helps parents pay for school fees and uniform costs from the money earned on the project. There is also strict monitoring of the work by Joining Hearts and Hands and RTC workers; who ensure that the work is done according to code. This project is a great example of how parents, families and care-givers are getting involved to provide the necessary infrastructure (buildings, decision making and material labor) to enable their children to go to and stay in school.

Improved literacy for mothers and fathers

Throughout Africa, the literacy rates for adults are relatively low. This is an obstacle for parental engagement in the actual content of education for their children. It is obvious from Table 1 that parents basically create the framework for educational work. According to Uwezo (2011),[7] the more literate the parent the higher the chances of the child performing well in school. The difference in grade average might be as high as 70%.

Mothers are the frontline of defense when it comes to life-saving and life-altering practices in their own home. They are also an ongoing influence on their children after they have left home. Well-educated mothers are more likely to have the skills necessary to help prevent germ and parasite infections, reduce the risk in a difficult childbirth, alleviate gender-bias attitudes within the family and stop the abuse of children and especially girls. As mothers educate themselves, they generally provide a safer and more stress-free environment in which their children can learn and grow.

It is important that fathers are the main providers for their families, when possible. When a father is educated, he is better prepared with the skills necessary to feed, clothe and educate his children. Fathers often sacrifice comfort in order to help their children be better prepared for the world ahead of them. Good fathers also protect their children and set an example of hard work and integrity. A father's role is one that cannot be replaced by any other. An educated father is a better protector and provider of necessities for his children.

The goal with regard to the lifelong-learning needs of youths and adults and adult literacy has, in a real sense, received great attention. There are encouraging trends of adults showing the desire to access education. There are adults who have literally decided to sit in class with their children or grandchildren in order to learn.

An educated parent not only provides more income for his/her family, but they also set an example of industry, responsibility and self-sustainability.

Reducing stress at home increases learning potential

Parents can also support the achievement of SDG 4 by providing an environment in which children can learn. According to the Michigan Department of Education, parents can establish a daily family routine that expresses the value of education. For example, they can set aside time and provide a quiet place for their children to study. They can also assign family chores to the children while taking into consideration the need to do homework. They can do all things in their power to provide a safe and stress-free environment in which children can function and learn.[8] One of the principles of child-centered learning, as stated by Aletha Solter PhD:

> Children are better learners when their lives are stress free. Distressing experiences can interfere with the learning process because painful feelings can lead to confusion, anxiety, lack of self confidence, and an inability to concentrate.[9]

Each day brings the reality that most African children, and many others, are exposed to a myriad of potential stressors. To name a few: the lack of food and clean water, the lack of proper medical care, the lack of hygiene and sanitation units, the myths associated with the girl child, the myths surrounding the HIV and AIDS pandemic . . . and the list goes on and on. These are issues parents should consider seriously because they are major inhibitors to learning.

Some may then ask: What can be done to help children bounce back from circumstances that might blight their emotional equilibrium and affect the potential of the moment to learn? There is much that can be done. Next are some examples showing what parents and other familial care-givers in Sub-Saharan Africa are doing so that their children can feel less stressed, more supported and ready to learn.

Storytelling and reading to children

Parents recognize the power in storytelling and reading to their children. Storytelling is therapeutic and has a powerful influence in bringing an individual's focus to the present moment, thus stimulating readiness to learn and to make learning more memorable and meaningful. Traditional family stories are naturally powerful and have a significant effect on emotions, thoughts and behavior. They are powerful not only because they are a communication tool but because they:
- Create and reveal strong emotions
- Are memorable and are used to teach morals and values
- Provide a greater context and understanding of a situation
- Are significant in alleviating stress and building learning interest
- Motivate the right attitude for language and moral development
- Create a strong bond between children and their parents, children and their teachers

In an effort to simulate the parental storytelling experience for children in Ghana and to provide access to traditional stories for teachers and children in school, RTC partnered with Books for Change, Inc., from New York, USA, in order to provide almost 600 culturally appropriate books that were written by Ghanaians, for 30 schools in the Lekma and Dangme West districts of Ghana. Now the beloved stories, old and new, are available in the classrooms and in community center libraries. Parents and teachers can use them to read to children and children can access them also. "Children whose parents read to them tend to become better readers and perform better in school."[11]

Helping girls obtain an education

Education plays a particularly important role as a foundation for girls' development toward productive and fulfilling adult lives. It is also an intrinsic part of any strategy to address the gender inequalities that remain prevalent in many African countries. The achievement of a girls' right to education can address some of societies' deeply rooted inequalities that disadvantage and expose girls to vulnerability. Basic education for girls leads directly to better reproductive health and improved family health, as well as lower rates of child mortality and malnutrition and is also a major key in the fight against the spread of HIV and AIDS. In addition, it has been proven that educating girls and women is an important step in overcoming global poverty. Girls' education and the promotion of gender equality in education thus become vital tools for accelerating rural development. Reproductive health challenges impact much more heavily on girls than on boys. The puberty stage of development, if not properly managed, can have severe negative effect on girls' performance and attendance in education.

The beauty of teaching or training the female members of families in any area is that the lessons learned are carried down through many generations. These girls will not only use these skills to keep themselves in class, but they will also share the skills with their peers, younger siblings (especially sisters), and even their own families after they finish school.

Feeding children helps them to learn

A starving child is not concerned with learning and will spend his/her day trying to find something to eat rather than attend school. Many children in Africa go without the nutrition necessary to allow them to learn. Parents and families spend a great deal of their waking hours trying to feed themselves. Many children are relegated to "work the streets' in order to survive. For families in Sub-Saharan Africa, having enough to eat is a daily concern.

More often than not the solution to persistent hunger lies not in the acquisition of more money, but rather, in the acquisition of more/better skills and knowledge. As the old Chinese proverb states, "Give a man a fish and you feed him for a day. Teach a man to fish and you feed him for a lifetime."

Most families served by RTC projects have learned the skills of family gardening in one form or another, in order to provide their children with a more balanced diet so they have a greater prospect of learning in school. The projects were started in the schools and communities to empower parents and children with the knowledge and

ability to plant vegetables and provide food for themselves. One of the gardening methods only occupies a small space and therefore those families with small pieces of land benefit greatly from using this method. A variety of vegetables can be grown in a small space, if proper methods are used. This exponentially increases a families' ability to provide for their children. Families work together towards a common goal and children acquire valuable management and work skills. A fam-

ily garden provides foodstuffs for the children to take to school for lunch. It also helps mothers and fathers to provide a balanced diet for their families. Each family member can actually choose the kind of vegetable they wish to have on a given day. It becomes easier and far less expensive for them to get vegetables without going to the market. The extra vegetables grown generate income that assists to sustain the project and pay for the children's school fees and other family needs. Many families use some of those funds to buy a few chickens; which add to their ability to eat better and provide more necessities for their children.

Quenching a child's thirst for education

Clean Water: Many organizations in African countries are working to provide access to clean drinking water, water harvesting and hand washing stations – to make sure children have access to these facilities. Not only does it greatly reduce the time needed for water collection (which allows children the time to go to school), but it greatly enhances personal hygiene and reduces the instance of water-borne illnesses.

Sanitation: Few schools in developing countries have adequate sanitation or hand washing facilities for girls or boys. For girls, communal toilet facilities are not suitable for changing sanitary towels due to the lack of water and a sanitary material disposal system. However, humanitarian organizations are working with parents in the communities to construct new toilet facilities and provide hand-washing stations so children can help prevent the spread of disease and stay in school.[10]

A healthy child can learn

The World Health Measles Immunization Campaign is coordinating with churches and NGOs to encourage communities to have their children immunized. Family volunteers (mothers and fathers, brothers and sisters) pass out flyers to their friends and neighbors and help during the immunization events with registration, crowd control, and other needed tasks.[21]

Many organizations also provide medical and dental clinics – to ensure the health of children so they can concentrate on learning and studying. These clinics provide lessons in personal and dental hygiene in addition to facilitating first-aid, general healthcare, emergency surgeries and referrals for additional medical attention. Parent volunteers are used to help in the clinics and also help teach the children, other parents and family members. Parents are learning ways to take better care of their children's health so they can stay in school.

HIV and AIDS prevention is of major concern in sub-Saharan Africa as well as other places around the globe. So many children live with the devastating effects of this deadly disease; either as innocent victims, unwitting participants in the causes of AIDS or as AIDS orphans who have lost one or more parents to the devastating disease.

Reach the Children is the administrative and implementing organization for the life-saving HIV / AIDS life-skills and prevention education program known as 'Stay Alive." The Stay Alive program, initially conceptualized and developed in Africa by Susan Roylance, was written and copyrighted by Wendy W. Sheffield, LCSW, and was originally developed in partnership with United Families International. The program

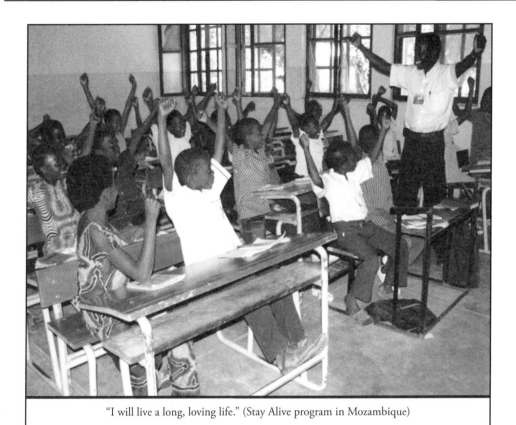

"I will live a long, loving life." (Stay Alive program in Mozambique)

has been updated and revised by Reach the Children, with permission of the author, to more succinctly address the current needs of children around the globe. (See page 98 for the Stay Alive program – www.stayalive.org)

How can schools help parents become engaged in their children's education?

A close-working relationship between the school and home helps parents to keep abreast with issues of their children's education. School-initiated activities to help parents change the home environment can have a strong influence on children's school performance. School officials who better understand their students' family situations are better able to assist in each child's best learning experience.

Epstein's "Six Types of Parent Involvement" (to be encouraged by the schools)

Research on parent involvement in education consistently underpins the perception that the degree to which parents are involved in their children's lives has a profound impact on their academic performance and thus quality education at macro level. Schools have a responsibility to actively engage parents and the community in the curriculum-implementation process.[13] Epstein's "Six Types of Involvement" provides a framework for schools to utilize in optimizing student performance, increasing parent involvement and encouraging community support. They are:

Parenting

Help all families establish home environments to support children as students.

Communicating

Design effective forms of school-to-home and home-to-school communications about school programs and their children's progress.

Volunteering

Recruit and organize parent help and support.

Learning at home

Provide information and ideas to families about how to help students at home with homework and other curriculum-related activities, decisions and planning.

Decision making

Include parents in school decisions, developing parent leaders as representatives.

Collaborating with the community

Identify and integrate resources and services from the community to strengthen school programs, family practices and student learning and development.[14]

Conclusion

The models discussed in this chapter depict a near-perfect conception of parental involvement in education. In the United States, according to the Michigan Education Department, 86% of the general public believes support from parents is the most important way to improve the schools. The 2011 Uwezo National Assessment of Kenya children concurs with this assertion and adds that appropriate parental involvement has a calculable positive influence on children's education – that limited parental involvement is the biggest problem facing schools and accounts for most of the poor achievement levels. This conclusion is a result of researchers interviewing almost 8,000 pupils in 328 primary schools in 76 districts.[15]

A close-working relationship between the school and home helps parents to keep abreast with issues of their children's education. School-initiated activities to help parents change the home environment can have a strong influence on children's school performance. School officials who better understand their students' family situations are better able to assist in each child's best learning experience.

The family unit is the center of a child's education, for good or for ill. The positive efforts of families everywhere, and especially in sub-Saharan Africa and Southern Asia, must be recognized, supported and lauded if every child in the world is going to receive a quality education.

Though much of the information in this article is about how Reach the Children is helping parents and caregivers provide an education for their children, stories like these can be told by hundreds of other organizations around the world who are doing the same.

Contributing Authors:

Mary M. Harris: Executive Director of Reach the Children, Inc. and Bountiful Resources Foundation – two sister organizations dedicated to helping underprivileged children. Reach the Children has facilitated numerous education programs and projects since its beginnings in 1998. Mary utilized the input from five African associates in writing this chapter. They are:

Lilian Odiero: Administrative Director for Inside Out Learning Education Program Kenya.

Evelyn Jepkemei: Senior Assistant Director, Research, Monitoring and Evaluation Division, Kenya Institute of Education; **Eric Onyango:** RTC Project Reporter; **Frederick Ashira:** RTC Project Reporter; **Moses Musasia:** RTC Project Reporter

Endnotes:

1. Watson, T., M. Brown, et al. (1983). "The relationship of parent's support to children's school achievement." Child Welfare 62: 175-180, Griffith, J. (1986). "Relation of parent involvement, empowerment, and school traits to student academic performance." *Journal of Education Research* 90: 33-41, Paulson, S. E. (1994); "Relations of parenting style and parental involvement with ninth-grade students' achievement." *Journal of Early Adolescence 14*: 250-267, Henderson, A. T. and N.; Berla, Eds. (1995). A new generation of evidence: the family is critical to student achievement. Washington DC, *Center for Law and Education*, Levine, D. U. and L. W.; Lezotte (1995). Effective schools research. Handbook of research on multicultural education. J. A. Banks and C. A. M. Banks. New York, Macmillan: 525-547, Yap, K. O. and D. Y. Enoki (1995). "In search of the elusive magic bullet: Parental involvement and student outcomes." School Community Journal 5: 97-106; Keith, T. Z., P. B. Keith, et al. (1996). "Effects of parental involvement on achievement for students who attend school in rural America." *Journal of Research on Rural Education* 12: 55-67; Cotton, K. (2000). The schooling practices that matter most. Portland, Northwest Regional Educational Laboratory.
2. Henderson, A. T. and N. Berla, Eds. (1995). A new generation of evidence: the family is critical to student achievement. Washington DC, Center for Law and Education.
3. Government of Kenya. (2007). Kenya Vision 2030. Nairobi.
4. William J. Bennett, author, politician, publicist.
5. Kenya Institute of Education. (2008). Analysis of Curriculum Implementation in the Context of FPE. Nairobi: KIE.
6. Tooley, J., Dixon, P., & Stanfield, J. (2008). Impact of Free Primary Education in Kenya : A Case Study of Private Schools in Kibera. Education management Administration and Leadership , 449-471.
7. Uwezo. (2011). Are our Children Learning? *Annual Assessment Report Kenya*. Nairobi: uwezo.net.
8. Michigan Department of Education. (2008). What Research Says About Parent Involvement in Children's Education. Michigan, USA.
9. Aletha Solter PhD. Aware Parenting Principles of Learning Copyright 1992.
10. U.S. Department of Education, National Center for Education Statistics. (2006). *The Condition of Education 2006*, NCES 2006-071, Washington, DC: U.S. Government Printing Office.
11. UNICEF, (2009), *Soap, toilets and taps*,
    http://www.unicef.org/wash/files/FINAL_Soap_Toilets_Taps.pdf
12. World Bank (2005), *Toolkit on Hygiene, sanitation and water in schools*, (the toolkit is part of the FRESH (Focus Resources on Effective School Health) initiative, a framework developed through a partnership of UNESCO, UNICEF, WHO, and the World Bank, and launched at the World Education Forum in April 2000). http://www.schoolsanitation.org/BasicPrinciples/GenderRoles.html
13. Hall, E., Wall, K., Higgins, S., Stephens, L., Pooley, I., & Welham, J. (2005). Learning to Learn with parents: lessons from two research projects. *Improving Schools, 8*:179-183. http://imp.sagepub.com/content/8/2/179
14. Epstein, J. L. (1990). School and family connections: Theory, research, and implications for integrating sociologies of education and family. *Marriage and Family* , 99-126.
15. *Uwezo National Assessment of Kenya*, op. cit.

Sustainable Development for Education

Mary Harris for Reach the Children

It is very difficult for a family in poverty to educate their children. Often families live in a cycle of poverty because they lack the "hand up" that allows them to move from that cycle. Free education does not include uniforms, books and school lunches. Families are still responsible to supply these things for their children to attend school.

Reach the Children (RTC) partners with local community-based organizations (CBOs) in an effort to build upon what Africans are already doing for themselves. One of these organizations is the Shiebu group of Western Kenya.

In an effort to help members of Shiebu lift themselves from poverty, provide the needful things for their families and educate their children, an innovative micro-enterprise project was developed wherein families were given a cow instead of cash.

As part of the Reach the Children sustainability program, that takes the first two heifer calves of each cow to help two other families, two other families are directly benefited and can also become self-reliant, thus providing the funds needed to educate their children. Then these two families give their first two heifer calves to two more families, and two more, and two more, etc.

In order for a family to receive a cow, they must meet certain "readiness" criteria. The two organizations provide training and oversight, and verify that the family is ready for the responsibility of caring for a cow.

In this situation a cow was given to the family. The cow was an "exotic" breed that guarantees a larger volume of milk. The milk provided much needed nutrition for the family and extra milk to sell for cash. The family was now able to begin the climb out of poverty.

With careful management of their resources the family was soon able to buy five chickens. These hens laid eggs and hatched

BEST PRACTICES

50 chicks. As these chicks grew, they began to increase the number of laying chickens. Their eggs supplemented the family diet with protein. In addition, all of the extra eggs were sold for more cash.

This enabled the family to pay for their younger children's school fees and uniforms, so they could all attend primary school. It also enabled the oldest daughter to attend secondary school and she is now two years away from high school graduation (which was not even expected before the gift of the cow).

The cow also produces a lot of manure; the family puts the manure on their kitchen garden and their fields of maize corn, ground nuts (peanuts) and their fruit trees. The manure greatly enhances the fertility of the soil and thus, the production of their crops.

Now the family has fresh fruits and vegetables to add to their diet and the extra produce is sold for still more cash. With the additional cash they can now buy clothing, shoes, medicine and all of the children can get an education.

The story just gets better and better. The cash from the sale of milk, chickens,

eggs and produce has provided the funds to start a commercial fish farm, where the family is now growing 600 tilapia fish, which they will sell to restaurants and local markets, thus improving the community.

This family is just one example of many families that now know what it feels like to drink a glass of fresh milk, eat fresh meat, vegetables and eggs, and put on a pair of real shoes to cover their feet from the dust and stones in the road.

They are just one family involved in this micro-credit venture who are now able to provide their children with a much desired education; an education that will virtually guarantee that future generations will not have to suffer the extremes of poverty faced by their ancestors.

They are just one family, but they represent the many families participating in micro-projects to improve the lives of family members.

Most families served by RTC projects have learned the skills of family gardening in one form or another, in order to provide their children with a more balanced diet so they have a greater prospect of learning in school.

Preparing the Brain for Education

Conceição de Sousa Solis for Purposeful Parenting™

Goal 4.2 of the Sustainable Development Goals is to ensure that all children have access to quality early childhood development, care and pre-primary education so that they are ready for primary education.

This lofty goal is particularly challenging because it includes children from all cultural and social backgrounds, many living in very difficult circumstances. Poverty and trauma negatively impact the developing brain. Children living in poverty experience higher levels of: developmental, learning and intellectual disabilities. Traumatic stress results in more problems related to: anger, aggression and lack of compassion and empathy. Beginning with the assumption that basic needs like food, shelter and safety are being met, achieving this goal will require that we focus on two things, the magnificent human brain and the family.

The brain – More than any other stage of development, the early years of a child's life determine who that child becomes as an adult. When we look at early brain development two factors stand out. First, the young brain develops at an astonishing rate. By the age of two-years-old, the brain is about 80% of the adult size! Second is the phenomenon called brain plasticity, the ability of the human brain to modify its structure in response to: sensory stimulation, the use of motor function and the presence of adequate nutrition.

Recognizing the importance of proper brain development in the first years of life is a critical first step in ensuring that children will enter school ready to learn.

The family – Given the importance of good brain development, it is fair to ask who is best suited to accomplish this? Based on 40 years of clinical and teaching experience at the REACH Family Institute, I know without question that the answer is the family.

Parents are the best coaches and teachers their children will ever have, provided they understand how the brain develops and how to apply that knowledge in practical ways in their daily lives.

Why are parents best at this? Because nobody else loves a child more than his parents and immediate family! This is the anthropological reality of the family bond.

In our work with parents throughout the world, we teach them how to parent with the brain in mind, an approach to parenting that we call "Purposeful Parenting™." When we combine parental love with knowledge included in "Purposeful Parenting™" the results are powerful, not just for

---

Conceição de Sousa Solis is an expert on the development of human functional ability. Conceição has nearly 40 years of experience teaching parents from all socio-economic levels how to transform their children's lives through enhanced brain development. She serves as the Vice Director of the REACH Family Institute.

BEST PRACTICES

that child and his family, but for the community and society in general. Our experience teaching "Purposeful Parenting™" shows that it is both effective and economical.

In Venezuela, where we worked with families from the low-end of the socio-economic spectrum, parents of children with developmental difficulties were highly successful at accelerating the development of not only their struggling child, but also the development of their other children. So there is a ripple effect that begins with one child, extends to others and eventually reaches an entire community.

Parenting with the brain in mind is not as complicated as it might seem. After all, parents successfully raised children for millennia until professionals took over. But it does require that the needs of the child be placed first and that all other needs follow, something that is not always easy or common in our modern society.

Professor James McKenna, former head of the Anthropology department at the University of Notre Dame and a leading expert on SIDS, says, "Selecting a pattern of social care for a baby is essentially selecting a pattern of physiological regulation for the baby. They're one and the same thing. There is no distinction." This is Dr. McKenna's way of saying that the child's needs come first – and how parents meet those needs matters.

Here are some simple, practical and easy to implement steps that will have a profound impact on your child's development.

Purposeful Parenting™ Best Practices

Newborn to 3 months

Often referred to as the 4th trimester, the first three months of life are a time for par-

ents to get to know and bond with their new baby. Newborn babies are completely dependent on their parents for the fulfillment of all biological and physiological needs. Nature simply assumes that the relationship between baby and mother, which begins in pregnancy, will remain throughout the first years of life. How a mother is able to fulfill her role as her baby's physiological regulating system affects how her baby's brain develops and thus affects the baby's future. Modern culture tends to rule in favor of decisions that separate mother from baby and the consequences of this decision may be greater than we think. The following best practices are particularly important in the early months of life, and ideally, should be extended for at least the first year.

Sleeping arrangements – Nature intends for mother to be in close proximity to her baby so that she can respond to the baby's biological and physiological needs in a timely and loving manner. Sleeping close to mother provides for this and promotes brain development. Sleeping with or close to baby is normal. It has been done for nearly all of human history, is done throughout the world and serves important biological purposes.

Breastfeeding – Breastfeeding provides the ideal nutrition for babies. In addition, it is an ideal opportunity for emotional bonding that involves extensive touch as well as mutual gaze. Mutual gaze is the term neuroscientists give to that special moment when mother and baby's eyes are locked in a dance of mutual admiration. Neuroscience research shows that the development of empathy and compassion is directly dependent on the number of mutual gaze experiences a baby shares with a

BEST PRACTICES

primary caregiver (usually mother) during the first year of life. Think about it, every time you and your baby are looking into each other's eyes you are growing his brain and helping him become more compassionate!

Skin-to-skin tactile stimulation – Touch is critical to the development of babies especially in the early months of life. Research shows that when premature babies are caressed or massaged frequently they gain weight faster, spend less time in the hospital and are less stressed. The most convenient time to provide this kind of stimulation is during breastfeeding. Infant massage is another great form of skin-to-skin tactile stimulation.

Respond to crying – The newborn baby's way of communicating is through crying. That is how they express their needs! It is very important to respond in a timely manner when a baby cries so he learns that he is safe, loved and cared for. You can also communicate at other times with your little one. Talk and sing to your baby. Let him know how much you love him, how tired you are and so on.

Tummy time – Human babies are designed to start moving on the tummy! Provide frequent brief moments throughout the day for your baby to spend time on the tummy. Every time your baby is awake and you are not changing, feeding or loving him, put him on his tummy. As baby grows and gets stronger you can increase the time he spends on his tummy. Complete freedom of movement is important, so make sure his arms and legs are free so he can easily move them. Make sure you are with your baby at all times while he is on his tummy. The first thing you

will notice is that your baby will resist the force of gravity and try to lift his head. Do this often and he will very quickly strengthen his neck and develop good head control.

3 to 6 months

Floor time – By three months of age the baby should have good head control, enjoy being on his tummy, be looking around at whatever is at his level and be making lots of arm and leg movements, trying to move. The more opportunities you give, the faster and earlier he will learn to crawl. Baby's arms, feet and legs should be bare and he should be on a smooth surface to make it

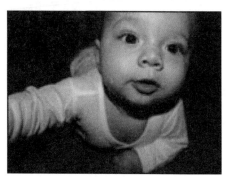

easier for him to move. At this stage you can place your baby on a clean, warm, smooth floor or a firm, smooth mat.

You should be on the floor with him, talking, singing, reading books and playing with him. As your baby gets stronger he will be able to play with toys while he is on his tummy. The baby will learn to roll from tummy to back and vice versa. Eventually, your baby will start to move.

At first, your baby may turn in circles or go backwards but eventually he should learn to go forward. Now he needs the opportunity to tummy crawl a lot! This is a very important stage of development and should not be skipped.

BEST PRACTICES

Sensory Development – Continue to provide baby with lots of pleasant tactile opportunities like: tickling, caressing, hugging and so on. Musical instruments are fun at this stage but if you don't have them, you can use whatever is around your house. Kitchen utensils, plastic dishes, and pots and pans make great instruments for you to play for your child. Talk a lot to your child. The more you talk the earlier he will understand language. Everything around your child is new to him. The environment you are in provides lots of new things for you to teach. Every time a child sees a new thing his brain is developing. Take advantage of this!

6 months to 1 year

Floor time – Now that your baby is arm crawling a lot, he should be very strong. The next important stage is called creeping. Creeping is when a baby moves on hands and knees! At this stage you want to give your baby lots of stimulation to develop balance - swinging, holding him close and spinning, rocking, etc. By now your baby should have good head control, but make sure this is done in a safe manner.

As balance improves he will get up on his hands and knees. At first, he might rock back and forth, but once he feels confident he will begin to move forward. At this stage a carpet or a firm mat is the ideal surface, but babies can creep on almost any surface. Now he needs the opportunity to creep a lot!

Sensory Development – As with the other guidelines, continue following the previous advice for providing: visual, auditory and tactile stimulation. Gradually make everything more sophisticated.

1 to 2 years

Floor time – If you have given your baby lots of opportunities to crawl on his tummy and creep on his hands and knees, he should be getting ready to walk. Keep doing lots of balance activities: rocking, swinging, spinning and so on. Your baby will walk when he is ready. It might be at 10 months, 1 year or 14 months. The important thing is not how early he walks but that he has he gone through all the important stages of mobility! If he has, from here on just keep giving him the opportunity to use his functions. He will keep getting better and better.

Sensory Development – Continue reading to your baby, talking and playing. Just keep increasing the sophistication of everything you do and HAVE FUN watching and being part of your baby's development!

Prevention within the family is key – the family is the strategic point of entry for eradicating multi-generational repetition of behaviors and beliefs found at the root of violence. The most effective prevention is forming and maintaining stable, loving families for raising children.

Lynn R. Walsh teaches sociology at the University of Bridgeport, with an emphasis on the family, gender and relationship education. Lynn serves as the Co-chair of the United Nations NGO Committee on the Family, NY. She is the Director of the Universal Peace Federation's Office of the Family.

5.2 - Gender Equality

Lynn R. Walsh, MSW

End violence against women

The task of ending violence and discrimination against women must be accomplished with broad efforts such as: education, economic opportunities, health care and female involvement in the political system. However, part of the challenge is transforming some deeply-ingrained unhealthy norms and relational patterns. This requires a "holistic and multidisciplinary approach," as recommended in the Beijing Platform, to not only address root causes of problematic male-female relationships, but also utilize and enhance the source of loving, respectful male-female relationships within marriage and the family.

Sustainability of Goal 5 will only be achieved by strengthening the family, which is the primal school of norms and the ability to love and be loved. It is precisely the relationship between a father and mother which can be a model of male-female harmony for children and society. Family is the seedbed for lasting gender complementarity, mutual respect and cooperation. The Beijing Platform for Action states:

> Developing a holistic and multidisciplinary approach to the challenging task of promoting families, communities and States that are free of violence against women is necessary and achievable. (Para. 119).

Limitations of solutions that ignore the family

Advocacy and awareness campaigns are often used to end violence against women in low- and middle-income countries. Such campaigns raise awareness and break the silence which, however important, are "generally ill-suited to the complex task of shifting social norms" (Heise, L., 2011:15). In fact, some Nicaraguan domestic violence-awareness programs over the last decade which involved only women, resulted in an increase in violence against women, not just an increase in reporting. It was observed that men retaliated with more violence to women's demands for changed behavior (Schopper, Lormand and Waxweiler, 2006; WHO, 2009:9).

Another example of the women-only approach is seen in micro-financing. These efforts can be monumental in beginning to lift women out of poverty, but unfortunately there is some evidence that without involving the male partners, domestic violence can increase (Heise 2011: 67-70; Koenig, 2003:269-288). Upon careful scrutiny of program outcomes, these women-only initiatives were found to be insufficiently intensive or focused to transform stubborn discriminatory and abusive norms and behaviors (Heise, 2011:16).

Laws and policies against partner violence are mandatory. Violence against women and girls absolutely must be universally illegal. But the Organization for Economic Cooperation and Development stated:

> Laws alone will not reduce violence against women. Discriminatory attitudes are significantly related to the prevalence of domestic violence, even when taking into account the existence and quality of domestic violence laws. Governments should introduce a combination of measures to change discriminatory social norms (OECD, 2013:1).

In the implementation of Goal 5 we cannot afford to ignore familial socialization and culture as part of the solution.

Marriage makes a difference in physical and sexual domestic abuse of women and children

It is heart-wrenching to review any of the data on physical and sexual abuse of women, such as in the World Health Organization's Multi-Country Study on Women's Health and Domestic Violence against Women. It is reported that:

> . . . overall, 15 to 71% of women who ever had a partner had been physically or sexually assaulted by an intimate partner. In most settings, about a half of these respondents reported that the violence was currently ongoing (WHO, 2005:5).

In addressing this egregious reality it is important to note family structure makes a difference.

After surveying 24,000 women from ten culturally varied countries, WHO recognized married women were less likely to be abused than unmarried women. Furthermore, separated, divorced and cohabiting women experienced much more partner violence during their lifetime than married women (WHO, 2005:8). US studies reveal the same global pattern: "Mothers who have never married – including those who are single and living either alone or with a boyfriend, and those who are cohabiting with their child's father – are twice as likely to be victims of violent crime as are mothers who have been married." Also, the severity of abuse experienced by unmarried women is five times more than that of married women (Rector, Fagan and Johnson, 2004).

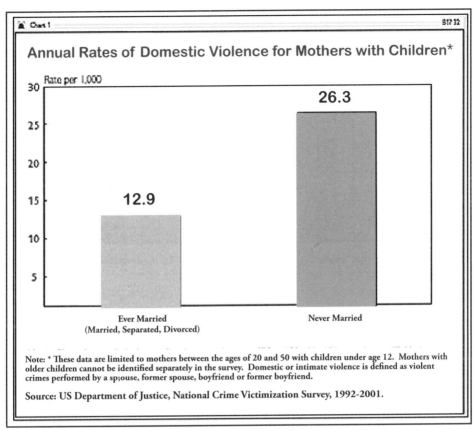

Annual Rates of Domestic Violence for Mothers with Children*

Note: * These data are limited to mothers between the ages of 20 and 50 with children under age 12. Mothers with older children cannot be identified separately in the survey. Domestic or intimate violence is defined as violent crimes performed by a sp;ouse, former spouse, boyfriend or former boyfriend.

Source: US Department of Justice, National Crime Victimization Survey, 1992-2001.

Furthermore, the rate of child abuse is correlated to the marital and biological ties of the abuser. According to the Fourth National Incidence Study of Child Abuse and Neglect in the United States, the non-biologically related romantic partner of the mother is more likely to abuse a child compared to the biological father. Children living with one parent having an unmarried, non-related partner in the household had the highest rate of incidence on the Endangerment Harm Standard – with eight times more abuse suffered than children living with two married biological parents (Sedlak et al., 2010:30-33).

Prevention starts with addressing family instability

SDG target 5.2 also focuses on prevention of abuse to girls. There is much evidence that boys and girls who are abused, or witness abuse, become abusers or victims themselves later in life. Obviously, we need to prevent abuse of girls and boys. Abused boys have a particularly higher rate of becoming perpetrators (Glasser et al., 2001:428-494).

Unfortunately much of the abuse, and that with the deepest psychological imprint, occurs in the dysfunctional home. Most male abusiveness originates from deepseated emotions from wounds inflicted early in childhood, leading to a fragile insecurity

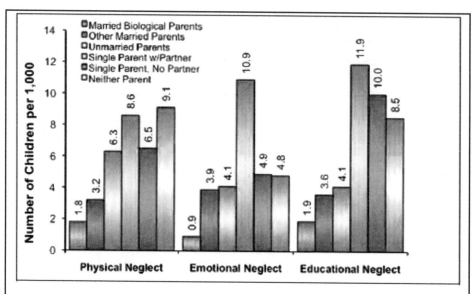

Incidence of harm standard neglect by family structure and living arrangement

US Congress from the National Incidence Study (Number 4) in 2010

and hyper-sensitive sense of masculinity. Without intervention, these boys can grow to become men who resort to physical violence when provoked by a threat to their insecure sense of masculinity (Dutton and Golant, 1995).

According to the Federal Bureau of Investigation's National Center for the Analysis of Violent Crime, "... the three most frequent factors in the history of a killer are physical or sexual abuse, a failure in emotional attachment to the mother, and a failure to use parents as role models" (US Federal Bureau of Investigation, 1990).

Building healthy gender relationships starting with marriage and parenting

We know male hormones and socialization have a significant influence on male attitudes and violence. Do marriage and parenting change men? Numerous studies in North America as well as Kenya have found that marriage decreases testosterone in males (Gray, Ellison, Campbell, 2007:5). Decreased testosterone correlates to decreases in aggression, promiscuity and violence.

Recent research on the influence of pheromones of pregnant women found fathers-to-be, who are in close proximity or live with the mother-to-be, experience an increase in oxytocin production. This "love hormone" is associated with an increase in bonding and protectiveness, readying a man to become a responsive father. Men's testosterone levels drop by about one third in the first few weeks after their children are born. Men and women, but especially men, receive a flood of the bonding hormone during sex. These biological changes make fathers more nurturing and emotionally connected to their babies and caring of their wives (Brizendine, 2011:80-86; Gettler et al., 2011:16194-16199). If we want to stop male violence, are we undermining nature's intended mate-bonding when we disregard the importance of a caring, marital commitment for the sake of women and children?

Within a culture that values traditional marriage, the conscious decision and public statement of commitment in marital vows creates more stability. Relational stability decreases emotional stress, which reduces some "bad" hormones and related reactive behaviors, while increasing other hormones which influence healthy relationships. For the husband and wife, commitment also creates a sense of long-term security, making it more worth investing into, and protecting, the relationship.

Committed spouses ideally are more willing to give more of themselves in order to work out the challenges and deepen the connection. As an analogy, compared to rentals, houses that are owned typically receive far more investment of: upkeep, improvements and beautification and generally increase in value. Just as homeowners gain new skills as they take on house projects, husbands and wives develop empathy and self-discipline as they live for the sake of their spouse and the marriage. The marital commitment to a higher purpose than self, cultivates significant personal and spiritual development. Marriage, in essence, raises the meaning of the relationship and the personal dedication to honor that value. Data affirms the stabilizing impact of marriage as studies reveal married couples stay together five times more than cohabiting couples (Binstock and Thornton, 2003: 432-443).

Marital commitment involves a promise of emotional fidelity and sexual exclusivity

Although marital infidelity does occur, married couples are more sexually faithful to each other than unmarried couples (Treas and Giesen, 2000:48-60). When relationships lack clear boundaries about fidelity, insecurities and conflict increase the stress hormone adrenaline, resulting in more emotional over-reaction. Jealousy created by concerns over infidelity, including previous partners, has consistently been associated with male-to-female violence (Nemeth et al., 2012:492).

In healthy marriages, fidelity facilitates a calming sense of trust and belonging. The best predictor for violence was the quality of the relationship (Bradley, Friend and Gottman, 2011: 97-116). Women in stable, healthy, married relationships, and their children, are the safest, most protected and happiest (Pardue and Rector, 2004).

One serious concern – as culture ceases to value marriage as a mutual commitment and the optimal environment for parents to raise children, males will fail to rise to the natural calling of their abilities and responsibilities as husbands and fathers. David Blankenhorn (Blankenhorn, 1991) reflects this in stating:

> In cultures across the world, the socialization of the male hinges largely, if not entirely, upon shared norms of fatherhood. In general terms, if we equate the essence of the unsocialized

man with violence, we can equate the essence of the socialized man with being a good father. At the very center of our most important cultural imperative, therefore, we find the fatherhood script: the story that describes what it ought to mean for a man to have a child.

Engaged fathers can end patterns of violence and protect their daughters

An involved father has an important impact of teaching the virtue of self-control and the management of emotions, especially anger. According to the Committee on Children and Families of the National Research Council ". . . children learn critical lessons about how to recognize and deal with highly charged emotions in the content of playing with their fathers. Fathers, in effect, give children practice in regulating their own emotions and recognizing others' emotional clues." A 26-year longitudinal study concluded fathers have a special impact on their children's development of empathy (Ray, 2015). Clearly, empathy and self-regulation of anger are prohibitive of violence.

Mothers impact the development of their daughters with great significance. However, psychological studies give compelling evidence that in a few areas fathers have more influence on daughters than the mothers. Adolescent girls reporting a strong relationship with their father suffer less depression, less substance abuse and are academically and socially more successful than those without a close father relationship (Videon, 2002: 498-502; Simons et al., 1999:1020-1030).

Daughters with involved fathers are more likely to have good self-esteem and report life-satisfaction as they emerge into adulthood (Allgood, Beckert and Peterson, 2012). Some studies show that fathers are better at instilling perseverance, a trait for developing skills, competence and attaining accomplishments such as academics (Padilla-Walker et al., 2013:433-455). From this foundational father-daughter relationship, a girl will more likely have the self-confidence and competence to overcome negative gender stereotypes and gain full participation in all levels of political, economic and public life. For the empowerment of every girl, the coach she most needs at her side is her responsible and devoted father.

Girls growing up without fathers

Another area where fathers clearly seem to have more of an impact than mothers is in relationships with other males. Girls who grow up without their father enter puberty younger than those raised by their biological father (Regnerus and Luchies, 2008:159-183). Fatherless girls are at greater risk for early sexual debut, adolescent pregnancy, single-parenting and difficulties in romantic relationships (Kline and Wilcox, 2010:40). Females who lose their fathers to divorce or abandonment tend to:

> . . . seek much more attention from men and had more physical contact with boys their age than girls from intact homes. They also tend to be more critical of their fathers and the opposite sex. These females seek refuge for their missing father and as a result there is a need to be accepted by men from whom they aggressively seek attention (Grimm-Wassil, 1994: 147).

Fatherless girls are far more vulnerable to becoming victims of sexual abuse and human trafficking.

In her paper, "Fatherless Women," Gabriella Kortsch, Ph.D., wrote: " . . . a little girl needs to see herself reflected in the love she sees for herself in her father's eyes" (Kortsch, 2014). A daughter learns what loving relationships are from how her father treats her and her mother. Given a healthy expression of fatherly love, including an appreciation for her looks and her body, girls expect to be treated respectfully and be genuinely valued by boys and men. Well-fathered daughters are much more likely to choose a mate wisely and build a happy, emotionally fulfilling marriage (Nielsen, 2013:151-160).

Fathers are not mothers

Fathers tend to bring to the child different gifts and traits than mothers. Children benefit receiving from the different natures of a mother and father. The fact that mothers in pregnancy, child birth and breast feeding are flooded with that "natural opiate," oxytocin, means mothers' role with infants is hard for fathers to replace.

Fathers can be wonderful caregivers and definitely bond with their babies, too. As the child gets older, fathers tend to be the fun parent. Fathers interact with play and stimulation while mothers generally are more concerned with caretaking, comforting and safety. Fathers' manner of play, which is more physical and exciting, encourages: risk taking, teamwork, cooperation and challenges children to learn new skills and abilities (Kline and Wilcox,2014: 11-13, 30 -36; Pruett, 2000:25-34.)

It is interesting that mothers tend to hold babies close and facing them. Fathers more often hold their babies facing outward. The analogy has been made that mothers are concerned how the world will treat her child, while the father is concerned how the child will fit into the world. Children need both comfort and push. Like yin and yang, the complementarities of mothers and fathers best nurture the whole child. Roles can be flexible. Mothers may work and fathers may stay at home, but experiencing the different feminine and masculine qualities of each parent helps children become well-rounded and appreciative of both genders.

The evidence is robust that children benefit the most when raised by their happy, married, biological mother and father. Two sociologists, Sara McLanahan and Gary Sandefur, expressed the merits of married biological parents in saying:

> If we were asked to design a system for making sure that children's basic needs were met, we would probably come up with something quite similar to the two parent ideal. Such a design, in theory, would not only ensure that children had access to the time and money of two adults, it also would provide a system of checks and balances that promoted quality parenting. The fact that both parents have a biological connection to the child would increase the likelihood that the parents would identify with the child and be willing to sacrifice for that child, and it would reduce the likelihood that either parent would abuse the child (McLanahan and Sandefur, 1994: 38).

Family-oriented programs for halting and preventing abuse and for building strong families

Family-oriented policies and approaches can reduce abuse and offer primary prevention of violence against females. As children witness healthy relationships within the family, any replication of discrimination and violence in the next generations can be ended. There are numerous programs around the world that have started to do this.

One successful program in the poorest areas in South Africa, the "Microfinance for AIDS and Gender Equity" (IMAGE) program, conscientiously engages men and boys. This program combines financial services with education and skill-building in several areas, including: communication, managing marital conflicts, gender norms and intimate violence. Rigorous evaluations produce encouraging results as:

> . . . participants reported 55% fewer acts of violence by their intimate partners in the previous 12 months than did members of a control group. . . . Women reported fewer experiences of controlling behavior by their partners, despite having suffered higher levels of this behavior than members of the control group before entering the program. In addition, participants were more likely to disagree with statements that condone physical and sexual violence towards an intimate partner. Furthermore, a higher percentage of women in the program reported household communication about sexual matters and attitudes that challenged gender roles (Pronyk et al., 2006:1973-83).

In addressing poverty eradication it makes sense to encourage husband-wife teamwork and cooperation, especially as it also reduces partner violence.

Programs that teach both partners effective communication skills for handling conflicts show a reduction in physical aggression and build relationship coherence (APA, 2004; Pardue & Rector, 2004; Bradley, Friend and Gottman, 2011). Involving men as an essential part of the couple/team enables couples to change problematic social norms together (Renay, Cleary and Gottman, nd.:17-20).

One program, "Stepping Stones," is used in over 40 countries around the world to improve sexual health. It was designed to include men and women. Results from program implementation in Gambia, which educated couples together, showed: " . . . participating couples over one year found that, compared to couples in a control group, they communicated better and quarreled less, and that the men were more accepting of a wife's refusal to have sex and less likely to beat her" (Paine et al., 2002:41-52). Another program administered in South Africa reported, "Male partner engagement in either the gender-separate or couples-based interventions led to modest improvements in gender power, adoption of more egalitarian gender norms, and reductions in relationship conflict for females" (Minnis et al., 2015:517-25).

Reaching new parents, strengthening fragile families and fathers' involvement

Women and girls can be better protected from abuse by strengthening fragile families through increasing positive father involvement. Several studies have demonstrated positive long-term benefits when fathers are involved with their baby. The best time to strengthen a father's commitment to the mother and his child is before and right after birth of his child. A program designed to take advantage of this opportune time can be more successful than programs trying to bring in a distanced father with a failed relationship with the mother.

One home-visiting program for new parents, "Welcome Baby," showed increased, positive father involvement with their child compared to fathers who did not participate in the program. Programs that teach care-giving of infants, couple communication skills and differences in genders help strengthen the couple-coping skills, co-operation and satisfaction. It is important to bolster the couple's relationship because often when the relationship becomes strained, the mother's "gate-keeping" obstructs the father's involvement – despite his sincere desire to help raise his child. With couple-enrichment programs parents are more likely to stay together and the father is more likely to stay positively involved with his children (Hawkins et al., 2008:49-58).

Parenting programs at any stage need to be encouraged and further developed. They could be added into other programs that lack a family-centered component. One program used in 25 countries around the world, the "Positive Parenting Program," was evaluated and found to "significantly reduce substantiated cases of child abuse in a large-scale community and actually prevent child abuse before it occurred." The study revealed strong evidence that parenting education is "effective at reducing conduct disorder and later antisocial behavior among children, both of which strongly predict future partner violence" (Prinz et al., 2009; Piquero et al., 2009:88-90). According to OECD, many programs being used in developing countries improve parent–child relations, reduce harsh punishment and strengthen the family unit (Heise, 2011:38-42).

Conclusion

As essential as the relationship between men and women is for the continuation of humankind, it has been troubled throughout history. Sadly, some of the worst maltreatment of women and girls happens within the home. But instead of ignoring the family, we need to focus on it – both to heal and strengthen it. The message from repeated global research findings is resounding: married mothers and fathers, committed in loving each other, create the optimum blending of gifts and teamwork for raising their children to grow – prepared to treat all people with equal dignity.

When this "natural and fundamental group unit of society" is protected and valued by the state and society, not only are women and girls safer and more likely to flourish, but men and boys are more likely to develop their greatest qualities also.

What can be more fundamental to sustainability? There are many resources, programs and policies that are already turning the tide by recognizing and uplifting the value of marriage, parents and the family. We will accomplish women's and girls' empowerment, but only when we support the family to do what only it can do best – nurture responsible, loving human beings.

References:

Allgood SM, Beckert TE, and Peterson C. (2012) "The Role of Father Involvement in the Perceived Psychological Well-Being of Young Adult Daughters: A Retrospective Study". North American Journal of Psychology. found at http://www.freepatentsonline.com/article/North-American-Journal-Psychology/281111794.html

American Psychological Association, (2004)"Marital Education Programs Help Keep Couples Together" October 8, found at http://www.apa.org/research/action/marital.aspx

Binstock, G & Thomton, A,(2003) "Separations, Reconciliations, and Living Apart in Cohabiting and Marital Unions," Journal of Marriage and Family 65, No. 2 , pp. 432-443. .

Blankenhorn, D., (1991) The Good Family Man, Fatherhood and the Pursuit of Happiness in America , Institute for American Values, found at http://www3.uakron.edu/witt/father/fanote3.htm

Bradley, R. P. C., Friend, D. J., and Gottman, J. M. (2011) "Supporting healthy relationships in low income, violent couples: reducing conflict and strengthening relationship skills and satisfaction" Journal of Couple & Relationship Therapy, vol. 10, pp. 97-116.

Brizendine, L., (2010) The Male Brain, New York: Random House, pp. 2- 8, 79- 94.

Dutton, D. and Golant, S., (1995) The Batterer: A Psychological Profile, New York: Basic Books

Fagan, P. and Hering, E., "The Incidence, Correlates, and Effects of Abuse: A working Paper," MARRI Research on Marriage and Religion, April, 2017.

Gettler L., , McDade, T.W., Feranil, A. B., and Kuzawa, C. W. (2011) "Longitudinal evidence that fatherhood decreases testosterone in human males". Proceedings of the National Academy of Science of USA, Sep 27; 108(39) pp. 16194–16199.

Glasser, M. , Kolvin, I., Campbell, D., Glasser, A., Leitch, I, and Farrelly, S. , (2001) "Cycle of child sexual abuse: links between being a victim and becoming a perpetrator " The British Journal of Psychiatry, pp. 482-494.

Gray, P, Ellison, PT, & Campbell, BC., (2007) "Testosterone and Marriage among Ariaal Men of Northern Kenya", Current Anthropology, vol. 48, p.5.

Grimm-Wassil, C., (1994). Where's daddy: how divorced, single and widowed mothers can provide what's missing when dad's missing. New York, NY: Overlook Press.

Hawkins, A. J., Lovejoy, K.R., Holmes, E.K., Blanchard , V.L., & Fawcett, E. (2008) " Increasing fathers' involvement in child care with a couple-focused intervention during the transition to parenthood". Family Relations, vol. 57, pp. 49–59.

Heise, L, (2011) What Works to Prevent Partner Violence? An Evidence Overview. Working Paper. STRIVE Research Consortium, London School of Hygiene and Tropical Medicine, London. found at http://www.oecd.org/derec/49872444.pdf

Heise, L, (2011) What Works to Prevent Partner Violence? An Evidence Overview. Working Paper. STRIVE Research Consortium, London School of Hygiene and Tropical Medicine, London. found at http://www.oecd.org/derec/49872444.pdf

Kline, K., and Wilcox, B., (2014) Mother Bodies, Father Bodies: How Parenthood Changes Us From the Inside Out, Institute for American Values. ISBN # 978-1-931764-36-0

Kortsch, Gabriella. (2014) "Fatherless Women: What Happens to the Adult Woman Who Was Raised Without Her Father?" Trans4mind. n.p., Web. 25 Nov. 2014 http://www.trans4mind.com/counterpoint/index-happiness-wellbeing/kortsch4.shtml

McLanahan, S. and Sandefur, G., (1994) Growing Up with a Single Parent. Cambridge: Harvard University Press. p. 38

Minnis, A., Doherty, I., Kline, T., Zule, W., Myers, B., Carney, T., and Wechsberg, W. , (2015) "Relationship power, communication, and violence among couples: results of a cluster-randomized HIV prevention study in a South African township", International on Journal Women's Health. vol. 7, pp. 517–525.

Nemeth JM, Bonomi AE, Lee MA, and Ludwin JM. (2012) "Sexual infidelity as trigger for intimate partner violence". Journal of Women's Health (Larchmt). Sep;21(9):942-9. doi: 10.1089/jwh.2011.3328. Epub 2012 Jun 29.

OECD (2013) "OECD Issues Paper: Transforming social institutions to prevent violence against women and girls and improve development outcomes", OECD Development Center.

Padilla-Walker L., Day, R., Dyer, J. D., and Black, B. C. (2013) "Keep on Keeping On, Even When It's Hard!: Predictors and Outcomes of Adolescent Persistence", The Journal of Early Adolescence, May, vol. 33, 4: pp. 433-457

Paine K ., Hart, G., Jawo, M., Ceesay, S, Jallow, M., Morrison, L., Walrave, G., McAdam, K., and Shaw, M. (2002) "Before we were sleeping, now we are awake: preliminary evaluation of the Stepping Stones sexual health programme in The Gambia". African Journal of AIDS Research, vol. 1, pp. 41–52

Pardue , M & Rector, R (2004) "Reducing Domestic Violence: How the Healthy Marriage Initiative Can Help" Heritage Backgrounder #1744 on Family and Marriage March 30. np. http://www.heritage.org/research/reports/2004/03/reducing-domestic-violence-how-the-healthy-marriage-initiative-can-help

Piquero, A ., Farrington, D., Welsh, B., Tremblay, R., and Jennings, W.,(2009) "Effects of early family/parent training programs on antisocial behavior and delinquency" National Institute of Justice, Office of Justice Programs, U.S. Department of Justice. found at https://www.ncjrs.gov/pdffiles1/nij/grants/224989.pdf

Prinz, R., Sanders, M., Shapiro, C., Whitaker, D. and Lutzker, J. (2009) "Population based prevention of child maltreatment: The US Triple P System Population Trial" Prevention Science, 10(1): p. 1-12. 125 found in http://link.springer.com/article/10.1007/s11121-009-0123-3/fulltext.html

Pronyk P.M., Hargreaves, J. R., Kim, J. C., Morison, L. A., Phetla, G., Watts, C., Busza, J., and Porteret, J. (2006) "Effect of a structural intervention for the prevention of intimate-partner violence and HIV in rural South Africa: a cluster randomised trial." Lancet, vol. 368, pp. 1973–83

Ray, W., (2015) "The Crisis of Fatherhood", Psychology Today" found at https://www.psychologytoday.com/.. June 7, https://www.psychologytoday.com/blog/wired-success/201106/the-decline-fatherhood-and-the-male-identity-crisis

Rector, RE., Fagan, P. and Johnson, K. (2004) "Marriage: Still the Safest Place for Women and Children," Heritage Foundation Backgrounder No.1732 on Family and Marriage, Heritage Foundation. np. http://www.heritage.org/research/reports/2004/03/marriage-still-the-safest-place-for-women-and-children

Regenerus, M. and Luchies, L. (2006) "The Parent-Child Relationship and Opportunities for Adolescents' First Sex," Journal of Family Issues 27, No. 2.

Renay, P., Cleary, B. and Gottman, J., (nd) "Reducing Situational Violence in low-income couples by fostering healthy relationship and conflict management skills". Relationship Research Institute, Seattle, WA, pp. 17-20

Schopper D, Lormand JD, and Waxweiler R (eds) (2006) Developing policies to prevent injuries and violence: guidelines for policy-makers and planners. Geneva: World Health Organization, in http://www.who.int/violence_injury_prevention/violence/gender.pdf

Sedlak, A.J., Mettenburg, J., Basena, M., Petta, I., McPherson, K., Greene, A., and Li, S. (2010). Fourth National Incidence Study of Child Abuse and Neglect (NIS–4): Report to Congress. Washington, DC: U.S. Department of Health and Human Services, Administration for Children and Families..

Simons, RL. , Lin, K, Gordon, L. C., Conger, R. D. and Lorenz, F. O..(1999) "Explaining the Higher Incidence of Adjustment Problems Among Children of Divorce Compared with Those in Two-Parent Families," Journal of Marriage and the Family , 61.

Treas, J. and Giesen, D. (2000) "Sexual Infidelity Among Married and Cohabiting Americans," Journal of Marriage and the Family 62, No. 1, February, pp. 48-60.

US Federal Bureau of Investigation, National Center for the Analysis of Violent Crime, Criminal Investigative Analysis: Sexual Homicide, (1990) found in Fagan, P., (1997) " Child Abuse Crisis: The Disintegration of Marriage, Family, and the American Community", Heritage Backgrounder #1115 on Family and Marriage May 15.

Videon, TM., (2002) "The Effects of Parent-Adolescent Relationships and Parental Separation on Adolescent Well-Being," Journal of Marriage and Family 64, No. 2, pp. 489-503

World Health Organization (2005) World Health Organization's Multi-Country Study on Women's Health and Domestic Violence against Women: summary report of initial results on prevalence, health outcomes and women's responses. Geneva: World Health Organization

World Health Organization (2005) World Health Organization's Multi-Country Study on Women's Health and Domestic Violence against Women: summary report of initial results on prevalence, health outcomes and women's responses. Geneva: World Health Organization

Equality of Women within the Chinese Society

Wendy Jyang

Observations of family and society's respect towards women

Chinese cultural societies have caused personal and family tragedies as they have not yet recognized the value of female family members. China has paid a great price to come to this day of understanding the challenges and inequality of the past few hundred years. It is not surprising to many scholars to find that the ancient systems honored their wives, mothers and daughters, more than in the last several hundred years. Those respected women gained their status mostly through their achievements at home and their field of work. The work-field performance also depended on the educational opportunities that were provided by the family. This article intends to provide some thoughts about the development of the increased value of women in the Chinese culture, especially in the Taiwan and China areas.

Since 1995, China's efforts in many fields have improved significantly – combined with international humanitarian groups' support. The leadership of women's organizations strives hard to allow effective events to happen in the rural areas – regardless of the challenges of the land. With government and Communist Party approval, international NGOs have been privileged to join efforts toward improving the quality of life for women, especially regarding their education and job skills training. In addition, the recent decades of internet usage in China, though not as liberal as other Chinese-culture-based societies, has provided significant legal information to females through Internet searches and news.

It is interesting to note that the status of women among the aboriginal people in Taiwan hasn't changed much over the centuries – due to their culture and tradition. However, most people without a matriarchal system have had more challenges in female gender rights.

Head-of-household

What causes a person in the family to be designated as the leader, or "head-of-household?" In both aboriginal people's lives and the lives of regular city people there is a respect for financial contributions. In city areas, more education also influences the leadership status for a person being designated "head-of-household." Yet, among aboriginal people the handing of family property to females is part of their culture and not totally dependent on her education.

The similarity in native people's lives, education and financial input contribute to the leadership status of the person in the family being designated "head-of-household."

Research during the 1990s showed that the increase of women as the head-of-household was mainly caused by two facts. First, a female in the head-of-household position in Taiwan depends heavily on her economic contribution, which is usually related to her educational preparation. Yet there is the suppressive fact of gender inequality in the Chinese culture.

Second, one of the most seriously damaging facts of marriage is the "mother-in-law vs. daughter-in-law." For many centuries, men had no ability to separate their married lives from their aging mothers' demands. The mothers of men had not been trained to support and increase their sons' happiness through being kind to both their son and their daughter-in-law. The inherited attitudes from many previous generations have made it very difficult for women, and even destroyed young families – by mistreating the wife if she was unable to provide a male child, or if she came from a poor family.

A royal man often divorced his wife if she was unable to produce a son. In some cases, royalty might choose to arrange another marriage, and still keep the first wife, but this would contribute to ongoing fights. This could even impact political instability. We hope history will teach this lesson – there must be respect for the wives, mothers and daughters in our families.

Regarding the unfaithful, married Taiwanese men's behavior, for many years most laws protected Taiwanese women; however, the differences of the legal systems between China and Taiwan have created serious family conflict. Taiwanese men may decide to cheat by choosing to not show they are married on their ID and then marry a woman from Mainland China. Notice that, again, people with religions that obey higher moral laws are more likely to protect their family and honor gender rights as a common practice.

There need to be laws in the Chinese-culture-based societies that prevent persecution and abuse of wives, mothers, daughters and daughters-in-law.

Due to the usage of the Internet among younger generations, more issues are being exposed through the media. The entertainment and media news reports have led youth to certain positive and negative statuses. While loud voices bring up more issues that have not been discussed by the public, too many images of unreasonable problem-solving skills causes the set-back of an intelligent younger generation. One significant challenge is pornography, combined with the traditional practice of looking down at a female's life-value. Young females are influenced to present themselves as objects to please men in order to secure their value as women, thus creating ongoing social burdens.

The following stories show gender equality and its development in the recent 60 years, as well as years of tradition.

1963-2016 – The story of Cindy

Cindy was born out of wedlock when her mother, June, was 20 years old. As a young girl she was the shame of the family, and was left to be cared for by her grandmother. Her mother worked in a garment production factory in a nearby town. When Cindy was 10, her mother married a soldier from China. She grew up feeling she was not valuable, although her father and mother were regular parents, just trying to make ends meet. However, she excelled at school and became a first-ranked high school student in the capital city of Taiwan. Many people discovered the talents within her. Before graduating from the university she had already obtained a high position in the news business. Several outstanding projects were directed by Cindy as she chose to use the news media to do good. Now, her family status is one of a well-loved wife, mother and influential media director. She has risen above what her childhood family thought about her future.

1985-2016 – The story of Trudy

Trudy, who lived in Taiwan, lost her husband and son during a three-month period – while living in Shanghai. Trudy learned her husband had cheated on her from 1985 until the day he died. The family is now wealthy in both Shanghai and Taiwan. However, Trudy married her husband when he was poor. Her ability as a wife and daughter-in-law (giving birth to more than one son), was well appreciated by her mother-in-law. Yet her father-in-law despised her due to the poor status of Trudy's family. Trudy took care of her husband's sick mother for years before her death – while managing the Taiwanese business. She fulfills the responsibly of a rich person's wife. She is the matriarch of her family, yet her life is left with sad memories, as she discovers more evidence of her husband's cheating that she did not have the courage to confront her deceased husband about.

1915-2015 – The story of Grandmother Zhou

One-hundred-year-old Grandmother Zhou, who recently passed away in China, is survived by 76 descendants. Zhou, her feet having been bound from a young age, went through poverty with her unselfish love, while nurturing her huge family of eight children. She was blind for 65 years. Her love and ability to watch out for the needs of her family, in spite of foot binding, blindness and poverty, will never be measured with a social standard. She lost her husband at age 60. The death was an accident (he drank industrial oil in the working area, thinking the pot he picked was water for the workers).

As their precious blind grandmother, she was able to take care of the little ones without making mistakes. Her hearing was such that she could tell which family member was approaching her or if a stranger had come to carry on a conversation. She was even able to weave and sew clothes for her family. Children loved her and always fought to be the one to thread the needles for her. It took little to please her: soft fruit, sugar cube treats and cotton candy were her favorites. Her high moral standard was such that her descendants were able to resist temptation in their own lives. Grandmother Zhou gained her family's respect by her traditions of value and love. They called her Great Dad and Great Grand Dad because referring to her as a mother or grandmother didn't give her the honor they wanted to give her as the head-of-household.

625-705 AD – The story of Wu Ze Tian, female king

Wu Ze Tian was the most famous female ruler of Chinese history. Her youth brought her to the position of wife to two kings. Her talents in ruling a nation gained her high respect in ancient times. The details in the following description will help modern people see that female rights in those days were not what we have assumed they were:

> After Gaozong's death she reigned through puppet emperors, her sons Zhongzong and Ruizong. She finally proclaimed herself Emperor, the first woman to do so. Wu ruled until her 80s when she was unable to thwart a coup. She died shortly after. Despite her ruthless climb to power, her rule was benign. Wu reduced the size of the standing army, and replaced aristocrats in the government with scholars. She was fair to the peasantry, lowering taxes, raising agricultural production, and strengthening public works. Wu also campaigned to elevate the status of women and had scholars write biographies of famous women (Angelia, 09).

Family-history records

In Chinese family-history records, most women did not have all their names recorded for hundreds of years. However, they had honorable titles as mothers of their children with their maiden names. This was a family-based motivation to get all adults married so they could be recorded in the on-going family records as someone who existed. They believed in the family bond and individual existence after death. If the husband died and the parents of the dead husband decided to marry the daughter-in-law off, this widowed daughter-in-law became a daughter as she stepped out of the family. Many of these marriages were performed out of love towards the young widows, while some of them could be a financial problem-solving solution.

If a family never had a son, the older generation would arrange a child from another family branch to be named after the family without a son. The child could still be raised by his own mother. This mother didn't lose a son. She actually gained a lot of respect from the other family plus the kind treatment of the older generation, unless the birth mother had moral problems. One reason they did this was they feared that without a son there would be no one to keep their family ancestor-worship and continue the records of family names.

Conclusion and suggestions

Since 2000, improvement has been more significant in the Chinese-culture-based island of Taiwan. The sacrifice since the Qing Dynasty has been tremendous. One of the most significant successes is the results of the Taiwan election of 2016; the 2016 election results in Taiwan showed successful gender-status improvement. Although Taiwan currently is not a member of the UN, as a formal UN senior member the government of Taiwan puts great effort into following significant UN declaration principles.

For all Chinese-cultural-based areas and governments, in order to help improve the quality of female affairs, here are some simple suggestions:

1. Use cultural objects such as Wu Ze Tian Dynasty temple national treasures and aboriginal festival activities, as symbols and tools to remind the younger generation globally about the achievement of, and respect for, women.

2. Allow women to participate in major purchasing decision. This can improve female rights significantly.

3. Consider creating new laws to prevent cultural-based gender-inequality practices.

4. Always take a closer look at family needs from a woman's point-of-view before making policies that influence the public. A woman's point-of-view should always be considered as plans are being drawn.

Loving girls, wives, mothers and female relatives is the best effort to increase joy in the world. History has told us this over and over again.

References

Qing Dynasty to May 4th Women's Right Observation
      http://ir.lib.nknu.edu.tw/retrieve/21848.pdf
Taiwanese Female Political Status Progress
      http://www.shs.edu.tw/works/essay/2016/03/2016032121435422.pdf
United Nations and China Since The Beginning
      https://zh.m.wikipedia.org/zh-tw
Taiwan Woman's Center
      https://drive.google.com/file/d/0BzrmvyxftmgHNlltMkRWYlZDSzQ/view?pref=2&pli=1
Taiwan Woman's Center - Exhibitions
      http://www.taiwanwomencenter.org.tw/en-global/New/Exhibitions/Content/1/2
Taiwan Woman's Center - Exhibitions/Development
      http://www.taiwanwomencenter.org.tw/en-global/New/Exhibitions/Content/1/1
Taiwan Woman's Center Video in Chinese
      http://www.taiwanwomencenter.org.tw/zh-tw/Video/Media/Content/video3
Charts Regarding Taiwanese Gender Equality Improvement
      http://www.taiwanwomencenter.org.tw/upload/website/twc_ef8cb87f-7598-4366-a4c1-717b831d1832.jpg
Gender Equality Committee of the Executive Yuan
      http://www.ey.gov.tw/gec_en/Default.aspx
Global Gender/WomenStatus In Taiwan
      http://www.globalgender.org/en-global/status_page/index/8
Angelia09, Wu Ze Tian,
      http://wenda.tianya.cn/question/48cca335c207314e

Note from Wendy Jyang: Special thanks to the people and photographers for sharing the pictures.

The Strength of a Woman
Myntillae Nash for Care for Life

Maria and her two children, before her daughter died, in front of her home.

Maria do Ceu became a single mother of two young children when her husband passed away unexpectedly. However, this was not the beginning of Maria's suffering, as she had previously lost her two-year-old daughter, Joaninha, to cholera. Looking back she now realizes that she had made no connection between the disease and everyone's poor sanitation habits in the village. If she could change anything, she wishes that Care for Life had come into her life sooner because, "If Care for Life had been here then, Joaninha would not have died," she says.

Before Care for Life entered the village, Motel Bispo was a typical village. The air was offensive with the foul odor of human waste and there was not a single latrine in the entire village. Naturally, the growing piles of refuse invited flies and mosquitoes to the already-contaminated environment, but none of the villagers understood the importance of sleeping with mosquito nets. As a result, cholera and malaria were persistent problems and took the lives of many prematurely.

With the truths learned through the alliance with Care for Life, the lives of all the villagers radically changed. Today, Motel Bispo is completely transformed – nearly unrecognizable from its previously unsanitary state. The village is clean and beautiful; there is no garbage or foul smell from human waste.

Family gardens promote a diverse, more nutritious diet and for some, like Maria, a means of income. In fact, Maria recently graduated from Care for Life's small business course and started growing vegetables in her garden, which she now

Maria showing her filled out chart with all the goals she accomplished.

BEST PRACTICES

sells at the market. In her future, she plans an expansion from the income gained.

Maria is also active in the development of her entire community. She helped to build a new well; she actively attends all her leadership meetings; and she is passionate about the Stay Alive HIV/AIDS prevention education program for youth. She loves being an instructor to the youth and believes the most important thing she can teach the younger generation is how to avoid getting HIV.

Maria knows she can't change the past, but is grateful to feel armed with the knowledge and skills necessary to protect her family's health and financial well-being for the future. She is an influential leader and example in her community, one who has helped promote tremendous change and is teaching lifestyle habits that will influence generations to come.

Maria and her son in front of her new latrine.

Maria selling her surplus at the market.

Progress toward the Sustainable Development Goals

Water

53. Striking inequalities are evident with regard to water, showing that half of humanity is still left behind. Access to basic sanitation is recognized as a key challenge in the twenty-first century. Global indicators to monitor the evacuation and treatment of wastewater and excreta are not in place. By 2025, two thirds of the world's population is expected to live in water-stressed regions owing to climate change, inefficient water distribution and its use and over-use by the agriculture, energy and other sectors. Global water withdrawals have tripled over the past 50 years. The scientific information available shows that water demands may reach "planetary boundaries" in the coming decades. There is therefore an urgent need for more sustainable water use and improved cooperation and synergies between sectors.
E/HLPF/2016/5, Economic and Social Council, 22 June 2016

Sanitation

47. In 2015, 4.9 billion people globally used an improved sanitation facility; 2.4 billion did not. Among those lacking adequate sanitation were 946 million people without any facilities at all, who continued to practise open defecation. In 2015, 68 per cent of the global population was using improved sanitation facilities compared to 59 per cent in 2000. Nevertheless, the unsafe management of faecal waste and wastewater continues to present a major risk to public health and the environment.
E/2016/75, Report of the Secretary-General, 3 June 2016

Timothy S. Evans, D.D.S.; Medical Biology, Spanish; Field Operations Manager, Cause for Hope (19 offices in 6 Latin American countries); managed micro-credit / micro-enterprise training/implementation programs; founder, president, CEO or board member of the following organizations: Ascend Alliance, Engage Now Foundation, CHOICE Humanitarian, Andean Children's Foundation, and Utah Bolivia Partners; part-time rancher; married with 6 children and 17 grandchildren.

6.4 – Clean Water

Timothy S. Evans, D.D.S.

The Rope Pump in Bolivia: Lessons learned while helping families move from meager to eager acceptance of important new innovations (Andean Children's Foundation).

Understandably, few men showed up for the demo: The drought had destroyed crops, the tin mines had shut down and the men were off in pursuit of what remained as their sole alternative for scanty cash—the arduous, dangerous and illegal work in the burgeoning cocaine traffic. They could find work as miserable trudgers and stompers in the coca vats of Bolivia's Chapare. Nevertheless, the women did come to the water-technology demonstration and brought their water samples. Felix smeared them over glass slides and the women peeked into the microscope.

It started out as another ho-hum event on Bolivia's Altiplano. While a few expressions of interest came at the sight of tiny "bichos" in their water supply, it was still not enough to convince anyone to change water-collecting routines. Felix turned the crank of the contraption fitted to the new well. His assistant filled a test tube with a sample of water and took it to the microscope. No bichos, but no enthusiasm either. Such had been the case over and over again.

The Thrasher Research Fund had provided a grant to the Andean Children's Foundation to develop groundwater technologies in hopes of finding simple, inexpensive solutions for families to overcome gastro-intestinal diseases caused by dirty water supplies. But so far there had been only meager acceptance of the wells and pumps.

While the health workers lectured about waterborne diseases, Felix tested the discharge rate of the newly installed rope and washer pump by filling a ten-liter bucket. The robust pump filled it in two easy turns. He pulled out a stop watch. With minimal effort the bucket filled in less than two seconds. Several tries confirmed a rate of about 350 liters per minute. Impressive! Let the women try....

Suddenly ho-hum became heave-ho. Rufina and her sister (working together, one on each crank) filled the bucket in 1.5 seconds yielding a whopping 400 liters per minute yield. The windlass flew around and around. Water splashed and ran in rivulets radiating from the well. The parched ground lapped it up.

Unnoticed by the happy crowd came a rag-clad man onto the scene. His pants, worn and torn above the knees, revealed ulcerated legs—the inevitable result of tromping in vats filled with kerosene and coca leaves. It was Ambrosio Mamani, Rufina's husband, returning from the Chapare. He jumped into the flowing water – soothing the sores on his legs, cupping his hands, drinking and shouting, **"Water! Water from the ground! This is my salvation!"**

No demo, no lecture, no revelation from on high could have been more effective at sparking interest in the wells and pumps developed by the Andean Children's Foundation. But it was not the water quality that impressed. It was the quantity.

Ambrosio knew immediately that with this well and pump he could save a crop during the frequent dry spells. He also knew he could save the family by keeping them together and not have to leave his farm and family behind while looking for work.

Such was the first of two poignant lessons learned by the Andean Children's Foundation—that people's perceptions must jive with interventions. In the case of diarrhea, for example, it is so common it is perceived as normal, even though children die. In the case of contaminated water sources, they are so common they are also perceived as the norm. Moreover, how do you prevent your children from drinking from those sources? Investing in wells and pumps, even though the new innovations were very cheap, was not perceived as worth the investment just for drinking. **But where starvation looms as a constant risk when crops fail, water for crops becomes a high priority.**

Ambrosio's home-made FLOM well and pump. If he can make it, he can fix it; thus it is more reliable than if he were dependent on outside technicians.

It did not escape the operatives of the Andean Children's Foundation that if families installed wells for watering crops they would also have clean water for drinking, and ample water for bathing and washing hands.

Yet there was one more lesson to learn. It came in the way of what had become a tradition whenever I flew into La Paz—a scrumptious, full course, white-glove dinner with wealthy friends before heading out to the Altiplano. On this occasion a wonderful salad bar had been added to the menu. I asked my hostess where she got such a varied array of fresh veggies, a near impossibility at the rarefied elevations of upper Bolivia.

She gushed about a recent **"green revolution"** among the Aymara Indians of the Altiplano. She told me how they had built greenhouses and captured the veggie market by claiming that greenhouse-grown is better, fresher, cheaper and more varied for the La Paz market than produce imported from the lower valleys.

The greenhouses introduced by the Andean Children's Foundation were not commercial, but for family production and consumption. Just as the pump and well interventions were self-help programs designed to eradicate waterborne disease for rural families, the greenhouses were self-help initiatives intended to eradicate nutritional deficiencies causing scurvy, eye problems and stunted growth.

The next day was a shocker! Donors for the Foundation's Greenhouse Initiatives Project and I beheld the glint of the morning sun off thousands of shiny surfaces in the distance—something we had not seen before. The staff was hardly able to contain the

Family with FLOM technologies – this system mitigates losses due to both drought and frost, providing food and cash security for families. This peasant farmer quadrupled family income by building a much larger greenhouse and placing the pump inside.

excitement to show off some stunning successes to our donors. We saw not only thousands of greenhouses shimmering in the sun and bursting with produce, but learned about what "Paquete Tecnologico Familiar" (Family Technological Package or FTP) which included not just one, but two kinds of wells and two kinds of pumps, one system for the cooking area in the living compound and another system for the family plot, a greenhouse, a stock watering receptacle, and an irrigation strategy for both greenhouse and non-greenhouse crops.

Of course we demanded an explanation for the obvious—a remarkable and unexpected transition from meager to eager acceptance, and we got it. The keys are several:

First: Family-level operation and maintenance (FLOM) – as opposed to the highly-touted VLOM (village-level operation and maintenance) innovations. ACF learned that community-level interventions are fraught with non-starters. For example, who owns it? Who works it? Who profits from it? Who maintains it? Village projects inevitably die once answers to these questions become apparent.

Second key: Accessible – true FLOM technology will be accessible. That means it will be affordable to poor families or simple enough to make with rudimentary tools and typical resources. Accessibility also means availability.

Third key: Utilitarian – FLOM innovations are always perceived as useful to typical poor families, either profitable in some obvious way or more convenient than other options.

This family with FLOM pump and well irrigates three acres; runs water 270 meters from well; sold onion crop off-season for double his usual income; and began a side business making pumps for sale.

Fourth key: Maintainable – again, FLOM means family-level operation and main-tenance. That means simplicity. It means cheap. It means sufficiently intuitive whereby a typical poor family can fix it when it wears or breaks. Maintainability also means reliability: If an innovation is available when needed by a poor family, it is re-liable. That does not pertain to durability. Rather, reliability should be measured by an availability criterion. Technology such as the rope pump, if it can be repaired eas-ily by the family even though it may break more often, will likely have a much better availability score (less down time) than if the family has to find and wait for a techni-cian to come fix it. Such a FLOM innovation, because it is maintainable by the fam-ily, is therefore more available and more reliable, even though it may be less durable.

Summary: Both water and greenhouse technologies were on the verge of being re-jected because project implementers were not on the same page as the users. On the one hand, implementers pushed health and safety in terms of microbes and micro-nutrients. On the other hand, the users were macro-oriented – they were worried about enough food to eat and enough money for necessities. First and foremost in that equation, were the overwhelming risks associated with drought and frost. Only when astute implementers and farmers perceived similarly that health, safety and econom-ics could be addressed on both macro and micro levels did the project succeed.

Interestingly, implementers measured success by a reduction of childhood mor-tality rates. The users measured success by increases in family income. Both metric systems showed overwhelmingly positive results from the adoption of the Family Tech-nological Package: a true FLOM innovation.

Three generations have watered stock with this pump installed in 1988 (picture taken 2015). Roberto says he has totally maintained it over the years on his own. He replaced one PVC tube once and the rope three times.

Water Purification in India
Naveen Pammi for Local Church Catalyst

We start with building a water plant for the village through the congregation of a church. It collects a very nominal fee for the water. The fee would be less than 1/3rd of what they would regularly pay and it is used in three different ways.

One – one third of it is used for maintenance of the water plant;

Two – one third of it goes to the congregation to provide funds to do other activities, like running medical camps for the community;

Three – one third of it is spent on the village for things like fixing roads.

Once the relationships are established (as the families are very poor), we always hear new needs and we try to raise funds to meet those needs. That was how we developed new activities – like sponsoring education for girls, caring for widows and providing medical care.

In some of the villages we build water plants that are directly hooked to ground water, because they run out of ground water in some very hot summer months. When that happens, the water is transported into the village with tanks on trucks. To accommodate such circumstances, we decided to build big sumps right next to the water plants that the plants draw water from. These sumps either draw water from the ground using a motor directly or collect water from a tank on a truck.

Providing clean water to drink is a very noble cause to work for and sounds very simple to do, especially when we have resources, including funds, available. But in reality it is very challenging. First, the circumstances of the culture make it difficult to provide the necessary information to the families. Second, because of their unfamiliarity with clean water, they usually do not know how to keep the water clean.

Understanding the challenges we faced in India in these areas could be helpful to others – to be prepared to better serve people not only in India, but also in other countries.

Community water filtration plant

BEST PRACTICES

Circumstances and culture

Because of the culture in the villages. the women generally stay inside. It is the men who participate in the training sessions to learn (1) how to use the equipment and (2) proper sanitization techniques. But in reality, it is the mothers who do all the work at home and use the water the most. So, it is important to insist on having women participate; and it is very helpful to have some women actually teach the training sessions – to encourage women's participation.

Unfamiliarity with clean water

Because the houses in the villages do not have taps to deliver the water, the water is collected in large containers. When they need water to drink, they dip a cup into the water container to collect the water to drink. Sometimes the hands might not be clean, and if they touch the water, bacteria might be re-introduced into the water container.

Large water-filtration tank with lid

Even though we try to educate on sanitization and the importance of washing hands every time, it is hard for them to keep following the instructions because that is how they have been doing things their entire life, and the day-to-day situations often demand urgency.

So, we built containers with lids and taps to collect the clean water from filters and water plants. This restricts them from dipping cups into the clean water and makes it easy to collect the water from a special tap.

Corruption and timing

Other circumstances to consider are corruption and a sense of timing. These two problems are very prevalent in third world countries. It is very important to be prepared for these concerns in the process of building equipment to provide clean water. It is also very important to obtain help from those very familiar with the local circumstances, yet themselves are very genuine and understand our expectations.

That is why when we are drawn to a village, we start working through a congregation that would provide them life skills and continuous relationships with the families that they will be continually serving.

Local families drive the work

A critical factor to keep the organization nimble and more effective is to keep local families as the face of the work in any village. They are the ones who live there and serve people in their village and no one understands the circumstances better than the local people. In addition, as soon as the system is installed, and functioning, it gives us the freedom to move on to the next village.

Protecting the Springs

Jastus Suchi Obadiah for Reach the Children

In the African culture, springs were thought to be a home to many spirits of ancestors – it was not acceptable for one to deny a villager access to spring water. This practice is still evident today, although due to private land ownership the owner of the land where the spring is located must confirm that he/she will not deny anyone from accessing water. Thus, accessibility of spring water is public and community owned.

Spring protection is the activity of protecting the sources of natural water from the ground due to natural pressure. If not protected, erosion, deposition or landslides can erase them and rob villagers of a reliable source of water. Most springs serve between 15 to 100 households and thus are very important in providing water in rural areas in Africa. In East Africa, it is estimated that more than 80% of rural households depend on spring water – especially in areas with high rainfall where springs run throughout the year, such as around: Kakamega, Bungoma, Busia, and Vihiga, etc.

Protecting springs assures rural people of a continual water source for a long time. It does this by preventing the contamination of water from fecal material, and the water from protected springs contributes to less infections – compared to the water from unprotected springs. (Unprotected spring water may also be infected by algae and fungus and provide a breeding ground for mosquitoes.)

During the protection project, families in local villages are mobilized, and they help achieve the goals of spring protection.

Some families participate further in a spring committee to ensure that the spring's protection is maintained after handover from Reach The Children Kenya.

The local people understand their problem. This project has the main objective of empowering them in a more sustainable way: First, to protect the springs so they can collect clean water; Second, to train them on the need to purify the water before being consumed. The government of Kenya has done a good work to empower people to use disinfectants. This is common knowledge to all Kenyans. The brand "Water Guard" is famous in Kenya, even among the illiterate.

Spring area before spring protection

BEST PRACTICES

Woman dancing near the new spout after the construction of spring protection

Trees for planting in spring catchment areas

The community and families contribute hard labor to protect the springs and also help transport materials to the site—some springs are far from where the material will be dropped from the supplier. Wheelbarrows are used. Some families will give lunch to the laborers. This is a good cultural practice among the Luhya communities, where families and community members show gratitude for protected springs. Most importantly, families will maintain and repair the springs after handover from Reach the Children.

In addition to spring protection, RTC has a project for tree planting – to ensure the protection of the catchment area of the springs. The children assist in planting the trees – teaching the importance of protecting the environment around the springs.

This project shows how the combined family capital of individual families can help all the families in the community.

Planting trees as part of the spring protection project.

The Importance of Sanitation
Family Preservation Program
careforlife.org

The Family Preservation Program provides meaningful learning opportunities through bi-weekly classes as well as personal visits. Through these interactions the families understand the importance of sanitation and implement:

1. The proper use of a latrine and a washroom;
2. Cleanliness of their property (including burning garbage and removing stagnant water and weeds); and
3. Proper housing of domesticated animals.

Diseases such as cholera and diarrhea are caused by the lack of proper sanitation and this problem is exacerbated during the rainy season. The use of latrines in Care for Life's villages is 40% higher than the national average. The Family Preservation Program includes the following goals:

Health & Hygiene
- Families will take sanitary measures to prevent infection and disease.
- Parents will follow prescriptions correctly when taking medicine.
- Parents will ensure yearly that children are current in their immunizations.
- Families will take care of their own sick members at the onset of illness.
- Families will visit health centers and hospitals for consultations and treatment.
- Pregnant women will have prenatal consultations and follow instructions.
- Toddlers will be taken to the hospital yearly to test growth pattern.

Sanitation
- Mothers will bathe their children daily.
- People will shower every day and know the advantages of personal hygiene.
- Families will drink only clean water.
- Families will wash dishes after each use.
- Families will have their own clean, functioning latrine.
- Families will have their own clean, functioning washing room.
- Families will have access to a water well or other water source within the community.

BEST PRACTICES

Building an approved latrine

Bathing the baby in clean water

Certeza water purification

BEST PRACTICES

Care for Life – Family Preservation Program

Goals for home improvement

- Roofs and walls of family houses will be built of adequate material and be in good condition.
- Family houses will have secure doors and screened windows.
- Floors of family houses will have a covering of cement or other material.
- Family houses will have their own latrine and washing room outdoors.
- Family houses will be clean inside.
- Family yards will be clean with marked boundaries.
- Families will eliminate stagnant water from their property.
- Families will keep their yard free of weeds and wild shrubs.
- Families will eliminate pests such as: rats, mice, cockroaches and other insects
- Families who raise animals will have them properly housed at all times.

Care for Life indicators measured & statistical progress

(In current communities)	Initial	Current
• Is there an adequate roof?	49%	86%
• Are the walls adequate?	52%	85%
• Does the house have a safe/secure door?	74%	94%
• Is floor cement or another covering?	33%	42%
• Does the family have a latrine?	26%	93%
• Does the family have a bathhouse?	56%	96%
• Is the yard clean?	95%	99%
• Pest free house (roaches, mice, worms)?	21%	59%
• Is garbage burned or buried?	44%	98%
• Have a tarimba (table for holding dishes)?	29%	91%

(In exited communities)	Initial	at Exit	Current
• Is there an adequate roof?	50%	88%	94%
• Are the walls adequate?	44%	85%	92%
• Does the house have a safe/secure door?	51%	81%	95%
• Is floor with cement or another covering?	35%	72%	80%
• Does the family have a latrine?	32%	94%	96%
• Does the family have a bathhouse?	65%	98%	99%
• Is the yard clean?	84%	99%	100%
• Pest-free house (roaches, mice, worms)?	15%	65%	75%
• Is garbage burned or buried?	58%	98%	97%
• Have a tarimba (table for holding dishes)?	31%	93%	92%

BEST PRACTICES

Old house and new house under construction

Luisa Antonio Mabe & Joaquina Antonio Mabe – bricks for latrine

---

Progress towards the Sustainable Development Goals
Report of the Secretary-General, 3 June 2016
E/2016/75

Goal 7. Ensure access to affordable, reliable, sustainable and modern energy for all

53. Energy is crucial for achieving almost all of the Sustainable Development Goals, from its role in the eradication of poverty through advancements in health, education, water supply and industrialization, to combating climate change.

54. The proportion of the global population with access to electricity has increased steadily, from 79 per cent in 2000 to 85 per cent in 2012. Still, 1.1 billion people are without this valuable service. Recent global progress in this area has been driven largely by Asia, where access is expanding at more than twice the pace of demographic growth. Of those gaining access to electricity worldwide since 2010, 80 per cent are urban dwellers.

55. The proportion of the world's population with access to clean fuels and technologies for cooking increased from 51 per cent in 2000 to 58 per cent in 2014, although there has been limited progress since 2010. The absolute number of people relying on polluting fuels and technologies for cooking, such as solid fuels and kerosene, however, has actually increased, reaching an estimated three billion people. Limited progress since 2010 falls substantially short of global population growth and is almost exclusively confined to urban areas.

56. The share of renewable energy (derived from hydropower, solid and liquid biofuels, wind, the sun, biogas, geothermal and marine sources, and waste) in the world's total final energy consumption has increased slowly, from 17.4 per cent in 2000 to 18.1 per cent in 2012. . . . The technologies making the largest contribution have been hydropower, wind and solar energy; together they account for 73 per cent of the total increase in modern renewable energy between 2010 and 2012.

Brad and Wendy Wixom:
Wendy Wixom, ASGS, UN Representative for World Congress of Families, former Administrative Chair of Sustainable Families Group. Her husband, Brad Wixom, MBA, BSBA, has 23 years as an executive in the energy field. Brad and Wendy have been married 29 years and have five children. They have visited 26 countries and collectively volunteered 42 years in leadership and teaching positions.

---

7 – Energy Efficiency

Brad & Wendy Wixom

Walking at dusk in the Alta Verapaz region of Guatemala, an unforgettable scene unfolds as the green hills ignite with orange flames and fragrant plumes of meandering smoke. The families' cooking fires often cause a slithering haze to roll over the hills. In 2014, 58% of the world's population had access to clean fuels and technologies for cooking.

> The absolute number of people relying on polluting fuels and technologies for cooking, such as solid fuels and kerosene, however, has actually increased, reaching an estimated three billion people.[1]

Regions of Guatemala are but a few areas of the world where open fires are used to: cook food, boil water, heat homes and survive. What are the side effects of these fuels for families? Are there healthier and more efficient ways families can conserve wood and other biomass fuels when cooking over fires? Are there things that families in more developed countries can do to conserve energy as well?

| Cooking over an open fire | *AP Photo* |

In February 2016, the World Health Organization posted:

> …around 3 billion people cook and heat their homes using open fires and simple stoves burning biomass (wood, animal dung and crop waste) and coal. Over 4 million people die prematurely from illness attributable to the household air pollution from cooking with solid fuels. More than 50% of premature deaths due to pneumonia among children under 5 are caused by the particulate matter (soot) inhaled from household air pollution. 3.8 million premature deaths annually from noncommunicable diseases including stroke, ischaemic heart disease, chronic obstructive pulmonary disease (COPD) and lung cancer are attributed to exposure to household air pollution.
>
> Inefficient cooking fuels and technologies produce high levels of household air pollution with a range of health-damaging pollutants, including small soot particles that penetrate deep into the lungs. In poorly ventilated dwellings, indoor smoke can be 100 times higher than acceptable levels for fine particles. Exposure is particularly high among women and young children, who spend the most time near the domestic hearth.[2]

Cleaner-burning cooking stoves

The good news is that various alternative cooking methods are emerging that are much safer, healthier and more energy efficient. Educating populations about these methods will have a positive impact on the development of sustainable communities, responsible consumption and improving family health.

There are more than 1500 organizations working to develop and produce healthier and more efficient cook-stoves within Africa, Asia and Latin America.[3] Many of these stoves are advanced variations of Rocket Stoves. Rocket Stoves use less biomass because of their highly efficient combustion.

This combustion burns more smoke and fewer particulates, releasing less waste pollutants into the home and air while producing a more concentrated heat source. Their high efficiency results in great energy conservation and increased health benefits.

A basic Rocket Stove can be made by strategically stacking as few as 16, 20 or 24 adobe/firebricks. Multiple internet websites have patterns for quick and affordable Rocket Stoves.[4]

Clean-burning cook stove, with chimney.
Photo by Deseret News

As families build more efficient stoves within their homes, they: lower health hazards, conserve energy, protect the environment and save time gathering fuel.

Purification of drinking and cooking water

The Secretary-General has said, "…water and sanitation are at the very core of sustainable development, critical to the survival of people and the planet."[5] Purification of drinking and cooking water is another use of biomass-fueled stoves. The World Health Organization claims:

> 663 million people rely on unimproved [water] sources, including 159 million dependent on surface water. Globally, at least 1.8 billion people use a drinking-water source contaminated with faeces. Contaminated water can transmit diseases such diarrhea, cholera, dysentery, typhoid and polio. Contaminated drinking-water is estimated to cause 502,000 diarrheal deaths each year.[6]

Economic growth and development require the production of goods and services that improve the quality of life. Sustainable growth and development require minimizing the natural resources and toxic materials, and waste and pollutants generated, throughout the entire production and consumption process.[7]

To help in this area, several companies are creating cost-efficient water filtration systems. Using water filters decreases the use of cookstoves for boiling water, thus indoor air pollution is greatly decreased and fuel resources preserved. Additionally, many filters can remove 99% of pathogens.[8]

In addition to the concern of biomass-fuel health and conservation, electricity is another conservation means where "family capital" can be a powerful resource.

The UN Secretary-General has stated that in 2012, 85% of the global population had access to electricity.[9] For that 85%, simple changes within families can have a significant impact on energy conservation.

Water filter system (India).
Photo by Naveen Pammi

Family practices to conserve energy

Gather and discuss which of these best practices can be implemented in your family today.[10]

Cooking

- Consider cooking meals with other families. Cooking larger quantities on fewer heat sources will conserve energy.
- Cook with lids on pots/pans to trap in heat and speed up cooking time.
- When using hot water, put a bowl under the faucet to gather excess water. Use it for watering gardens, washing dishes, hands, etc.
- Do not boil more water than needed. This reduces heating time and energy use.
- Keep lids and doors on pots, pans, slow cookers and ovens shut while cooking to maintain temperature.
- If electricity is used for cooking, use small appliances like slow cookers, microwaves and toaster ovens rather than conventional ovens.

Suggestions for families in more developed countries

Homes – General

- Take shorter and cooler showers.
- Turn off water while brushing teeth.
- Do not let water run for long periods while preparing food or doing dishes.
- Turn computers off or set to sleep rather than screen saver mode.
- Unplug small appliances, chargers and computers when not in use.
- Keep fireplace flues closed.
- Installing glass doors on fireplaces can keep warm/cool air from escaping out – or sneaking in – the chimney.
- Keep furniture and blankets off vents so air can properly circulate.
- Decorate with lighter colors to better reflect light and require less lighting and/or lower wattage bulbs to light the room. It also allows lights to be turned on later in the day.
- Use LED or fluorescent lighting rather than incandescent.
- Turn off lights when leaving a room or home.
- Keep garage doors shut to provide another barrier between the house and outdoor temperatures.

Heating/cooling

Simple and routine checks around the home can lessen carbon dioxide emissions into the environment and reduce heating/cooling expenses.

- Check for air drafts around windows and doors. If found, seal with proper filler, sealant, weather stripping or thresholds. Doors with larger gaps can be covered with blankets, bags of sand, etc.
- Replace furnace filters every month.
- Have furnace/air conditioning unit checked yearly to insure efficient operation.
- Turn thermostats down (in cool climates) or up (in warm climates) 8 degrees when leaving.
- Invest in a programmable thermostat that automatically turns down temperatures at night or when the house is vacant.
- While on vacation, adjust thermostat so it is not heating/cooling the house to more than minimal needs.
- In cool climates close window blinds or draperies at night.
- Rather than turn heat up, use throw rugs, socks, shoes or sweaters to keep warm.
- Close air vents in rooms that are not being used.
- Install ceiling fans to circulate air and keep cool.
- Turn off air conditioning at night and open windows.
- Trees or shrubbery on the sunny side of homes provide shade from exterior heat.
- Add insulating foam gaskets behind plug/light switches. Never insulate around recessed lighting.
- Add insulation to roof, all exterior walls and exposed floor joists.
- Put insulation on the back of attic doors. Install weather stripping around openings.
- When possible convert to solar or geo-thermal heating.

Appliances

- Turn water heaters down to 60 degrees Celsius/140 degrees Fahrenheit to save energy and prevent burns.
- Install a timer or turn water heater off when home is not occupied.
- When replacing appliances, buy energy efficient appliances and ones that use less water, if available.
- Turn off "heat dry" setting on dishwashers.

- With laundry and dishwashing machines, wash only full loads.
- Doing laundry in cold water saves energy and money.
- Hang clothing to dry. If using a dryer, do not over-dry loads.
- Clean lint filters in clothing dryer. Lint can be used for kindling to start fires.
- Vent dryer outside the home unless added heat and humidity are wanted inside.
- Keep stove heat-reflector trays clean so more heat is reflected back at the pots.
- Use the appropriate sized pot for the burner.
- Turn off kitchen and bathroom fans when not in use.
- Check seals on refrigerators and freezers. If cold air is escaping, replace seals.
- Assure refrigerators and freezers are level so doors don't come open unexpectedly.
- Let food cool down before putting in refrigerator/freezer.
- Dust light fixtures regularly to insure light is optimally disseminated.
- Do not put lamps near thermostats, as the heat may affect accurate thermostat reading.
- Place humidifiers and dehumidifiers away from walls for proper air circulation.

Family activities

- Dedicate one night a week to turning off, or putting aside, all electronics—enjoy an activity with your family: go for a hike or walk; play a board, card, circle game or sport; visit extended family, friends or neighbors; read a book together; go to a park; ride bicycles or scooters.
- Rather than driving, when possible walk, carpool and make use of public transportation.

Conclusion

Integrating more efficient cooking and water purification methods into the homes of developing countries conserves energy for the planet, and provides greater health to our most valuable resource, the family. In any community, working together as families rather than individuals can greatly impact the conservation of the world's energy resources. Family capital plays a key role in educating future generations on how to implement best practices for energy conservation and healthier lifestyles.

Endnotes:

1. Moon, Ban-Ki, (2016), "Report of the Secretary-General: Progress Towards the Sustainable Development Goals", High-level segment, 2016 session, para 55.
2. World Health Organization, "Household air pollution and health," July 8, 2016, http://www.who.int/mediacentre/factsheets/fs292/en/.
3. Global Alliance for Clean Cookstoves, "The Clean Cooking Catalog: Product and Performance Data for the Cookstove Sector," July 12, 2016, http://catalog.cleancookstoves.org

4. Sustain A Blog, "How to Build a Rocket Stove Plans," July 12, 2016, http://sustainablog.org/2011/09/how-to-build-a-rocket-stove/

5. Moon, Ban-Ki, (2016), "Report of the Secretary-General: Progress Towards the Sustainable Development Goals," High-level segment, 2016 session, para 46.

6. World Health Organization, (2015), Drinking-water, Fact Sheet No. 391, July 9 , 2016, http://www.who.int/mediacentre/factsheets/fs391/en/.

7. Moon, Ban-Ki, (2016), "Report of the Secretary-General: Progress Towards the Sustainable Development Goals," High-level segment, 2016 session, para 84.

8. The Carbon Neutral Company, "Guatemala: Water Filtration and Improved Cookstoves", July 12, 2016, http://www.carbonneutral.com/images/uploads/projects/Guatemala_Water_Filtration_Improved_Cookstoves_Jan15.pdf.

9. Moon, Ban-Ki, (2016), "Report of the Secretary-General: Progress Towards the Sustainable Development Goals," High-level segment, 2016 session, para 54.

10. Many of these items are listed on multiple websites. Therefore, instead of specifying a specific reference per conservation activity, the various websites used to create this conservation list are below:

    a) Energy.gov, (2016), "6 Smart Energy Resolutions for 2016," July 8, 2016, http://www.energy.gov/articles/6-smart-energy-resolutions-2016

    b) Energy.gov, (2015), "Are Energy Vampires Sucking You Dry?," July 8, 2016, http://www.energy.gov/articles/are-energy-vampires-sucking-you-dry

    c) National Wildlife Federation, "Conserving Energy In Your Home," July 8, 2016, https://www.nwf.org/How-to-Help/Live-Green/Energy-Conservation/In-Your-Home.aspx

    d) Duke Energy Progress, 2015, "100 Ways to Save Energy at Home," July 8, 2016, https://www.progress-energy.com/carolinas/home/save-energy-money/energy-saving-tips-calculators/100-tips.page

    e) California Energy Commission, 2016, "Saving Energy," July 8, 2016, http://www.energyquest.ca.gov/saving_energy/

    f) Didier, Suzanna, Demand Media/SF Gate, "How My Family Can Conserve Energy," July 8, 2016, http://homeguides.sfgate.com/family-can-conserve-energy-78712.html

    g) Alliant Energy, 2016, "101 Ways to Save Energy," July 8, 2016, http://www.power-housetv.com/Energy-EfficientLiving/Energy-savingsTips/027471

    h) Ecomall, "20 Things You Can Do To Conserve Energy," July 8, 2016, http://www.ecomall.com/greenshopping/20things.htm

Four key links between families and the economic welfare of states across the United States:

- **Higher levels of marriage, and especially higher levels of married-parent families, are strongly associated with more economic growth, more economic mobility, less child poverty and higher median-family income at the state level in the United States.** When we compare states in the top quintile of married-parent families with those in the bottom quintile, we find that being in the top quintile is associated with a $1,451 higher per capita GDP; 10.5 percent greater upward income mobility for children from lower-income families; a 13.2 percent decline in the child poverty rate; and a $3,654 higher median family income. These estimates are based on models that control for a range of factors—from the educational and racial composition of a state to its tax policies and spending on education, and to unchanging characteristics of states—that might otherwise confound the family-economy link at the state level.

- **The share of parents in a state who are married is one of the top predictors of the economic outcomes** studied in this report. In fact, this family factor is generally a stronger predictor of economic mobility, child poverty and median family income in the American states than are the educational, racial and age compositions of the states.

- **The state-level link between marriage and economic growth is stronger for younger adults** (ages 25–35) than for older adults (36–59). This suggests that marriage plays a particularly important role in fostering a positive labor-market orientation among young men.

- **Violent crime is much less common** in states with larger shares of families headed by married parents, even after controlling for a range of socio-demographic factors at the state level. For instance, the violent crime rate (violent crimes per 100,000 people) sits at 343 on average for states in the top quintile of married parenthood, whereas those in the bottom quintile average a rate of 563. This is noteworthy because high crime rates lower the quality of life and real living standards and are associated with lower levels of economic growth and mobility.

Available at: https://www.aei.org/wp-content/uploads/2015/10/IFS-HomeEconReport-2015-FinalWeb.pdf
by W. Bradford Wilcox, Joseph Price, and Robert I. Lerman

W. Bradford Wilcox, Ph.D., Associate Professor of Sociology of the University of Virginia, directs the National Marriage Project at the University of Virginia and is Visiting Scholar at the American Enterprise Institute. He is coauthor of *Soul Mates: Religion, Sex, Love, & Marriage Among African Americans and Latinos.*

8 – Strong Families, Prosperous States

W. Bradford Wilcox Ph.D.

I want to begin by talking about the conventional wisdom. From Hollywood to the halls of academia, we often hear the message that marriage doesn't matter. Kids and families, we are told, need not enjoy the shelter and security of a married home to thrive. Take, for instance, Jennifer Anniston, who said, "Women are realizing it more and more: knowing that they don't have to settle with a man just to have that child." Or in the book *Raising Boys Without Men: How Maverick Moms Are Creating the Next Generation of Exceptional Men*, which celebrates women who have had boys without fathers, the Cornell psychologist Peggy Drexler said "Women possess the innate mom-power [sic] that in itself is more than sufficient to raise fine sons." And this Pollyannish message is also taken up by some in the media. Last year, for instance, Matthew Yglesias at *Vox* gave explicit voice to the idea that the decline of marriage isn't a problem for women, children and the country as a whole.

Of course, the only problem with this new conventional wisdom about marriage and family life is that it's not true. This is indicated by some of the highlights from the newest research I've done with economists Joseph Price and Robert Lerman, research that underlines the connection between marriage and the economic health of states across the country.[1]

Marriage matters

Let's begin this conversation by considering how it is that marriage matters in this country of ours [the United States of America]. A publication just out from Princeton and Brookings demonstrates how marriage is connected to the welfare and well-being of our kids. More specifically, "reams of social science and medical research convincingly show that children who are raised by their married biological parents enjoy better physical, cognitive, and emotional outcomes on average than children who are raised in other circumstances."[2]

Clearly, social science is telling us that kids are more likely to flourish when they are raised in intact married homes. And I say this to you as someone who was raised by a single mother. Many kids like me and my sister turn out "just fine," but I am also speaking as a social scientist, and on average, our kids are more likely to flourish, as this new publication from Princeton and Brookings tells us, when they have the benefit of an intact married-parent family behind them.

But I want to turn our thinking away from just the kids and towards thinking about how family structure matters for the larger society. How is what is happening to our marriages in our states linked to what is happening in state economies? As we were exploring this issue, Lerman, Price and I found that virtually no research had been published on the connection between the health of marriage and economic growth.

Connection between health of marriage and economic growth

This is ironic because the term *economics* is rooted in the Greek term *oikonomia*, which means "the management of the household." It is for that reason that Joseph Price, Robert Lerman, and I set out in our report "Strong Families, Prosperous States," to study the link between marriage and economics at the state level. What was the connection between the health of a state's marriage culture and its economy?

What we found is that when families are stronger in a state, when there are more married-parent families in a state, you see higher levels of economic growth, you see

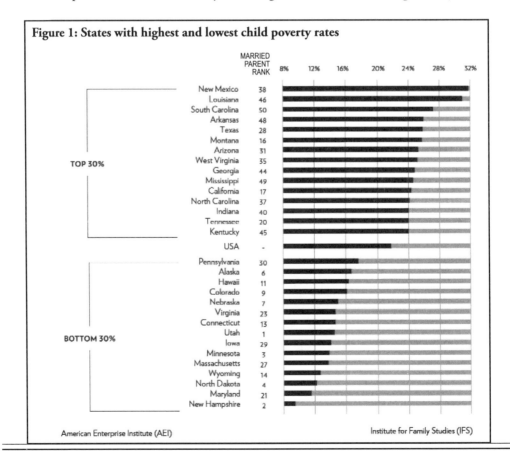

Figure 1: States with highest and lowest child poverty rates

less child poverty, you see higher levels of median-family income, and you see that the American Dream is more likely to be realized by poor kids.

So if you look, for instance, at Figure 1, what you see is that states like New Mexico, Louisiana and South Carolina have some of the highest levels of child poverty in the country, in part because these states have comparatively few married parents in them.[3] By contrast, states like New Hampshire, Minnesota and North Dakota have comparatively low levels of child poverty, in part because so many of the families in those states are headed by married parents; these parents can bring more economic resources to the table, in part because they are married. There is a connection at the state level between child poverty and the health of the married-parent family.

The odds of moving up

We also see a very similar story when it comes to the American Dream (see Figure 2).[4]

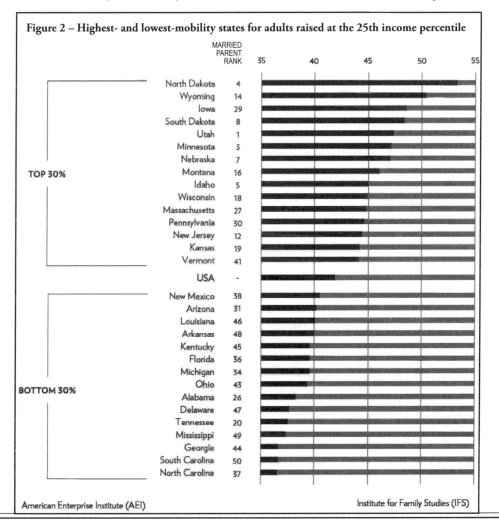

Figure 2 – Highest- and lowest-mobility states for adults raised at the 25th income percentile

Looking at the odds that a child growing up in a poor family—the 25th percentile—moves up to a higher percentile as an adult, we see that some states are more likely to make that American Dream come true. But states like New Mexico, Louisiana and South Carolina, again, are not doing so well. Kids from these kinds of states are less likely to move toward the middle class (toward the 50th percentile) as adults. By contrast, kids in states like Utah, for example, which has the highest share of married-parent families in our nation, are more likely to move toward that 50th percentile as adults, because they benefit from growing up in a community, neighborhood and area where there are lots of married parents in the mix. Again, there is a connection between the health of the American Dream for poor kids and the health of the married-parent family in our states.

If we think about this in a broader sense, what would the economic profile of our states look like if our states enjoyed, on average, 1980-levels of married parenthood? We would see state per capita GDP about 4 percent higher. We would see child poverty rates about 17 percent lower. And we would see family median income resting at a level about 10 percent higher. **There is clearly a connection between what is happening in our families and what is happening in our state economies.**

Family structure a better predictor of outcomes

In our culture today there has been a lot of discussion in policy circles, in media circles and in academic circles, about the impact of education and race on the economic arena. These are important factors, but what is striking about this new report is that we find, at least at the state level, that family structure is a better predictor of outcomes like economic mobility, child poverty and median family income than are race or education. Family matters here; it seems to be a very powerful factor when it comes to the health of our state economies.

The bottom line is if you care about growth and child poverty, family income and the American Dream, you should care about the health of the family, both for the country at large and in your state and community more particularly. So why does marriage matter? Why it is that there is such a strong connection between healthy families and healthy state economies? Let me begin by taking a point that was elucidated by Jason Carroll, which is that men especially are affected by marriage and family life (see Figure 3).[5] This is a point not unique to me. It was articulated back in 1998 by Nobel Laureate George Akerlof (who is married to our Fed chair Janet Yellen), who said, "Men settle down when they get married."[6] His basic argument is that the responsibilities attendant to being a married father are likely to motivate men to be more responsible and more directly engaged in the labor force.

Married men work more strategically

The research indicates that men who are married tend to work more hours than their single peers. They tend to work more strategically. They are less likely, for instance, to

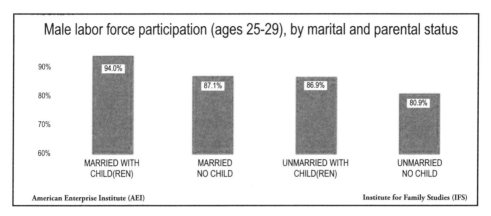

Male labor force participation (ages 25-29), by marital and parental status

MARRIED WITH CHILD(REN): 94.0%
MARRIED NO CHILD: 87.1%
UNMARRIED WITH CHILD(REN): 86.9%
UNMARRIED NO CHILD: 80.9%

American Enterprise Institute (AEI)

Institute for Family Studies (IFS)

be fired than their comparable single peers. And they work more successfully—they make more money—than their comparable single peers.

We can see this at the level of labor force participation. Married men with kids are 13 percent more likely to be in the labor force than their comparable, single peers. Again, there is a connection between marriage, men and work in our society.

Money management

The organization of the household also matters. We know that married families have more money to manage, and they tend to manage it more prudently than families headed by single parents and cohabiting couples. They draw on economies of scale. They pool income. They have higher rates of saving. They get more financial support from their kin. And they are more likely to stay together, which also reinforces their economic position. So, again, there is a connection between what is happening in the household and what is happening in the checking account. We see a family-income premium for African Americans, Hispanics, Whites, less-educated Americans and for college-educated Americans that are married.

Fostering human capital

Finally, we know that strong families foster the accumulation of human capital. We know that kids who come from married families tend to graduate from high school, then graduate from college at higher rates. They are more likely to be gainfully employed as adults and to work more hours. This is true for both young men and young women; if you are concerned about women's professional opportunities you should be concerned about their family structure growing up.

At the state level we see states that enjoy higher levels of married parenthood also have higher levels of high-school completion. So again, both at the household level and at the state level, there is a connection between education and strong families.

In our report, then, we hypothesize that there is a connection between strong families and state prosperity, because marriage and family life deepen men's connection to the labor force, they boost income and assets and they improve the accumulation of human capital.

The retreat from marriage

Which states have been more affected by the retreat from marriage, and why? When progressives are thinking about these questions they tend to gravitate towards what is called "social structure explanations," usually economic explanations. For example, in talking about this issue Annie Lowrey wrote for the *New York Times* that "from the economist's perspective, our collective allergy to matrimony might be a macro-economic issue. In order to save marriage, we'd have to end poverty."[7] Or in more simple terms, "It's the economy, stupid." Economic factors are driving this retreat from marriage, especially in states with large numbers of working class and poor people.

A different perspective would say it is about more than money – that culture matters, that public policy matters. Isabel Sawhill at the Brookings Institution wrote, "A purely economic theory falls short as an explanation of the dramatic transformation of family life in recent decades."[8] There is evidence from the last century to back up Dr. Sawhill's observation. We know, for instance, that at the height of the Great Depression in the 1930s, when the economy was in terrible shape, we had much higher levels of family stability, much lower levels of divorce and much lower levels of single parenthood than we do now. Clearly, what is happening in the family is not simply about economics.

Structural and cultural explanations

What does that say about what is happening today in states across the country? What we find in this new report is that some states, primarily in the north, from Utah across to New England, are doing pretty well on the married-parent front. By contrast, states in the south, states like Georgia and Louisiana, are not doing so well, as Figure 4 sug-

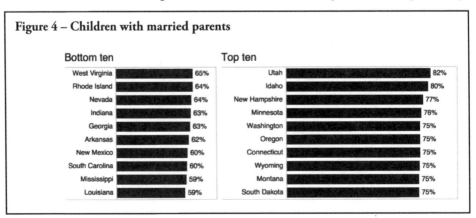

Figure 4 – Children with married parents

Bottom ten		Top ten	
West Virginia	65%	Utah	82%
Rhode Island	64%	Idaho	80%
Nevada	64%	New Hampshire	77%
Indiana	63%	Minnesota	76%
Georgia	63%	Washington	75%
Arkansas	62%	Oregon	75%
New Mexico	60%	Connecticut	75%
South Carolina	60%	Wyoming	75%
Mississippi	59%	Montana	75%
Louisiana	59%	South Dakota	75%

gests.[9] This leads us to consider social, structural and cultural explanations regarding what is happening to marriage and family life in our country today. I think there is something to this progressive idea that economics matter, that education matters, that states like Mississippi and Louisiana are doing not so well, for example, in part because they have low levels of education. By contrast, states like Minnesota and New Hampshire are doing comparatively well on the married-parent front, in part because they have higher levels of education. So this set of findings is broadly consistent with a more progressive view on family life in America.

But if we turn to a different set of states, states like Idaho, South Dakota and Utah, we see even middling or even lower levels of education coexisting with higher degrees of marriage. Here I think a cultural explanation about the way in which these states and these communities value marriage, is more compelling. I echo the words of David Leonhardt of the *New York Times*, who has written about this subject three times in *The Upshot*: "…the more respect and even reverence for the idea of marriage [found] in conservative communities [may] affect people's behavior and attitudes" in ways that reinforce the strength and stability of married life in more conservative communities and states.[10] Putting all of this together, our bottom line is that structural and cultural factors explain why some states—largely in the north—have proven to be more successful in resisting the nation-wide retreat from marriage.

Where do we go from here?

Given all of this, where do we go from here? What is to be done? One key point to make here is that given the structural realities mentioned, we need to think more about how we can shore up the economic foundations of working-class and poor families and communities across the United States. One area we can do this is in the arena of educational policy.

We need to recognize that even today most Americans will not get a college degree. Yet our educational system tends to focus solely on that as the primary goal. We need to serve our kids who are not on the "college track" much better, with better vocational and apprenticeship training, for instance. That would improve their sense of identity, their economic prospects, and down the road, their marriage prospects as well.

Do no harm

A second point when it comes to public policy is we need to take very seriously this idea of "doing no harm" when it comes to marriage and family life. An unfortunate reality is that too many of our public policies targeting lower-income Americans unintentionally penalize marriage. That matters, because a third of Americans are receiving some kind of means-tested benefit, from Medicaid to food stamps. Because these policies penalize marriage, they may also be undercutting the value of marriage in working-class and poor communities.

Creative cultural and civic strategies

We also need to realize what is happening in our families is affected only at the margins by what is happening in Washington or Salt Lake City or Sacramento, in our federal and state capitals; public policy only matters so much. We need to be thinking about creative cultural and civic strategies to change marriage and family life, to change relationships in our culture. I think we can take some comfort from the successful campaign that was inaugurated in the early 1990s by the National Campaign to Prevent Teen and Unplanned Pregnancy. Working with a range of partners, from Hollywood to religious institutions to schools, they have helped to bring down the rate of teen pregnancy by more than 50% since 1990. This is the kind of example that we should use as we think about ways to reintegrate or resurrect what Jason Carroll called "the success sequence," encouraging adults to put education, work, marriage and parenthood in that order, as a newly reinvigorated public norm.

Conclusion

Let me conclude: given the central role that marriage plays in fostering growth, prosperity and the American Dream, the nation needs to renew the economic, policy, civic and cultural foundations of marriage and family life for the twenty-first century. Clearly, there is no magic bullet when it comes to dealing with marriage and families. Some will doubt the justice and even feasibility of such a project. But this report demonstrates that some states have achieved a measure of success in resisting the nation's retreat from marriage.

If more states could get behind public policies that do not penalize marriage, educational efforts that strengthen the earning power of working-class and poor young men, and civic efforts to make the culture more marriage-friendly, we just might see a renaissance in marriage and family life in America. And that would bring about improvements not only in the state of our unions, but also in the wealth of our states.

Endnotes

1. W. Bradford Wilcox, Robert I. Lerman, and Joseph Price, "Strong Families, Prosperous States: Do Healthy Families Affect the Wealth of States?" American Enterprise Institute and the Institute for Family Studies, October 19, 2015, available at https://www.aei.org/publication/ strong-families-prosperous-states/.
2. David C. Ribar, "Why Marriage Matters for Child Wellbeing," *The Future of Children* 25.2 (Fall 2005): 11-23, at 12, available at https://www.princeton.edu/futureofchildren/publications/docs/Fulll%20Journal%20Marriage%20Revisited.pdf.

3. Wilcox *et al.*, figure 8. Tabulations by authors from the Current Population Survey, 2012-2013. Married parent rank is based on the share of parents with children under 18 that are married, according to the 2013 Current Population Survey. Ages restricted to 25-59. All states included.

4. *Ibid.*, figure 6. Tabulations by authors from the Equality of Opportunity Project's absolute upward mobility data by county, collapsed to the state level. Married-parent rank is based on the share of parents with children under 18 that are married, according to the 2013 Current Population Survey. Ages restricted to 25-59. Mobility is from the 1980-1982 cohort.

5. *Ibid.*, figure 11. Tabulations by authors from the Current Population Survey, 2010-2013. All states included.

6. George A. Akerlof, "Men Without Children," *The Economic Journal* 108.447 (March 1998): 287-

7. Annie Lowrey, "Can Marriage Cure Poverty?" *The New York Times Magazine*, February 4, 2014, available at http://www.nytimes.com/2014/02/09/magazine/can-marriage-cure-poverty.html?_r=0.

8. Isabel Sawhill, "The Economics of Marriage, and Family Breakdown," *Opinion*, July 15, 2014, available at http://www.brookings.edu/research/opinions/2014/07/15-economics-of-marriage-family-breakdown-sawhill.

9. Wilcox et al., "Share of Children With Married Parents" interactive graphic. Data from the Current Population Survey, a 2014 Gallup Poll, and the American Presidency Project (% voting Republican).

10. David Leonhardt, "Republicans Say They Are Happier In Their Marriages," The Upshot, *The New York Times*, August 17, 2015, available at http://www.nytimes.com/2015/08/18/upshot/republicans-say-they-are-happier-with-their-marriages.html.

> *If more states could get behind public policies that do not penalize marriage, educational efforts that strengthen the earning power of working-class and poor young men, and civic efforts to make the culture more marriage-friendly, we just might see a renaissance in marriage and family life in America. And that would bring about improvements not only in the state of our unions, but also in the wealth of our states.*
>
> —*W. Bradford Wilcox*

**Progress towards the Sustainable
Development Goals**
Report of the Secretary-General, 3 June 2016
E/2016/75

**SDG 9. Build resilient infrastructure, promote inclusive and
sustainable industrialization and foster innovation**

65. An important component of physical infrastructure is air
shipping and air travel. In 2014, 45 per cent of all air passengers
originated from developing regions; 55 per cent originated from
developed regions. However, in the least developed countries,
landlocked developing countries and small island developing
States, air passenger volume was extremely low, making up only
0.8 per cent, 0.8 per cent and 1.4 per cent . . . .

66. Manufacturing is a foundation of economic development, employment and social stability. In 2015, the share of manufacturing
value added in terms of GDP of developed regions was estimated
at 13 per cent, a decrease over the past decade owing largely to the
increasing role of services in developed regions. . . . . While manufacturing job numbers have fallen in industrialized countries,
they have steadily increased in developing countries. In the least
developed countries, agricultural and traditional sectors remain
the main sources of employment.

70. Total official flows for economic infrastructure in developing regions reached $59.5 billion in 2014. The main sectors re-
ceiving assistance were transport and energy.

71. Infrastructure and economic development also rely on information and communications technology. . . . By 2015, the
percentage of the population living in areas covered by mobile
broadband networks stood at 69 per cent globally. In rural areas,
the share was only 29 per cent.

Jastus Suchi Obadiah is a Masters of Agriculture and Rural Development student at Kenya Methodist University
(KeMu). He has a degree in community development and rural development from Daystar University in Kenya and
Institutional management and Business Planning (International) from Plymouth University in the UK. He works
for Global Outreach Alliance, Reach the Children in Kenya, and Rafiki Wa Maendeleo Trust.

9 – Infrastructure

Jastus Suchi Obadiah

Good infrastructure empowers the family

One of the best ways government can strengthen and empower the family unit is to provide the necessary infrastructure for the family to utilize their resources, talent and energy to become self-sufficient, and contribute to the community. The 2016 UN Secretary-General Report on Sustainable Development states:

> SDG 9 encompasses three important aspects of sustainable development: infrastructure, industrialization and innovation. Infrastructure provides the basic physical systems and structures essential to the operation of a society or enterprise. Industrialization drives economic growth, creates job opportunities and thereby reduces income poverty. Innovation advances the technological capabilities of industrial sectors and prompts the development of new skills.[1]

Infrastructure assessment

In a self-assessment project in Makueni County, Kenya, communities were asked to evaluate ways to alleviate their own poverty. The families in the community proposed the following: (1) improved infrastructure such as: roads, electricity and provision of water; (2) free education, especially for primary and secondary schools (Until 2003, education was not free in primary schools in Kenya – now primary education is free and secondary schools have been subsidized.); (3) land policy changes so both men and women may own land and use it for agriculture. They also proposed: irrigation, machinery, subsidized inputs (fertilizer, seeds, etc.) and land to be used for public projects such as construction of a market place, etc.

A good infrastructure is essential to empower families to contribute toward the achievement of the Sustainable Development Goals.

SDG 1: End poverty

A good infrastructure is a key for eradicating poverty – for several reasons. Very basically, without roads it is difficult to transport produce to market. Some may need electricity to develop rural industries. Good infrastructure also fosters good health, as people can easily access health facilities. Healthy people become more productive.

SDG 2: Sustainable agriculture

A good example comes from Mumias, in western Kenya. It was a very poorly-developed community before the Mumias sugar factory came into existence. Local farmers now have markets for their crops, with most farmers still engaged in sugarcane planting. Since then the area has seen many developments in the infrastructure. The main roads are now tar marked, and there are numerous schools, banks, hospitals and colleges. All these have contributed to the income of the local people, as more people have been attracted to the town. Numerous shops in the town allow local people to engage in enterprise.

SDG 3: Health

Good health facilities (doctors' offices, clinics, hospitals) are also part of the infrastructure needed – providing easy access to health care. Again, when people are healthy, they become more productive.

SDG 4: Education

Basic social services, such as schools and hospitals, are included in a community's infrastructure. Just like a human skeleton, if all of the parts are not linked together, the body cannot perform all of the desirable functions. All components are necessary to help the community run smoothly.

SDG 6: Water and sanitation

Cities and other rural settlements can increase the availability to fresh water through drilling wells or building systems to transport clean water for their citizens. Proper waste management facilities also contribute to a healthier family and community.

SDG 7: Energy

A good example of how an improved infrastructure spurs growth and development is the government initiative of Kenya to electrify rural areas. With electricity available, people are now able to develop commerce in rural areas. This, in turn, attracts small industries, which attracts people and other facilities, such as hospitals, schools, etc.

SDG 8: Economic growth

Without a strong infrastructure a society cannot progress. The *Oxford Dictionary* defines infrastructure as: "the basic physical and organizational structures and facilities (e.g., buildings, roads, and power supplies) needed for the operation of a society or enterprise."[2] Viewed functionally, infrastructure facilitates the production and distribution of goods and services.

SDG 11: Cities and human settlements

Infrastructure is the framework that makes it possible for all the systems within the society to function. It includes: roads, utilities such as water supplies and electricity, communication structures, etc.

The "core to our quality of life"

Liesbeth Casier of the International Institute for Sustainable Development, describes infrastructure as the "core to our quality of life," with the following description:

> Population growth, migration and urbanization trends demand an increase in infrastructure development, especially in emerging economies and developing countries. For example, energy-related infrastructure and an expansion of the electricity grid is necessary to provide energy access to urban and rural areas. Transportation infrastructure— such as roads, railways, ports, airports—is key for people's mobility from home to work, and for connecting rural areas to domestic and regional markets, contributing to a country's economic development. Sustainable water infrastructure will improve people's lives by providing access to water and help managing scarce resources in a sustainable manner.[3]

A good infrastructure empowers the family unit

Each family unit empowered by an adequate infrastructure – and thus can use their combined family capital to provide a greater contribution toward achieving all of the Sustainable Development Goals.

Endnotes

1. "Progress towards the Sustainable Development Goals," Report of the Secretary-General, para. 64, 3 June 2016, E/2016/75
2. Definition of infrastructure, Oxford Dictionaries, http://www.oxforddictionaries.com/us/definition/american_english/infrastructure
3. Casier, Liesbeth, "Why Infrastructure is Key to the Success of the SDGs," September 9, 2015, https://www.iisd.org/blog/why-infrastructure-key-success-sdgs

10.7 Facilitate orderly, safe, regular and responsible migration and mobility of people, including through the implementation of planned and well-managed migration policies

UNHCR Refugee Report
The UN Refugee Agency

"Global Trends: Forced Displacement in 2015"
http://www.unhcr.org/576408cd7

Global forced displacement has increased in 2015, with record-high numbers. By the end of the year, 65.3 million individuals were forcibly displaced worldwide as a result of persecution, conflict, generalized violence, or human rights violations. This is 5.8 million more than the previous year (59.5 million).

. . . .

In recent years, UNHCR and States have increased efforts to expand beyond traditional resettlement programmes. Other humanitarian pathways such as private sponsorship programmes, humanitarian visas, and admission on medical grounds can also provide protection and solutions for refugees at risk. Family reunification programmes, labour mobility schemes, and academic scholarships and apprenticeships also can provide opportunities for refugees in a third country. These pathways have been promoted to complement existing resettlement programmes, mainly to assist Syrian refugees urgently in need of assistance to move elsewhere safely.

. . . .

It is important to note that not all cases for resettlement are submitted by UNHCR and that a number of States accept family reunification cases independent of a UNHCR referral.

Mariah Fralick spent years living internationally with her family in her youth. She founded an Interfaith Music Association, facilitated youth leadership classes, and served as Vice-President of a local school board. Currently, she is Director of Events and Outreach for the Sustainable Families Group. Mariah is married to Gordon Fralick. They have 4 children.

10.7 – Families Helping Families

Mariah Fralick

Empowering the refugee family through social and economic inclusion

For refugee families, the long road to becoming assets in their new communities is rife with unforeseen challenges and unexpected solutions. While food, shelter and clothing programs are necessary to sustain life, the most resilient refugees benefit from an array of comprehensive services addressing the needs of the whole family.

Beyond basic education for children and adults, additional solutions that allow for refugee families to empower themselves include: accessible health care interventions, mental and emotional support programs, nurturing family relationships, family literacy, vocational training and creating meaningful work. Fostering resilience in refugee families through promoting social, economic and political inclusion for all is crucial to reducing inequalities within and among countries, and building sustainable communities.

Refugees by the numbers

- More than 15 million of the uprooted are refugees who fled their home countries.
- Children constitute about 41 percent of the world's refugees, and about half of all refugees are women.
- About two-thirds of the world's refugees have been in exile for more than five years, many of them with no end in sight.
- More than half of the world's refugees are in urban environments, not in camps.[1]

Beyond beneficiaries

My family's introduction to people seeking to restore their sense of strength within a community came when we chose to foster the Shongole family, refugees from Somalia, in their first year of transition in the United States. Our initial efforts to help were presumptuous, misguided and comical. We were instructed to go to the Shongoles' home and then, "Find a need and fill it." We brought a dining table, chairs and beds to a family whose cultural observance was to eat their meal sitting on mats around a common bowl, and sleep on roll-away pads so floor space could be put to other uses during the day.

They didn't need the things we thought they did. However, with communication, and understanding that they knew their needs a lot better than we did, we eventually learned what our most important role was. After food, shelter, vocational and educational needs were met, what the Shongoles most desired was a sense of social inclusion in their new community. And, most importantly, what we had to offer was true friendship.

We spent our year with the Shongoles teaching English and learning Somali culture; attaining library cards for all and attending events; playing at the park and

Shongole Family – Refugees from Somalia

"These are our friends."

learning to swim; and visiting local farms and community gardens. One of my daughters recently said, "Isn't it so cool that we were all just kids when we met our refugee family. We didn't know anything about why they were refugees, or what was going on in their part of the world. All we knew was, 'Hey, these are our friends!'" To me, the complete acceptance and friendship that transpires between children who don't know any better is one of the best examples of how to foster social inclusion.

Key success factors

Years later, at the sixtieth session of the United Nations Commission on the Status of Women, I helped organize an event with the Howard Center for Family, Religion and Society. Presentations centered on strengthening refugee families and other vulnerable populations worldwide. A panel of experts brought important solutions to the forefront, including: the need for social connection, community-based problem-solving, financial literacy and relying on family members in times of crisis and strength.

As part of the event, I interviewed two sisters, Kri and Jenny Paw, who provided their harrowing, firsthand account of repeated flight and resettlement over a 20-year period as refugees. After their hurried escape from their homeland, the family was uprooted three additional times when the refugee camps they settled in were attacked and burned.

With each expulsion, the family hiked through the jungle for days in search of food, shelter and safety. Throughout their ordeal they worked together to meet their needs and to help those around them. In their final camp, both girls graduated from high school and proactively sought additional education. Kri Paw became a teacher in the primary school and Jenny Paw was a nurse's assistant at the medical clinic.

When the opportunity arose for members of the family to make a new home

Kri Paw and Jenny Paw with their family, as refugee children

Three sisters with their families, re-settled in Utah

Kri Paw and Jenny Paw preparing to speak at the UN

in the United States, Kri Paw, with her husband and children, was the first to go. Her courage and example paved the way for the others to follow. Once here, all of them took advantage of vocational and language training, working their way through a succession of jobs that have led to their families' self-sufficiency and increased economic participation. For the last nine years they have been assets in their new community, and are now raising families alongside their siblings and their families.

Three key factors for successful transition in new country

Kri Paw and Jenny Paw report that their transition was made successful because of three key factors. Authorities in refugee reunification and integration validate their experience:

1. **They identified as members of a strong family unit.**

   > UNHCR [the UN refugee agency] stresses the important role that family plays in the specific situation of refugees. Family reunification is a fundamental aspect of bringing normality back to the lives of persons who have fled persecution or serious harm and have lost family during forced displacement and flight . . . . It is a generally agreed-upon fact that the family is the fundamental unit of society, entitled to protection by society and the State. Following separation caused by forced displacement, such as from persecution and war, family reunification is often the only way to ensure respect for a refugee's right to family unity . . . .[2]

2. **They chose to access services provided through welcoming community organizations,** new-found friends, local families and volunteers – addressing the needs of the whole family. A Canadian model shines the light on the best-practices of local families and organizations fostering Syrian refugee families, as reported in *The New York Times*:

   > The *Toronto Star* greeted the first planeload by splashing 'Welcome to Canada' in English and Arabic across its front page. Eager sponsors toured local Middle Eastern supermarkets to learn what to buy and cook and used a toll-free hotline for instant Arabic translation. Impatient would-be sponsors . . . have been seeking more families. The new government committed to taking in 25,000 Syrian refugees and then raised the total by tens of thousands . . . . Advocates for sponsorship believe that private citizens can achieve more than the government alone, raising the number of refugees admitted, guiding newcomers more effectively and potentially helping solve the puzzle of how best to resettle Muslims in Western countries. Some advocates even talk about extending the Canadian system across the globe.[3]

3. **They resolved to remain intact as a family unit** (even as adults), to work together for successful integration in their host country, and to become social and economic assets in their new communities.

UNHCR considers that integration should not require refugees to forgo their own culture . . . . As such, Executive Conclusion No. 104 calls on States to facilitate, as appropriate, the integration of refugees, including, as far as possible, through facilitating their naturalisation. As such, integration in the refugee context is the end product of a multifaceted and on-going process, of which economic independence is but one part. Integration requires preparedness on the part of the refugees to adapt to the host society. From the host society, it requires communities that are welcoming and responsive to refugees, and public institutions that are able to meet the needs of a diverse population . . . . Measures should be taken and developed to foster an inclusive society without discrimination . . . ."[4]

Conclusion

Through the strength of their family capital, new friendships, access to resources and the encouragement of other families, Kri Paw, Jenny Paw and their siblings are thriving in their new lives. Their families have enjoyed so much success that they were able to arrange for their youngest sister to attain citizenship in Thailand – where she received scholarships to attend Bangkok University. She will graduate in the spring of 2017. Kri Paw, Jenny Paw and other family members will be in attendance.

Endnotes

1. "Refugees: The Numbers," Resources for Speakers on Global Issues, United Nations, Accessed July 7, 2016.
   http://www.un.org/en/globalissues/briefingpapers/refugees/index.shtml
2. UNHCR, Refugee Family Reunification, Bureau for Europe, February 2012, pp 1-3. Retrieved July 7, 2016 from: http://www.unhcr.org/4f54e3fb13.pdf.
3. Kantor, Jodi and Einhorn, Catrin (2016, June 30), "Refugees Encounter a Foreign Word: Welcome," The New York Times. Retrieved from
   http://www.nytimes.com/2016/07/01/world/americas/canada-syrian-refugees.html?_r=0.
4. UNHCR, Integration of Beneficiaries of International Protection in the European Union - Recommendations to the European Ministerial Conference on Integration, Zaragosa (15 and 16 April 2010), April 2010, paragraph 7, available at:
   http://www.refworld.org/docid/4bc862412.html [accessed 7 July 2016]

> *Families have an important role to play as supporters and allies of family members with disabilities. Families and individuals with disabilities themselves should develop strong and well-organized cross-disability networks and alliances to ensure the 2030 Agenda will be truly inclusive by promoting accessibility and inclusion of persons with disabilities as a precondition for inclusive, sustainable and equitable development and poverty eradication for all.*

Victor Santiago Pineda, Ph.D., is a global expert on disability policy and the Senior Research Fellow at the Haas Institute for a Fair and Inclusive Society at the University of California Berkeley. He teaches courses on planning theory, policy evaluation and development. He proudly serves on the US Access Board.

Galyna Korniyenko is a City and Regional Planning PhD student at Ohio State University, with a Masters in Urban Planning at the University of Kansas, supported by Fulbright. Galyna is an Edmund S. Muskie program alumna. Her previous experience includes facilitating international conferences for the Ukraine-USA Foundation and working for the city of Cherkasy. She has a special interest in the use of information technology in governmental and corporate planning and practice.

Stephen Meyers is an Assistant Professor of Law, Societies & Justice and International Studies at the University of Washington in Seattle, where he is also a contributing member of the Disability Studies Program. His previous research has focused on grassroots disabled-persons organization integration into the global disability rights-movement.

John Paul is a research associate for World Enabled and a senior analyst for the Global Initiative for Inclusive ICTs. He was a Fulbright visiting fellow at the University of California, Berkeley School of Law. He holds an MA in Comparative and International Disability Policy from American University, Washington, DC.

Molly A. Martínez, Ph.D., serves as Director of Special Projects for World Enabled—an educational non-profit organization that promotes the rights and dignities of persons with disabilities. Previously, she worked as a consultant to the International Disability Alliance—the largest network of international disability-rights organizations as acknowledged by the United Nations.

11.2 – The Inclusion Imperative

Victor Santiago Pineda, Stephen Meyers,
John Paul Cruz, Galyna Komiyenko,
Molly A. Martínez

Introduction

About 6.25 billion people, 15 per cent of them persons with disabilities, are predicted to be living in urban centers by 2050. Urbanization provides both challenges and opportunities for individuals with disabilities and their families. This chapter focuses on inclusive urban development, and illustrates how Habitat III has the potential to redress the current lack of environmental accessibility faced by people with disabilities in many cities of the world. It is included in this book on the SDGs and Family Capital because the structures of urbanization do not affect the individual alone, they affect the entire supportive structures that allow persons with disabilities to live meaningful and productive lives – and **a major source of that support comes from families working together, sharing responsibilities and coordinating activities for mutual support.** This chapter was written with the premise that all families should work towards the ultimate goal of enhancing the participation of persons with disabilities in every aspect of public life. This includes supporting persons with disabilities to be engaged in the multiple and complex national, regional and international processes of global governance. The purpose of this chapter is to demonstrate that persons with disabilities should be speaking for themselves, and families have a unique role in helping that happen.

Inclusion in the urban century

Over the next 35 years, cities will shape virtually every aspect of global development, including the manner in which rights to housing, health, and education are won or wasted, implemented or ignored. The urban century can transform the productive capacity and outcomes of the estimated 400-600 million urban citizens who live with disabilities. This number is set to increase dramatically by 2050 when 66% of the global population will be living in cities. Of the projected increase of 2.5 billion urban dwellers,[1] 15-20% are expected to be persons with disabilities.[2] Well-planned cities have dramatically improved the social and economic outcomes for individuals with a range of disabilities, their families and the larger communities they participate in. Well-planned cities take into consideration the widest range of needs and incorporate design standards that assume a significant portion of the population may have difficulty seeing, hearing, or moving around without assistance.

The most pressing issue faced by millions of persons with disabilities

A growing body of research now shows that the most pressing issue faced by millions of persons with disabilities worldwide is not their disability, but rather social exclusion. Poor planning and unregulated urban development can have devastating consequences for persons with disabilities. According to the United Nations CRPD Committee, "Without access to the physical environment, to transportation…and to other facilities and services open or provided to the public, persons with disabilities would not have equal opportunities for participation in their respective societies."[3] The committee also states that "Accessibility is a precondition for persons with disabilities to live independently and participate fully and equally in society."[4]

Gender, ethnicity and poverty compound existing exclusions for persons with disabilities, limiting their access to opportunities. According to Nobel Prize winning economist Amartya Sen, the lack of access too often deprives persons with disabilities of their right to mobility, education and healthcare.[5] Cities are under immense pressure to ensure that urban development is inclusive and responds to the needs of marginalized groups, including persons with disabilities. What steps can urban planners, development practitioners and scholars take to promote a better understanding of access and inclusion for people with disabilities in cities?

The main goal of this chapter is to review the global status of disability rights in urban development and offer a set of recommendations to ensure that local city initiatives respond to the needs of persons with disabilities. The paper starts with a baseline review of the progress made in recent years and highlights good practices alongside the voices of persons with disabilities. The report also offers technical and policy recommendations derived from extensive research on disability-inclusive urban policy. The recommendations provide practical steps and guide immediate and bold measures to (1) account for and report progress on the rights of persons with disabilities in urban planning, policy and development, and (2) ensure that key issues in the New Urban Agenda, such as accessibility and equality, truly address the needs of everybody, including persons with disabilities.

Disability in global development

Globally, more than half of all people with disabilities now (2016) live in towns and cities and by 2030 this number is estimated to swell to between 750,000 - 1 billion.[6] Persons with disabilities face technical and environmental barriers such as steps at the entrances of buildings, the absence of lifts in multi-floor buildings and a lack of information in accessible formats. The built environment always relates to social and cultural development as well as customs; therefore the built environment is under the full control of society.[7] The Convention on the Rights of Persons with Disabilities (CRPD) includes accessibility as one of its key underlying principles — a vital precondition for the effective and equal enjoyment of civil, political, economic, social and cultural rights of persons with disabilities. Accessibility should be viewed not only in the context of equality and non-discrimination, but also as an integral part of the sustainable development agenda.[8]

The international community, in the Outcome Document of the UN High Level Meeting on Disability and Development, reaffirmed its commitment to advancing a disability-inclusive development agenda, emphasizing among other issues, the importance of accessibility and inclusion for persons with disabilities in urban development contexts.[9] As the international community embarks on implementing the Sustainable Development Goals (SDGs), it is important to make cities and human settlements inclusive, safe and sustainable. This means actions and measures must ensure: universal access to safe, inclusive and accessible green and public spaces; adequate and affordable housing; urban and peri-urban transport; and basic services for all urban dwellers, whether or not they live with a disability.[10] It also means that persons with disabilities are included as full and equal participants in the social, political and economic life of cities and urban dwellings, including: representation in civil society, political decision making, access to employment and income-generating activities – on an equal basis with others.

The processes leading to the formulation of the 2016-2030 Sustainable Development Goals recognize the critical need to include people with disabilities more broadly in development.[11] Forms of inclusion are explicitly mentioned in Sustainable Development Goal No.11, stating that cities should be 'inclusive, safe, resilient and sustainable.' This goal should explicitly engage universal design principles and encourage cities to develop regulations and building codes that comply with the principle of universal design.[12] Social inclusion thus is understood to be a central aspect of a global, and increasingly urbanized, form of development.

Although disability-inclusive development has influenced the Sustainable Development process, its coordination and administration on the local level require additional specifications and guidelines. Like other urban issues, tackling accessibility will require assessing and responding to shortcomings in: infrastructure management, municipal codes, land use, transportation planning, housing and community development, mobility, social services and broader monitoring of human rights on a local level.

Calls for an ambitious New Urban Agenda have gained momentum on a global stage. A disability-inclusive New Urban Agenda has the potential to transform geographies of exclusion, dependence, isolation and despair[13] into thriving active communities that according to Nobel Laureate Amartya Sen, afford disabled citizens the "capabilities to live the type of lives they have reason to value."[14] More inclusive communities are forming at global, regional, national and local levels. By creating a barrier-removal plan or a plan for accessibility, cities, towns and villages can implement the CRPD and other internationally adopted agreements concerning the human rights of people with disabilities.[15]

At all levels there continues to be a lack of reliable data on disability. This hinders the ability of development actors to assess progress and take action.[16] For example, urban indicators measuring accessibility of the built environment, mobility barriers or budget allocations for local community based programs that support the implementation of Article 19 of the CRPD "Community and Independent Living" are rarely measured.[17]

Multidimensional and cross-sectional analysis is needed

The World Report on Disability Summary, published in 2011 by the World Health Organization and the World Bank (within the framework of the largest consultation on disability to date and with the active involvement of hundreds of professionals in the field of disability), stresses that the built environment, transport systems and information and communication are often inaccessible to persons with disabilities (p. 10). Persons with disabilities are prevented from enjoying some of their basic rights, such as the right to seek employment or the right to health care, owing to a lack of accessible transport and inaccessible buildings and infrastructure. The level of implementation of accessibility laws remains low in many countries and persons with disabilities are often denied their right to freedom of expression and full political participation in their communities, owing to the inaccessibility of information and communication.[18]

Poorly planned cities create a series of interconnected barriers that limit mobility options, increase environmental hazards and ultimately prevent persons with disabilities from enjoying their right to accessible housing. Such barriers put persons with disabilities in a precarious, often challenging, position whereby the rights to education, employment and security of tenure are denied due to a lack of adequate housing. Urban centers in all developing nations struggle to control the expansion of informal and inaccessible housing. Informal housing and unplanned growth often result in housing that has limited access to: latrines, water, sanitation, electricity, other energy sources and affordable transportation. Many informal developments increase the marginalization of their resident populations by crowding them together and restricting their mobility. These very urban issues are also the main factors that deprive persons with disabilities of well-being, dignity and the benefits of social and economic development on an equal basis with others.

Cross-cutting identities imply varied experiences in urban environment

The enjoyment of rights and full participation by persons with disabilities are often differentiated on the basis of other identities they share. For example, some women with disabilities in Bandung, Indonesia, have adopted the concept of self-determination and independent living in the face of a patriarchal culture and inaccessible environment. This group, however, is made up of women of middle- and upper-class backgrounds who can afford chauffeurs, personal assistants and so forth.[19] Other factors also determine the utilization of rights and services. A study of families that include persons with disabilities in urban Australia found that in Melbourne, where 25% of the population is foreign-born, migrant parents of children with disabilities were far less likely to access respite care and other forms of support offered by the municipality than native-born Australians.[20]

Cross-cutting identities, however, also offer opportunities for promoting disability inclusion. For example, a project in Israel was successful in using mosques in Jerusalem and other urban centers as venues for inclusion. Imams, who were introduced to disability rights, emphasized Islam's commitment to equality and disability inclusion, raising disability inclusion throughout the community and drawing significant numbers of new congregants with disabilities into their communities.[21] These examples reinforce the need to think more holistically. Current approaches fail to highlight the powerful ways that cross-cutting social identities can either be harnessed for inclusion or contribute towards social isolation and exclusion.

Transforming good intentions into measurable actions

Effective solutions are often inhibited by policy fragmentation, poor accountability and lack of political will. Legal reforms can create new incentives, elevating accessibility and stimulating new investments in infrastructure and innovations in design. New ways of engaging the private sector will be needed to address supply and demand for accessibility.

In addition, the lack of a cohesive disability policy at both the local and national level limits the impact of existing efforts to include accessibility requirements in planning, policy, and design. This is compounded by gaps in: local leadership, budget allocation, local capacity, lack of engagement with targeted groups and by limiting beliefs about persons with disabilities. For example, in many countries such as: Ethiopia, China, Qatar and the United Arab Emirates, local governments are utilizing language of equal opportunities and rights-based development, yet still limit the ability of persons with disabilities to form their own associations, organize awareness-raising campaigns and fundraise to strengthen their organizational capacity, at both the national and local levels.

Accessibility of the built environment is not seen as a priority by local and municipal governments in many parts of the world. In Cape Town,[22] Kampala,[23] and Nairobi[24] efforts to promote accessibility often get pushed aside by other important priorities such as: poverty alleviation, provision of affordable housing and upgrading decaying infrastructures. Efforts should focus on engaging the local authorities to set: zoning, land use, transportation and building regulations in these cities to ensure that persons with disabilities, as members of a marginalized community, are prioritized and included within these larger initiatives.

Voluntary measures towards accessibility, however, will not bring about needed changes. Mandatory regulation is necessary for lasting urban transformation to occur. For example, Australia set a goal that all new housing will meet a basic level of visitability by 2020. Visitability is defined as the capacity for a dwelling to facilitate inclusion and participation of all people in family and community activities. A study of Australia's voluntary national guidelines on visitability showed that voluntary practices failed to ensure the right of adequate housing. As such, new construction of accessible housing has not been realized because there is no legal mandate. Australia will fail to reach its accessible housing targets.[25]

Gaps exist across sectors and scales. To fill these gaps, governments are beginning to incentivize innovation across the board. Innovations in urban development allow for new broad-based local coalitions to form around: equity, access, walkability, bikeability and broader ecological sustainability. Such coalitions can further a disability-inclusive message and spark new dialogues between: urban planners, architects, policy makers and other groups, to jointly develop detailed technical guidance for inclusive-urban development efforts and develop a coalition to overhaul existing approaches.

Cities successfully implementing programs are still few and far between. For example, in Kampala, disability-inclusive laws protect the rights of persons with disabilities – and people with disabilities participate in the public policy process. Too often local administrative agencies lack the capacity to deliver services and implement laws. Likewise in Lima, Peru – laws and public attitudes match international norms, but low political will and administrative and coordinating failures limit progress. In other cases, a city may need to develop policy programs to bolster efforts in all five sectors.

Very few governments can do this successfully without the active engagement of civil society or the private sector.

Conclusion

There exist numerous challenges to enhancing the active and effective participation of persons with disabilities in global, national and local discourses. The provision of sign-language, Braille and personal assistance supports to persons with disabilities is important to facilitate their full participation.

Families have an important role to play as supporters and allies of family members with disabilities. Families and individuals with disabilities themselves should develop strong and well-organized cross-disability networks and alliances to ensure the 2030 Agenda will be truly inclusive – by promoting accessibility and inclusion of persons with disabilities as a precondition for inclusive, sustainable and equitable development and poverty eradication for all.

Endnotes

1. The proportion of the world's urban population is expected to increase to approximately 57% by 2050. African Development Bank, http://www.afdb.org/en/blogs/afdb-championing-inclusive-growth-across-africa/post/urbanization-in-africa-10143/.
2. Approximately 90% of this increase will be concentrated in African and Asian cities like Shenzhen, Karachi, Lagos, Guangzhou, Dhaka, Jakarta, and many others that have urbanized at a rate of 40-60% between 2000-2010
3. CRPD/C/GC/2
4. The International Convention on the Elimination of All Forms of Racial Discrimination guarantees everyone the right of access to any place or service intended for use by the general public, such as transport, hotels, restaurants, cafes, theatres and parks (art. 5 (f)). Thus, a precedent has been established in the international human rights legal framework for viewing the right to access as a right per se.
5. Sen. Disability and Justice. 2004 retrieved August 5, 2015: http://siteresources.worldbank.org/DISABILITY/214576-1092421729901/20291152/Amartya_Sen_Speech.doc
6. Utilizing 5 billion urban dwellers, we calculated that 15-20% of these would be persons with disabilities. Data sources derived from WHO World Disability Report (2011) and "Urbanization | UNFPA - United Nations Population Fund." Accessed May 3, 2015. http://www.unfpa.org/urbanization.
7. CRPD/C/GC/2
8. CRPD/C/GC/2
9. General Assembly Resolution 68/3.
10. Report of the Open Working Group of the General Assembly on Sustainable Development Goals , see http://www.un.org/ga/search/view_doc.asp?symbol=A/68/970&Lang=E
11. Rio+20 promised to strive for a world that is just, equitable and inclusive, and committed to work together to promote sustained and inclusive economic growth, social development and environmental protection and thereby to benefit all, in particular the children of the world, youth and future generations of the world without distinction of any kind such as age, sex, disability, culture, race, ethnicity, origin, migratory status, religion, economic or other status.
12. See targets 11.2 'By 2030, provide access to safe, affordable, accessible and sustainable transport systems for all, improving road safety, notably by expanding public transport, with special attention to the needs of those in vulnerable situations, women, children, persons with disabilities and older persons' and 11.7, 'By 2030, provide universal access to safe, inclusive and accessible, green and public spaces, in particular for women and children, older persons and persons with disabilities'.
13. Likewise, in developed countries, rapid urbanization can result segregation ordinances, privatized spaces, and exclusions of undesirable or destabilizing social groups. Cities will increasingly be looking for ways to turn the tide on increasing concentrations of poverty, inequality, and social marginalization.
14. Amartya Sen. 1999.
15. The United Nations, and other organizations such as the World Bank, UNICEF, UNDP, WHO, UNDESA have undertaken important work in the area of disability inclusive development.
16. The World Development Reports and the World Development Indicators have only begun to consider disability.
17. Sweden, Norway, Denmark, and Finland support municipal programs that allow people with significant disabilities to have the support needed to live safely in their own homes and communities.
18. CRPD/C/GC/2
19. Komardjaja, Inge. "Independent Living and Self-Determination of Women with Physical Disabilities in Bandung, Indonesia." Disability Studies Quarterly 24, no. 3 (2004). http://www.dsq-sds.org/article/view/509/686.
20. Stevens, Carolyn S. "Disability, Caregiving and Interpellation: Migrant and Non-Migrant Families of Children with Disabilities in Urban Australia." Disability & Society 25, no. 7 (2010): 783–96.
21. Mizrachi, Nissim. "Translating Disability in a Muslim Community: A Case of Modular Translation." Culture, Medicine, and Psychiatry 38, no. 1 (2014): 133–59.
22. Maart, S., A. H. Eide, J. Jelsma, M. E. Loeb, and M. Ka Toni. "Environmental Barriers Experienced by Urban and Rural Disabled People in South Africa." Disability & Society 22, no. 4 (2007): 357–69.
23. "AYWDN: Med Ssengoba, Uganda - YouTube." Accessed May 7, 2015. https://www.youtube.com/watch?v=if0rmVwyyJ0&list=PL407C8373BB7BE5C3&index=12.
24. "AYWDN: Rose Kwamboka, Kenya - YouTube." Accessed May 7, 2015. https://www.youtube.com/watch?v=BZm8emJaLDU&list=PL407C8373BB7BE5C3&index=5.
25. Ward, Margaret, and Jill Franz. "The Provision of Visitable Housing in Australia: Down to the Detail." Social Inclusion 3, no. 2 (2015): 31–43.

Accessible Playgrounds
Katrina Bleyl

My name is Katrina Bleyl. I am married and have three children. Our daughter is 8 years old and has a disability that requires use of a wheelchair. Getting out and doing things as a family has been a struggle, as a lot of places are not accessible to wheelchairs. An example is the playgrounds and play areas in our community.

When we go to the playground my daughter, Brinley, was never able to play because we couldn't use her wheelchair with the playground. She would have to sit off to the side of the playground with me, while the

Children with disabilities playing in the leaves at the edge of the playground, since they couldn't play on the playground. They made their own play and people joined in.

others played. This is really hard for her. She wants to be included and make friends. However, children do not come to talk to her or play with her because she is outside of the playground.

In 2015, our city asked what the citizens would like to see done in the community. Another mom, who also has a daughter in a wheelchair, and I both asked them to build a playground that could be used by able-bodied children as well as children with disabilities. Being able to play side-by-side creates an opportunity for new friendships to be built and for children and adults to become more aware of others. We presented our idea to the city and they loved it! They dedicated an area to start planning and building for our "All-Together Playground."

We are currently raising money to build the playground with the build date set for the first week in September, 2016. A design company is going to supervise the construction, but this is going to be a community build, which means that involved families and other concerned community members will build the playground. Everyone will have a part in making this project happen. Children in the city were part of the design of the playground. They were told that it would be a place where all types of children could play together. It was incredible to hear the ideas that the children came up with. This process, from inception to end, provides an opportunity for people to come together in our community to show unity, support and inclusion for everyone – able-bodied and disabled all

BEST PRACTICES

together as one. This all came about because we spoke up and let the city know about a need in our community.

As people learn about this important project and how they can help, it has been wonderful to see how excited they are for the playground to be built. Families have a sense of ownership and are trying to make this a wonderful, accessible and inclusive place in our community.

The idea of an accessible, inclusive space can be modified for many situations around the world. A community can take ideas from families with disabled members and develop ways for all to participate. Roads without rocks, so wheelchairs can be used on them; ramps into buildings, so they can get inside buildings with ease; curbs with wheelchair access, so families can travel a city together.

The possibilities are endless. **We just need to ask where we can make changes to include everyone.** And the best place to start is with our own families – in the communities where we live.

NBA and BYU basketball player Jimmer Fredette after his 3-point shootout to raise money for the playground. It was almost $25,000!

The plan of the playground that will be put in. The kids of the city of Orem, Utah, helped design this playground!

> *People are both producers and consumers and need to function within a sustainable environment. The concept of sustainability arises at the family level where children are taught fundamental values and ethics that will guide them later in life as producers, consumers and good stewards of the environment.*
>
> *— Vincenzina Santoro*

Vincenzina Santoro is an international economist, consultant and former Vice President of JPMorgan and Co. She is a volunteer at the Charity Accountability Program of the New York Better Business Bureau, represents the American Family Association of New York at the United Nations and writes frequently about international economic and social issues. Ms. Santoro is a native New Yorker, a graduate of Hunter College, City University of NY (BA, MA in economics) and is fluent in five languages.

12 – Sustainable Consumption & Production

Vincenzina Santoro

Consumption and production are first and foremost economic concepts. Personal, and to a lesser extent government, consumption are principle components of gross domestic product (GDP). Consumption is the "market" for production. Without production and consumption there would be no economic development or growth and no means of eradicating poverty.

People are both producers and consumers and need to function within a sustainable environment. **The concept of sustainability arises at the family level where children are taught fundamental values and ethics that will guide them later in life as producers, consumers and good stewards of the environment.**

Sustainable consumption

A glance at any country's GDP shows personal consumption expenditures at the top. These expenditures comprise durable goods such as: motor vehicles, household furnishings and equipment – goods that last many years; nondurables such as: food, beverages, clothing, footwear and gasoline; and services including spending for utilities, health care, transportation, recreation, restaurants, and lodging, as well as financial and insurance services. Personal consumption accounted for 68% of GDP in the United States in 2015. This percentage is typical of developed countries but is generally lower in developing countries.

Food and water are indispensable for life itself. Yet an estimated 40% of food is wasted[1] despite advances in food preparation and storage, while part of the global population goes hungry. This situation can be reversed at the local level. In New York City a diligent, concerned individual in 1983 created City Harvest, a nonprofit company that rescues surplus food and redistributes it to community centers that feed the hungry.[2] Each day the organization's trucks make rounds to collect food from restaurants, supermarkets, food shops and even the surplus production from local farms, then delivers the excess supply to community food banks. This undertaking helps indigent people while preventing food waste in landfills. In many developing countries food may be lost at the production stage if basic infrastructures, such as roads and transportation, are lacking.

In developed countries obesity has become a problem, especially among children who may lack adequate family supervision as they overindulge in excessive calorie and fat-laden prepared foods and snacks. Obesity often leads to medical complications and health problems.

Responsible consumer choices apply not just to food but to vehicle purchases and especially clothing. The availability of cheaply priced apparel has encouraged excess purchases. To prevent discarded clothing and textile products from landfills, both donation and recycling opportunities already exist.

Some fast-fashion companies are becoming more proactive in trying to help control the growing mountain of used garments. Swedish multinational H&M offers customers discounts on new products if they return used clothes. Some are recycled in-house to make new garments but most of them are sold in the international market.[3]

Some of the same developing countries, such as India, that produce cheap clothing for the developed world also receive their discards – which are sorted and resold to even poorer countries in Africa or reprocessed into other products. Similar global recycling networks exist for discarded technology products such as computers and cell phones. Metal cans, plastic and glass bottles, newspapers and other paper products also are recycled as indicated in Targets 12.5, 12.6 and 12.7.

In developed countries public service advertisements by consumer, business and government associations are mainstream and encourage the public to consume healthy foods; recycle packaging, paper and plastics; and otherwise be mindful of environmental considerations – including prevention of disasters such as forest fires.

Carbon-based fuels are finite and will have to give way at some point to more alternative types of energy generation including solar, wind and water. Aircraft and auto producers are experimenting with more fuel-efficient options and carbon tax proposals are being considered.

Sustainable production

Before goods and services can be consumed they must be produced. Sustainable production is a challenge that can be met through innovation and creativity, even while mindful of risk and reward. Businesses are constantly improving production processes by reducing or changing inputs to operate more responsibly, efficiently and assure viability. Many businesses seek out ISO (International Organization for Standardization) accreditation to demonstrate that they comply with strict industry standards.[4] ISO has developed over 21,000 international standards.

Target 12.8b singled out tutelage of sustainable tourism, which has already made its mark. International travelers exceeded the 1.1 billion mark in 2014 and generated over $1.2 trillion in tourism spending on transportation, lodging and food. Recent developments include agritourism and ecotourism. Agritourism has saved numerous family farms and estates that have been transformed into lodging and recreation facilities especially for urban dwellers to experience rural life and sample locally-produced foods.

Ecotourism allows vacationers to enjoy nature, promote conservation, assist local communities and leave only footprints. Some countries, such as Costa Rica, have set an example in this increasingly popular industry. In both endeavors, property and a way of life are being preserved profitably and sustainably.

Through creativity and innovation in production and consumption, businesses and families will continue to play a key role in sustainability. Examples already abound.

Endnotes

1. National Resources Defense Council (NRDC), "Wasted: How American is Losing Up to 40 percent of its Food from Farm to Fork to Landfill," NRDC Issue Paper, August 2012.
2. https://www.cityharvest.org/programs
3. Fashion Feeds a Recycling Network," Wall Street Journal, June 27, 2016.
4. http://www.iso.org/iso/home/standards.htm

When families in the community are prepared, they are able to respond to the emergency situation and recover from it more easily and more quickly than would otherwise be possible. More importantly, they can reduce the amount of suffering people endure and make their community a better, healthier place.

–Rick Birrell

Rick Birrell has a Bachelor of Science degree from the University of Utah and a Master of Science degree from the University of Phoenix. He also holds several certifications and a licenses from the United States Federal Emergency Management Agency, the United States Federal Communications Commission and the American Red Cross in community emergency response, incident command, amateur radio, first aid and emergency shelter management. Rick actively works to educate individuals and families in his community about emergency preparedness concepts as well as how to function as volunteers in an emergency situation.

13 - Emergency Preparedness for Natural Disasters

Rick Birrell

Emergency situations and natural disasters can occur anywhere in the world. Earthquakes, hurricanes, typhoons, volcanoes, tsunamis and other extreme conditions can strike a village, town or city with little or no warning – resulting in significant destruction and mass casualties. Contaminated water, unhealthy food and disease can spread rampantly in the days and weeks that follow the disaster. If the people who survive have not stored enough clean water, good food and other emergency supplies, they may suffer from the want of those things long after the disaster has gone. Families can be vulnerable to the impact of a disaster. Young children and older adults are especially sensitive to disease and malnutrition. If emergency supplies are not available during the recovery from the disaster, then children and seniors may be affected before other healthy adults. This chapter is designed to help families identify and obtain the emergency supplies they will need in recovering from a disaster situation.

I – Planning and Preparing for Emergencies

Family emergency plan

When a disaster strikes, people naturally want to connect with family and friends. An emergency plan can help people make those connections. Deciding in advance where to go, who to talk to and what to do, will help them to reunite with loved ones.[1]

Action:

- The plan should be simple, concise and tailored to address personal needs. Disaster situations are rarely predictable. So, the family should build some flexibility and adaptability into their plan. For example, if the family chooses to designate a prearranged gathering place outside their home, they may also need to designate one or two alternative locations in case the primary one is not accessible.

- The gathering place should be safe and present an alternative location for shelter if the family residence is no longer suitable for habitation.

- The family might choose to periodically practice using the plan with a fictitious scenario. Practicing the plan can help identify weaknesses and flaws in its design that can be rectified before a real disaster situation occurs.

Community emergency plan

A large scale disaster can impact everyone in the community. Services like: electricity, gas, water, telephone and other essential supplies may be cut off. Damaged roadways can add to the problem by preventing emergency responders from reaching the community or a particular neighborhood in time to help. As a result, cooperation with neighbors is necessary when a disaster strikes – to alleviate suffering. Neighbors can do so by working together to build a community emergency plan.[2]

Action:

- The scope of the plan should be built upon a scalable, flexible framework capable of addressing the types of disasters most likely to occur in the community.

- The framework should define the roles and responsibilities of community leaders, responders and volunteers – along with the logistical procedures, protocols and other considerations they need to follow and implement.[3]

- The plan should specify how community leaders and responders will help families prepare for disasters (e.g. by providing guidance, education and support regarding topics and issues relevant to the community).[4]

Al-Amin lives in Bangladesh. His grandmother taught him about the importance of emergency preparedness in their community. Al-Amin said he "…learned about many precautions that can be taken to face a disaster, like constructing houses and animal pens, by taking into account the high flood level and avoiding wetlands, preparing a banana-tree raft and keeping a portable burner for emergency travel, planting bamboo and banana trees around the house to face cyclones and always storing some dry food and clean water for emergencies."[13]

Picture by World Vision International

Water storage

Adequate water storage is critical for disaster preparedness. In the aftermath of a disaster, community water supplies can become contaminated with bacteria and other pathogens that may lead to serious illness if they are consumed. Water is essential to survival.

Water tank storage with filter (India).
Photo by Naveen Pammi

A normally active person needs to drink at least two quarts of water each day. Hot environments can double that amount. Children, nursing mothers and ill people will need even more. You will also need water for food preparation and hygiene. Store a total of at least one gallon per person, per day. You should store at least a two-week supply of water for each member of your family.[5]

Action:

- Families can reduce the risk of illness by storing clean water. A two-week supply of water for the family represents a minimum of fourteen gallons of water for each person living in the household. The water should be stored in sealed containers kept in a cool, dry place away from sun light.

Food storage

When a disaster strikes, food supplies in the community may be quickly exhausted. If private companies and government agencies are unable to replenish food supplies in the days and weeks that follow the disaster, people may suffer from hunger and dehydration. Consequently, the family should create a food storage plan that identifies the kinds of food they want to reserve in case community supplies vanish. A family may include "…food items such as wheat, dry beans, rice, and other products that have been prepackaged for longer-term storage…" in the plan.[6]

Action:

- Families should carefully consider the types of foods they want to include in their storage. The food's nutritional value, ease of preparation, hydration requirements, etc., are all considerations that may impact its usefulness.

- The food storage plan should describe how often to rotate, use and replenish food supplies.

- The family should periodically review their storage plan and ensure the foods they store are current and appropriate for the needs of those in the household. Over time the family's needs may change. For example, a family made up of young children may have different dietary needs than a family made up of teenagers and older adults.

A family walks through their flooded property to recover belongings, following Hurricane Dolly (Texas, 2008).
FEMA News Photo

Fuel storage

If utility services in the community are interrupted or disabled, then the means to cook and prepare food may be unavailable. Families who depend on utilities to create heat for cooking should stock pile alternative fuel sources, such as wood and charcoal.[7]

Action:

- Families should periodically practice preparing and cooking food from their storage, with alternative fuels, in order to become proficient and effective at using what is stored.

Emergency kits

Families should ensure that each member of the household has an emergency kit that is easily accessible and ready to use at a moment's notice. "A disaster supplies kit is simply a collection of basic items your household, and/or individuals, may need in the event of an emergency."[8]

Action:

- Each kit should contain items like food, water, medication, first-aid supplies, a flashlight, extra clothing, etc.

- The kit should be tailored for the needs of the person who is expected to use it. No two kits need to be exactly the same. For example, an adult's kit may include the food, supplies, clothing, medication, etc., they personally need while a child's kit may include diapers, baby food, etc.

Personal hygiene

Disease can spread rapidly throughout the community in the aftermath of a disaster when people come in contact with contaminated water or food. Illness and disease can often be managed successfully when family groups in the community work together, with the goal of preventing contamination of drinking water. The ECHO Factsheet (European Commission), discussing Disaster Risk Reduction, states, "By improving planning and placement of temporary sanitation facilities (latrines, leaching fields) the contamination of groundwater used for human consumption, which is especially critical in areas of high ground water tables, can be prevented or limited."[9]

Action:

- Families can reduce the risk of disease and infection by deciding how they will practice proper hygiene and then documenting those strategies in their family emergency plan. In turn, they can help other families in the community become educated about disease prevention and integrate the ideas into the community emergency plan.

"Cambodia suffered six major floods and three serious droughts in the last decade to 2013, a history convincing enough to establish a nationwide strategy for natural disasters to avoid and mitigate the risks of disasters and plan responses. World Vision is training regional leaders to improve disaster preparedness at the local level."[12]

Picture by World Vision International

First aid and other medical supplies

Medical supplies and treatment options may be limited after a disaster occurs. If a family member needs ongoing medical treatment or prescription medication, they should work with their medical doctor before a disaster occurs to decide how to address it because, " . . . all drugs are perishable. After the expiration date, they begin to lose their potency, and some (especially tetracycline) may contain toxic byproducts. This means that supplies should be rotated . . . ."[10] Adequate planning can ensure access to critical medical supplies for individuals and families in an emergency situation.

Action:

- Families can adapt to the scarcity of medical supplies by building their own first aid kits.
- They can also supplement licensed medical professionals by learning how to treat minor medical problems and injuries.

II – Responding to and Recovering from Emergencies

Family emergency plan

If the family has been affected by a disaster situation, the first step in their response is to implement the family emergency plan. At a minimum, it should account for everyone in the household, assessing their well-being and administering any help they need. After everyone in the household is considered to be safe and cared for, family members are free to carry out other acts of service needed by neighbors in the surrounding community.

Community emergency plan

When an emergency situation occurs, community leaders should assess it and determine if their community emergency plan should be implemented. If they do so, the leaders should implement the portion of the plan that is designed to address the scope of the problem currently affecting people.

Shelter

If a disaster occurs and results in widespread damage, the family should activate their emergency plan. They should also assess the structural stability of their home. If the structure is stable and the disaster appears to be over, then the family should plan to shelter at home unless directed otherwise by community leaders. At home, the family has full access to the food, water and other supplies they have reserved for such an occasion. However, if the home is no longer safe to live in, then the family should evacuate to another safe location. If evacuation is needed, the family should take their emergency kits along with the amount of food and water they can carry.

Shelter represents a key asset for any family, and its loss or damage can result in increased vulnerability and exposure. A lack of adequate and safe shelter presents major risks to people affected by disaster. Shelters which are poorly located, designed, constructed and/or maintained are a leading cause of death during natural hazards such as earthquakes, floods or typhoons.[11]

Regardless of whether families shelter at home or an alternative location, the recovery process is the same. They implement their family plan, reserve water, prepare food, help their neighbors, mitigate the spread of disease and care for the wounded. When families in the community are prepared, they are able to respond to the emergency situation and recover from it more easily and more quickly than would otherwise be possible. More importantly, they can reduce the amount of suffering people endure and make their community a better, healthier place.

Endnotes

1. "Make An Emergency Plan: Tailor Your Plan To Your Needs," official website of the Department of Homeland Security, https://www.ready.gov/considerations.
2. "Disaster Preparedness Tokyo: 02 Let's Get Prepared Disaster Preparedness Actions (P80-141)," Tokyo Metropolitan Government, page 124, http://www.metro.tokyo.jp/ENGLISH/GUIDE/BOSAI/.
3. "Sendai Framework for Disaster Risk Reduction 2015-2030," The United Nations Office for Disaster Risk Reduction, Sendai, Japan, March 2015, 1st Edition, page 17, paragraph 27-f, http://www.unisdr.org/files/43291_sendaiframeworkfordrren.pdf.
4. "Sendai Framework for Disaster Risk Reduction 2015-2030," The United Nations Office for Disaster Risk Reduction, Sendai, Japan, March 2015, 1st Edition, pages 21-22, paragraphs 33-d, 33-f, 33-h, 33-i, 33-m, 33-n and 33-o, http://www.unisdr.org/files/43291_sendaiframeworkfordrren.pdf.
5. "Emergency Water Storage," Homeland Security News and Information, http://www.nationalterroralert.com/safewater/.
6. "Provident Living: Home Storage Centers," The Church of Jesus Christ of Latter-day Saints, https://providentliving.lds.org/self-reliance/home-storage-centers.
7. "Safely Stored Fuel is a Preparedness Essential," LDS Living, Emergency Essentials, October 4, 2011, http://www.ldsliving.com/Safely-Stored-Fuel-Is-a-Preparedness-Essential/s/66120.
8. "Build An Emergency Supply Kit," official website of the Department of Homeland Security, https://www.ready.gov/build-a-kit.
9. "ECHO Fact Sheet - Disaster Risk Reduction," European Commission's Humanitarian Aid and Civil Protection department, April 2014, page 4, http://ec.europa.eu/echo/files/aid/countries/factsheets/thematic/disaster_risk_reduction.pdf.
10. Orient, Jane M., "Doctors for Disaster Preparedness: A Basic Medical Kit For A 10 – 20 Person Shelter," http://www.ddponline.org/medkit.htm.
11. "ECHO Fact Sheet - Disaster Risk Reduction," European Commission's Humanitarian Aid and Civil Protection department, April 2014, page 4, http://ec.europa.eu/echo/files/aid/countries/factsheets/thematic/disaster_risk_reduction.pdf
12. Nonkes, Mark, "Knowledge for life: 11 Ways families across Asia prepare for disasters," World Vision International, October 2015, http://www.wvi.org/asia-pacific/article/knowledge-life-11-ways-families-across-asia-prepare-disasters.
13. Biswas, Richa Silvia, "Knowledge for life: Tips to predict and prepare for a disaster from a 9-year-old", World Vision International, October 2015, http://www.wvi.org/bangladesh/article/knowledge-life-tips-predict-and-prepare-disaster-9-year-old.

Progress towards the Sustainable Development Goals

Report of the Secretary-General, 3 June 2016

E/2016/75

Goal 14. Conserve and sustainably use the oceans, seas and marine resources for sustainable development

95. Oceans, along with coastal and marine resources, play an essential role in human well-being and social and economic development worldwide. They are particularly crucial for people living in coastal communities, who represented 37 per cent of the global population in 2010. Oceans provide livelihoods and tourism benefits, as well as subsistence and income. They also help regulate the global ecosystem by absorbing heat and carbon dioxide from the atmosphere and protecting coastal areas from flooding and erosion. In fact, coastal and marine resources contribute an estimated $28 trillion to the global economy each year through ecosystem services. However, those resources are extremely vulnerable to environmental degradation, overfishing, climate change and pollution. The sustainable use and preservation of marine and coastal ecosystems and their biological diversity is essential to achieving the 2030 Agenda, in particular for small island developing States.

Mark Matunga has made contributions to many policy and strategy formulations in education in many African countries while at Microsoft Corporation for 10 years. Currently, Dr. Matunga leads Corporate Programs for Intel Corporation in East Africa. A devoted Christian and community organizer, He has spent his life transforming communities through education and other socio-economic interventions. Mark has helped build schools, roads and much more. He is patron of many organizations and schools, including the Mark Matunga High School (public school named in his honour). He is married to Josephine, and is a father to Darleene, Furaha, and Daddy (Wema).

14 – Oceans, Seas & Marine Resources

Mark Matunga

Goal 14. Conserve and sustainably use the oceans, seas and marine resources for sustainable development

14.1   by 2025, prevent and significantly reduce marine pollution of all kinds, particularly from land-based activities, including marine debris and nutrient pollution

14.2   by 2020, sustainably manage and protect marine and coastal ecosystems to avoid significant adverse impacts, including by strengthening their resilience, and take action for their restoration, to achieve healthy and productive oceans

14.3   minimize and address the impacts of ocean acidification, including through enhanced scientific cooperation at all levels

14.4   by 2020, effectively regulate harvesting, and end overfishing, illegal, unreported and unregulated (IUU) fishing and destructive fishing practices and implement science-based management plans, to restore fish stocks in the shortest time feasible at least to levels that can produce maximum sustainable yield as determined by their biological characteristics

14.5   by 2020, conserve at least 10 per cent of coastal and marine areas, consistent with national and international law and based on best available scientific information

14.6   by 2020, prohibit certain forms of fisheries subsidies which contribute to overcapacity and overfishing, and eliminate subsidies that contribute to IUU fishing, and refrain from introducing new such subsidies, recognizing that appropriate and effective special and differential treatment for developing and least developed countries should be an integral part of the WTO fisheries subsidies negotiation *

14.7   by 2030 increase the economic benefits to SIDS and LDCs from the sustainable use of marine resources, including through sustainable management of fisheries, aquaculture and tourism

14.a   increase scientific knowledge, develop research capacities and transfer marine technology taking into account the Intergovernmental Oceanographic Commission Criteria and Guidelines on the Transfer of Marine Technology, in order to improve ocean health and to enhance the contribution of marine biodiversity to the development of developing countries, in particular SIDS and LDCs

14.b   provide access of small-scale artisanal fishers to marine resources and markets

14.c   ensure the full implementation of international law, as reflected in UNCLOS for states parties to it, including, where applicable, existing regional and international regimes for the conservation and sustainable use of oceans and their resources by their parties

The reality

All of the above articulation of the SGD 14 sounds great, but until it makes sense to the local fisherman and to families around marine areas, sustainability will remain a mirage. The SGDs must be broken down to the family unit, making sense to those who survive from the proceeds of the waters. It must make sense to all whose lives and livelihoods depend on an aquatic environment, either as: fishermen, traders or residents whose natural and/or ancestral dwelling is around the waters, be it: rivers, lakes, oceans, dams and swamps.

Putting SDG 14 into perspective

Living on Mfangano is subsistence living. The only sustainable way to survive and to put food on the table is to till the land, fish in the lake and raise capital for the family.

Then someone comes to read all the great sentences and clauses of SDG 14 and tell us this is what global leaders have said. I still have to feed, clothe and educate my children – so maybe one day they can also be a global leader. The best way to do it is to do what I am doing now, put my family first – fish and till the land – anything else is not important. The families in our village need money to feed, clothe and educate the children by relying on the marine ecosystem around them. Without their combined "family capital" these resources are out of reach. To achieve SDG 14, there is need to reflect on how family capital sustains marine dwellers.

My home on the island

This item is as personal at it can get. I was born on a small island in Lake Victoria known as Mfangano Island. On the island it was, and is, organic – any young man learns how to till the ground for family use, but most importantly he learns how to fish for both his family and subsistence.

Growing up, as young as 10-years-old, I had no choice but to ensure that I knew how to fish, till the ground, and maintain my schoolwork. I also had to assist my parents with home chores and running all sorts of errands. I know child-rights organizations would have my parents arrested for what qualifies today as child-labour. The reality is that this was the way of life, and although it sounds like child-labour, there were zero options if we wanted to survive. A good bit of such a situation still exists for many, many families.

Fishing villages on Mfangano Island of Lake Victoria.

Allow me to go granular here and give a practical case in point from my village. Mfangano Island is in Lake Victoria, on the Kenyan waters. My ancestors named our village Mauta, which is a Suba word for caves, because in the foothills of the village there are many caves in which my forefathers lived. But that is on the hilly side of the village. On the southern end of the village is the lakeshore of Victoria. The two subsistence activities that my village is involved in are completely different from each other – tilling the land and fishing.

The way of life in the village

Early morning, the movement of people is predictable. You either walk to the lake to search for fish caught by fishermen in the night, or climb the hill to till the grounds in the small gardens on the upper plateau. Children are also walking to school (situated near the lake shore). Men and women do both activities in the same day, using the early morning hours to check the fish catch as a buyer, trader or fisherman, and then proceed into the hills to till the soil.

Fishermen spend the whole night in shallow- or deep-sea fishing (using various techniques), then bring their catch to shore in the morning. The rest of the community comes to the shore to buy fish to consume or for preservation to resell later – to the other fish mongers. At the end of the transactions (about an hour), the villagers melt from the lake front into other chores.

As you can see from the above photo, the morning lake activities also include women doing the dishes from the previous night, even as they fetch water for home use. Those who buy fish also use the abundant lake water to wash the fish in preparation for cooking at home.

Fishing techniques

Fishing is done in many forms and versions. There would be instances when we went to fish the whole night, especially over the weekends. Fridays and Saturdays the children my age and above would go for overnight fishing to catch "Omena" (the small fish in the photo below). You catch them by floating a bright light into the water, they gather around and you scoop them out with nets. That is the fishing technique that would largely require night fishing. We also had other forms of fishing, such as Rimba, where you throw a net into the waters and then pull it out immediately, so as to net any type of fish that lingered in that general area. The main catch would be "Mbuta," Nile perch, and some stray tilapia, but the main target usually is Nile perch.

Other techniques of fishing include simply dropping gill-nets into the deep sea overnight and in the morning checking on any fish entangled in the nets. The main target fish with that was Nile perch. In another fashion, we would use overnight sink-line

Omena fish

The Nile perch (Mbuta)

hooks that in the early days targeted mudfish, but later on targeted Nile perch. But there was also single hook type of fishing that would be done on the lake shores and the river-banks that targeted mainly tilapia. As a child of 10 years and as a young adult, these are the types of fishing activities I participated in to bring food to the table for my parents and siblings – but occasionally we sold any extra fish to raise money for other family uses, including paying school fees for our family members.

Fishermen preparing nets to launch into the waters later in the afternoon for an overnight stay.

Mfangano Island

Mfangano Island is one of several sister islands found in Lake Victoria. It is bordered by Tanzania to the south, Kenya to the east, and Uganda to the west. The population is approximately 45,000 people. Olusuba is spoken on Mfangano.

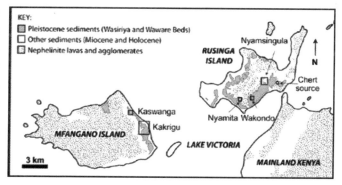

Sustainability of marine resources

Sustainability is very important to the Mfangano way of life. Families are involved in making sure our resources are used wisely and replenished so as to maintain our way of life on this beautiful island.

Using Family Capital to Improve Soil Fertility

The success of any family farming operation is directly related to the fertility of the soil. Family members can combine their talents and abilities to halt and reverse the problems of land degradation, and improve soil fertility, by accomplishing the following:

1. Leave the residue on the field and plant directly into the soil.

2. If the residue is incorporated in the soil, the plant residues will tie up nitrogen in the decomposition and nitrification processes. Therefore, in order to avoid yield depression, extra nitrogen must be applied.

3. Never remove plant materials from the field unless it will be returned in the form of compost, manure, etc.

4. Discontinue burning crops. There are usually short-term benefits with crop burning but the long-term impact is disastrous.

5. Use crop rotations that have high tonnages of crop residues.

6. Enhance the production of crop residues by utilizing organic and/or inorganic fertilizers and pesticides.

7. Utilize human biomass in order to enhance organic-matter levels in the soil. This is important in regions where soils are in a state of degradation.

8. Track annual organic-matter trends by field, farm and country.

9. Rotation plans should include legume-producing nitrogen crops.

10. Utilize no-till precision planters as much as possible

Robert C. Roylance: As General Manager for Farm Management Company, Robert managed numerous corporate farms in theU.S., UK, Mexico and Canada. After retirement he and his wife, Susan, spent eight months of the year, for four years, in Kenya and Uganda, targeting poverty alleviation, orphan care and HIV/AIDS prevention. These targets included: the organization of community associations, export and local marketing, drilling boreholes (deep wells), laying pipelines, hand digging shallow wells, advising farmers on crop production, micro-credit, building schools, establishing a home-based community orphan program and the development of the Stay Alive HIV/AIDS prevention education program for children. He also provided agriculture consultations for farms in Egypt, Paraguay, Guatemala and Haiti.

15.3 – Halt & Reverse Land Degradation

Robert C. Roylance

Goal 15: Protect, restore and promote sustainable use of terrestrial ecosystems, sustainably manage forests, combat desertification, and halt and reverse land degradation and halt biodiversity loss.

It all depends on the soils

It is becoming more apparent that the plight of African society is closely tied to the health of their soils. The Montpellier Panel, made up of agricultural experts from Europe and Africa, warned: ". . . land degradation reduced soil fertility, leading to lower crop yields and increased greenhouse gas emissions . . . . In Africa, the impacts are substantial where 65% of arable land, 30% of grazing land and 20% of forests are already damaged."

> *We spend a lot of time talking about crops and we spend a lot of time talking about livestock. We have big debates about all kinds of agriculture, yet we tend to ignore that it all depends on soils.*

Panel chairman Sir Prof Gordon Conway, Imperial College London, told BBC News: "We spend a lot of time talking about crops and we spend a lot of time talking about livestock. We have big debates about all kinds of agriculture, yet we tend to ignore that it all depends on soils" (BBC, 2014).

The reality of soil degradation

The reality of soil degradation is finally starting to move to the forefront of African issues. There may now be an opportunity to do something meaningful to correct the problems. This article will focus on practical solutions that can play a major role in correcting this roadblock toward solving poverty alleviation and the destruction of natural resources. The solution will require a major effort from all stakeholders – especially prominent universities that can provide the technical expertise. There are a number of important steps to be taken; however, this effort will require the adoption of one major practice change – using a new planting system. This practice will systematize the processes necessary to increase the organic matter percentages of soil. This planting system will be described in greater detail later in this article. It is important to gain an appreciation for the benefits of this system and also understand the basic biological factors that make this system so effective.

The natural setting

In a natural setting of undisturbed soils, an ecological equilibrium is maintained over time. This is known as a closed cycle. This cycle is found in forests and deserts allowed to stay in their natural state. Even in cases where cattle have over-grazed, the soil will stabilize and reach an acceptable equilibrium. The main characteristic of the soils' equilibrium is the percent of organic matter. Some of these soils are somewhat infertile, which is usually due to low rainfall. Others have reached a high state of fertility, usually the result of high levels of moisture–normally in regions of high rainfall. The difference between the fertility in high- and low-rainfall regions is a result of the amount of plant residues produced and returned to the soil each season.

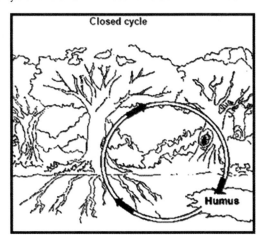

Destabilizing the natural setting

As residues (plant materials) are removed for food, cattle feed, bedding and fuel, the equilibrium is disturbed. When these elements of the soil are removed, the depletion levels of the soils' elements gradually erode and over time the soil becomes unproductive. This is what has been going on in Africa for the past several centuries. It is a very slow, imperceptible process that is currently jeopardizing the economic well-being of the African community. To a large extent it is the result of an uneducated society – in a life or death struggle to secure the basic necessities of life – that does not understand their predicament.

Most advanced societies have recognized the need to maintain or enhance this biological balance. They have taken steps not only to stabilize the soils but to enrich them. However, in many developing countries the peasant farmers seem to lack the will or understanding to take advantage of these practices that will improve crop production. Their focus is usually on the short-term need of growing enough food to feed their families. In addition, they don't understand the serious problem of soil degradation – as a result of their archaic systems of tillage and cultivation.

It is not unusual to see peasant farmers trying to plow a field with a hoe and finding the soil too hard to penetrate. Many times when the rains come the water cannot penetrate the soil's surface and it runs off, carrying sediment into the rivers, lakes and reservoirs. When the rain water cannot reach the root zones, further yield losses are inevitable. This leads to a reduction in crop residues to return to the soil – and the downward spiral continues.

In the case of maize, the first thing that is taken is the ear, used primarily for food. In order to clear the land for the next planting, the corn stalk is hauled away and either burned, used for livestock bedding or cattle feed. It is very seldom that any of the plant material is returned to the field. (It would be most beneficial if these residues would be returned in the form of manure or compost.) And finally, there are times when the roots are pulled for fire wood.

How to rectify damaged soils

Asian farmers are so conscious of the principal of returning more to the soil that it has become part of their culture, and their production levels are constantly improving. They

not only fertilize (animal manure and commercial fertilizers) crops to generate more crop residue, but they also return the crops' spoils in the form of human waste. The picture to the right is a facility at the edge of a field – in hopes that travelers will deposit their bio-waste in the toilet, thus increasing the amount of organic matter the farmer can add to his field.

In addition to the principle of returning high levels of residue to the soils, many farmers are using no-till principles to maximize the impact of residue management. This technique has become so successful that the number of farmers in the U.S. using no-till is approaching fifty percent—whereas in Africa, it is only one third of one percent, and most of that acreage is in South Africa.

This no-till technology appears to be ideally suited to the African crop-residue dilemma. However, the peasant farmers in many developing countries find it very difficult to embrace the principles associated with crop-residue management techniques. This is primarily due to the lack of heavy equipment, motivation and a desire to put in the extra time and effort to make it work.

A farmer near Kitale, Kenya, has embraced the principle of utilizing crop residues to build up his soil-production potential. He actually gathers up the corn stalks from his neighbors' fields and spreads them on his fields. His crops are much better, but that still does not seem to impact or change his neighbors' farming techniques. The challenge to stop soil degradation in Africa is a difficult problem.

The following quote on the yield of maize is particularly alarming due the amount of effort already exerted to improve crop yields over the past fifteen years.

> Maize yields are decreasing in Morocco, Chad, Somalia, Kenya, Zambia, Zimbabwe, Rwanda, Burundi, and Democratic Republic of Congo. Elsewhere, rates of yield improvement are lower than population growth, suggesting that production per capita is likely to decline (Ray, 2013).

Another issue that clouds the interpretation of crop yields is the atmospheric CO_2 levels. Commercial greenhouse operators pump high levels of CO_2 into their growing areas in order to increase the quality and yield of various fruits and vegetables. So, the question has to be asked, what kind of increase in crop yields is the world experiencing under high atmospheric CO_2 levels? Some agronomists say it is around 21%. Others are not so sure. Since it is likely yields are enhanced with CO_2, the African yields are artificially tabulated and the conclusion is that yields would be significantly lower if it were not for high CO_2 levels. This means the cultural practices of the African farmers are more damaging than raw statistics indicate. This is especially disturbing because population growth alone already fuels the need to find additional farm land in order to reduce hunger. Add depleted soils and even more land must be found to produce food. This leads to further destruction of forests and deserts.

Why are organic levels so important?

Organic matter in the soil accomplishes a number of essential functions pertaining to crop production; these include (1) enhancing the water-holding capacities of the soil, (2) generating nitrogen and sulfur that is available to the plant, (3) reducing soil compaction, (4) increasing soil aeration, (5) increasing soil biological activity, (6) improving tillage activities, (7) assisting in the regulation of the soils' acidity and alkalinity,

(8) reducing soil erosion, and (9) assisting in restricting chemical pollution. This is an impressive list and should command a great deal of attention.

Understanding the role of organic matter is key to the resolution of deteriorating soils in Africa or elsewhere. Enhancing organic matter is simply a matter of increasing the amount of plant material that is applied to the soils. This will be discussed in greater detail in the following segments. One of the positive aspects of this critical aspect of combating soil degradation is the ease in which organic matter can be determined and tracked.

(See SDG Target 2.3: "Double Agriculture Production," page 39.)

Specific and critical steps to revive African agriculture

Ways to revive African agriculture must include discussion on different farming systems. It is suggested the farming systems of GAP (Good Agriculture Practices) and BAP (Best Agricultural Practices) become the central focuses on reforming African agriculture. Organic certification is certainly an option, but limited markets preclude it from becoming a macro-solution. This is simply an economic reality.

GAP is a set of production standards requiring extensive preparation and a set of difficult certification procedures. This program has been adopted by major food retailers of the world in an effort to ensure customers have safe food. In addition, these regulations require farmers to take care of the natural resources. This is extremely complicated and has become a major barrier with the small peasant farmers in Africa. The GAP program has many excellent features, but it has gone too far with inconsequential consumer benefits. Many of these pointless requirements have put numerous African farmers in a very difficult situation, thus many of them have reverted back to subsistence farming. Because it is the accepted practice of the food industry, farmers are going to have to find ways to include it in their production and marketing programs.

The GAP programs embrace the following productions systems:
- IPM (Integrated Pest Management)
- ISFM (Integrated Soil Fertility Management)
- Integrated irrigation management systems
- Marketing

In addition to these productions systems, GAP has intense sanitation standards and a traceability feature to allow consumers to trace produce back to the exact field.

The one critical step

With the understanding of: (1) some of the basic rudiments of soil fertility, (2) yield possibilities, and (3) the psychology of African farm families, it is time to reveal the one technology or practice that could make a huge difference in African corn yields, stimulating positive side-effects on all levels of social and economic issues.

This is the introduction of a highly-effective planter, which has a lot to do with the incredible yield-surge in the U.S. (see photo to right). Many companies produce high-tech planters. Even though it had an amazing impact on U.S. corn production, it will have an even larger impact on African farms. Its unique contribution to the African agricultural situation is its ability to reverse the land degradation trends. The degradation reversal is due to the following:

John Deere Maxemerge Corn Planter

- The planter can **seed through previous crop's plant residues**, thereby: (1) retaining all plant materials so they can return to the earth's organic matter pool, and (2) minimize the amount of crop residues that would tie up nitrogen if this material was mixed in the soil.

- This planter is called a precision planter because it **accurately spaces seeds** at the right depth and in an ideal seedbed.

- The planter can **minimize the use of fertilizers** (organic and/or inorganic) by placing the fertilizers in the right location with ideal access to the plant's rooting system.

- This planter can also **minimize the use of pesticides** (organic and inorganic) by making minimal quantities work effectively.

The proper use of high-tech planters will greatly increase the production of crop/plant materials that are an addition to the grain crop. This extra plant material will, over time, end up as organic matter – a major contributor to highly productive soils.

It is understood that most peasant farmers will not have access to these high precision planters, therefore the following practices will go a long way in the development of soils that are rich in organic matter.

The chart **"production practices" on page 225** illustrates the extremes between the current operating procedures and future possibilities.

The following practices can improve the productivity of the soil.

Compost bins and piles

There has been a great deal of effort in trying to get the peasant farmer to use the technique of composting, however it has been met with limited success. Here again it requires a great deal of effort and short-range benefits are difficult to see.

Ridge composting

Ridge planting is another way of keeping crop residues in the field while standard conventional seed bed operations can be retained. This requires more work but some farmers prefer a trash-free seedbed. Simply dig a trench and fill it up with the crop residue (leaves, stems, etc.). Cover the crop residue with soil and this portion of the row will result in an excellent seedbed for the coming year.

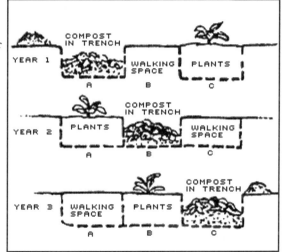

Return cattle manure to fields

Returning crop residues to the fields in the form of composted animal manures is an essential part of soil management. This practice will go a long way to restore the balance of giving more back to the soil than you take from it.

Return human waste to fields

Some farmers in Asian countries have set up outhouses to collect human waste, in hopes that travelers will stop and use it, giving the farmer more bio-mass to return to the soil. This represents an important mindset that Asian farmers have in regard to soil improvement principles. Other more sophisticated systems for the collection, treatment and distribution of human waste are being used in Asian and South American countries.

Jab planting

The jab planter is a tool that is designed to reverse the current trend of land degradation – by allowing the crop residues to stay in the field. This helps increase soil organic matter and is an effective aid to increase water-use efficiency. This method has been used in Africa on a limited basis and could become an effective way to preserve crop residues

Crop rotations

Rotating crops is essential in maximizing crop production. A good crop rotation will accomplish the following:
　　(1) Increase crop yields,
　　(2) Reduce the quantity of pests,
　　(3) Improve the soil long-term,
　　(4) Reduce the need for fertilizers,
　　(5) Improve water infiltration and
　　　　retention rates, and provide
　　(6) Provide higher quality produce.

Organic matter extremes

The next chart illustrates the extremes between the current operating procedures and future possibilities.

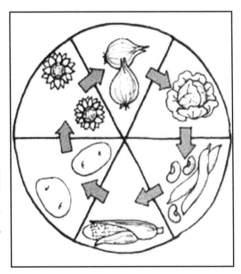

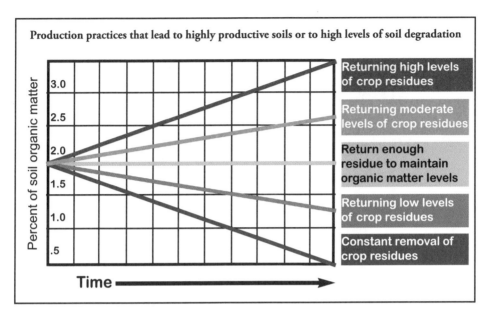

Production practices that lead to highly productive soils or to high levels of soil degradation

Percent of soil organic matter

3.0
2.5
2.0
1.5
1.0
.5

Time ➡

Returning high levels of crop residues

Returning moderate levels of crop residues

Return enough residue to maintain organic matter levels

Returning low levels of crop residues

Constant removal of crop residues

It is important to point out the starting point of 2% organic matter is an arbitrary number and represents average conditions. It is likely that many of the existing fields in Africa are already below 1%.

As previously stated, organic matter is an excellent predictor of soil productivity; however, there are more accurate indicators that this article will not address at the present time. These more sophisticated indicators are designed for high-production regions of the world and would be somewhat irrelevant in Africa.

The organic-matter soil test is very simple and inexpensive and would accommodate a program where a standardized testing program could be implemented on all farms. This would give the farmer and extension agents a measure on how well specific farms are doing.

High organic-matter soils have the following benefits:

- The soil has a **mellow texture** that enhances seedbed preparation.

- Each percent of organic matter will produce from 30 to 70 pounds of nitrogen per crop. (The length of the growing period dictates the number of nitrogen pounds that can be utilized by the crop.)

- High-organic soils will not only accept water at a faster rate but will **hold more water.**

- High-organic soils will **increase aeration in the soil**, an important feature for maximizing the functions of roots.

- Organic matter encourages the **development of beneficial microorganisms**.

The following is a list of steps to help family farmers overcome land degradation:

- **Develop cooperative associations between strong agricultural universities in developed countries and similar universities in developing countries.** This could facilitate the transfer of scientific agricultural information.

- **Expand and improve research farms** – in different countries and in different growing regions within a country.

- **Increase the availability of extension services.**

- **Encourage cooperatives or community development centers** in various agriculture communities – to provide the following to farmers:
    1. Training.
    2. Marketing services.
    3. Financial services.
    4. Mechanization services.
    5. Cropping supplies.

- **Provide effective supervision of farmer organizations** to assure transparency and sound financial management.

- **Organize a cooperative system to acquire precision planters** with financial assistance from the World Bank or other financial institutions. In order to overcome the land degradation problems in the developing countries, the World Bank needs to reallocate a significant portion of their budget to this cause. Currently, allocations to agriculture are less than 1% of the World Bank's budget and their actual allocation to agriculture is on the decline (while the overall budget is on the rise). This is indicative of the lack of understanding that exists in the upper levels of the UN and the World Bank about the importance of a good agricultural program.

- **Strengthen the African Union Advisory Board on Corruption.** Corruption is a huge deterrent to outside intervention. Eliminating corruption would encourage investment in agriculture in developing countries.

Conclusion

There is no question about the extensive farmland degradation happening in many parts of Africa. Unfortunately, most of the farmers are totally oblivious to that fact. This problem has an impact on almost every aspect of the African society. With programs to provide the proper education and support, this degradation can be halted and turned around to make the land sustainable for families and communities. It is time to educate to ensure a sustainable future.

Resources

BBC News, "African soil crisis threatens food security," Mark Kinver, 4 December 2014
http://www.bbc.com/news/science-environment-30277514

Brady, N. C.; Weil, R. R., The nature and properties of soils. 1966 Prentice-Hall Inc. USA
http://www.cabdirect.org/abstracts/19961906536.html;jsessionid=587B373AD9824A12D8250FF
EEEC0D013

Sanginga, N. and Woomer, P.L., 2009. Integrated Soil Fertility Management in Africa: Principles, Practices, and Developmental Process, Tropical Soil Biology and Fertility Institute of the International Centre for Tropical Agriculture (TSBF-CIAT), Nairobi, Kenya

Ray, Mueller, West, Foley, "Yield Trends Are Insufficient to Double Global Crop Production by 2050," Public Library of Science, 2013.
http://journals.plos.org/plosone/article?id=10.1371/journal.pone.0066428

FAO, Title: Land and environmental degradation and desertification in Africa.., The magnitude of the problem http://www.fao.org/docrep/x5318e/x5318e02.htm

Soane, B.D. The role of organic matter in soil compactibility: A review of some practical aspects. Soil and Rillage Research Volume 16, Issues 1-2, Netherlands 1990

Staton, Mike, Corn residue management begins in the fall, Michigan State University Extension, 2011
http://msue.anr.msu.edu/news/corn_residue_management_begins_in_the_fall

Farming as a Family Business
Uganda Busoga Program – Foods Resource Bank (FRB)

Godfrey and Jessica's farm is a family business in FRB's Uganda Busoga Program – led by Lutheran World Relief and local partner Namubuka Grains Cooperative.

Godfrey and Jessica are now running their farm together as part of FRB's Uganda Busoga program – Farming as a Family Business – that focuses on gender equity and conservation farming.

Married for 32 years, the couple and their 12 children were subsistence maize farmers who saw decreasing yields on their 3-acre plot of land due to depleted soils and changing weather patterns. Farming methods they and other farmers in the region had been using for generations no longer worked.

Farmers in the community have received training in conserving water and replenishing soil fertility by using ground cover and minimum or no-tillage techniques that also minimize runoff and erosion. Planting in holes allows them to concentrate compost and rainwater around the base of each plant.

Godfrey and other farmers were encouraged to include their wives in the training and planning. According to Jessica, this was the first time she had a say in how their farm's proceeds would be used. "This program has changed everything! I now sit with my husband and we plan how to use what the farm produces in terms of food and income."

Godfrey and Jessica – Uganda

BEST PRACTICES

They have seen a reduction in on-farm costs because of savings in time, labor and machinery. "Can you imagine? We have prepared three acres this season for the same cost we used to pay for one acre," Godfrey says. Thanks to instruction in household-level business planning, they can now make calculations and budgets based on their projected yield. They expect to get 600 kgs of maize from the same acre of land that yielded 200 kgs just a few months ago. With the increased income, they plan to pay school fees for their children and buy two goats.

They also plan to increase their maize acreage, and Godfrey is confident that this **will not increase Jessica's workload. "First of all, we work on the field together, and the new system of zero tillage means less work,"** says Godfrey. Jessica adds, "It takes me half the effort to do more acres. All I have to do is dig one hole per plant instead of tilling the entire acre."

Godfrey and Jessica are happy with the new way of managing their farm and home. Jessica says it's her decision how much food they store for family consumption and how much they sell as surplus." When she expresses a hope that they continue farming as a family business, Godfrey assures her, "It will not change."

Uganda Busoga encompasses two communities: 1500 households, and 5500 individuals. Godfrey and Jessica's farm is a family business in Uganda FRB's Uganda Busoga Program #1306, led by Lutheran World Relief and local partner Namubuka Grains Cooperative This program has been funded in part by FRB's Community Growing Projects. For more information please visit the Overseas Program page on the website: www.foodsresourcebank.org.

Godfrey in his maize farm

Progress towards the Sustainable Development Goals
Report of the Secretary-General, 3 June 2016
E/2016/75

Goal 16. Promote peaceful and inclusive societies for sustainable development, provide access to justice for all and build effective, accountable and inclusive institutions at all levels

106. **Peace, justice and effective, accountable and inclusive institutions are at the core of sustainable development.** Several regions have enjoyed increased and sustained levels of peace and security in recent decades. But many countries still face protracted armed conflict and violence, and far too many people struggle as a result of weak institutions and the lack of access to justice, information and other fundamental freedoms.

107. The number of victims of intentional homicide worldwide remained relatively stable from 2008 to 2014. The worldwide number of victims of intentional homicide was estimated to be between 4.6 and 6.8 per 100,000 people in 2014, a slight decrease with respect to previous years. Yet during that period, the homicide rate in developing countries was twice that in developed countries, and increased in the least developed countries. Moreover, despite the lack of harmonized data, fatalities and injuries related to armed conflict appear to be increasing in some countries, causing unprecedented population displacements and enormous humanitarian needs.

J. Ruel Haymond is married to Tresa Marshall Haymond and they are the happy parents of seven children and he is a grandfather. He teaches political economy, economics, constitutional law, history, literature and debate to wonderful students at American Heritage School in American Fork, Utah.

---

16 – Peace and Justice

Ruel Haymond

For the past ten years, I have been honored to serve as a teacher of 17-18 year-old young men and women from a variety of different countries, religious faiths and world-view perspectives. As an instructor, my goal is to inform their minds and more importantly, inspire and change their hearts so each student will have a greater desire and commitment to do the following: feed the hungry, clothe the naked, educate the ignorant, heal the sick, comfort the lonely, spread beauty and liberate the captive.

Our class time is daily filled with intense and often rigorous research discussions on topics such as: economics, roles of men and women, religion, all levels of government from individual to international, slavery, debt, poverty, political economy, fidelity, marriage, family, constitutional law, pain, suffering, moral law, ethics, values, history and the list goes on. We look at challenges in countries in Europe, Africa, Asia, North America and Central and South America, such as: incoming and outgoing refugees, human trafficking, corrupt government, uneducated populace, child abuse, droughts, famine and war. Together we reason through the who's, what's, where's, how's and when's, but when the why's finally enter the debate (as they should), the difficulty and pain begins. Some of their questions and comments (and often tears) start to pour from them:

- Mr. Haymond, why is there such violence in the world?
- Why can't people just get along? It seems so simple.
- There should be a way to feed everyone on this planet.
- Is there no way to stem the progression of, or completely stop, child abuse or trafficking? Why?
- The vast majority of people on this earth, with their differences in religion, culture and landscape pretty much want the very same things – peace on earth. Why is this so hard? I am so tired of the suffering.

With tender feelings of love and affections for those that suffer injustices in this world, these young men and women look to me for the answer to the same critical question each one of us asks: "What can we do?"

The room quiets down and the aching of their hearts and minds drowns out the silence. I ask them gently, "What do we do? What do you do?" Soon hands begin to rise and sound and thoughtful suggestions emerge:

- Become more aware of suffering around us.
- Serve with humanitarian trips.
- Support an orphanage.
- Donate money for micro-loans.
- Sponsor the education of a child.
- Serve in local food banks.
- Donate clothing and other needed items to homeless shelters or charitable organizations.
- Become a mentor or teacher.

I admire the love and concern they feel for people throughout the world they have never met and for hardships and difficulties they have rarely seen or experienced. Their desire is sincere but their current experiences and resources are limited. They want the truth, pure and simple, and they look to me as a trusted adult to give them straight answers that will work.

I humbly look them straight in the eyes (with assurance and confidence) and say that the answers to all of these human challenges can be best solved using family capital – or the most basic and essential unit in society, the family.

This chapter will focus on the irreplaceable need for family capital, particularly the unique roles of father and mother capital (especially father capital) in helping to solve the problems that face so many human beings on this earth. Specifically, the focus of this writing is to show the government closest to a child, the family government, is the most effective and efficient form of government to meet and surpass the following Sustainable Development Goal and targets.

SDG Goal 16 promotes peaceful and inclusive societies for sustainable development, the provision of access to justice for all, and building effective, accountable institutions at all levels. This includes:

- Promote the rule of law at the national and international levels and ensure equal access to justice for all
- Significantly reduce all forms of violence and related death rates everywhere
- End abuse, exploitation, trafficking and all forms of violence against, and torture of, children
- Ensure responsive, inclusive, participatory and representative decision-making at all levels

SDG Goal 16

The sixteenth goal of the United Nations Sustainable Development Goals advocates the "promotion of peaceful and inclusive societies for sustainable development, the provision of access to justice for all, and building effective, accountable institutions at all levels."[1] At the foundation of this goal is the stated importance of men and women learning how to govern themselves at every level of government in a manner conducive to peace, respect, accountability and justice for all. There is no better training ground for the development of these essential values and characteristics than at home with a family.

UN: Family has primary responsibility

The World Declaration on the Survival, Protection and Development of Children (1990) states:

> The family has the primary responsibility for the nurturing and protection of children from infancy to adolescence. Introduction of children to the culture, values and norms of their society begins in the family. For the full and harmonious development of their personality, children should grow up in a family environment, in an atmosphere of happiness, love and understanding. Accordingly, all institutions of society should respect and support the efforts of parents and other care-givers to nurture and care for children in a family environment.[2]

The ability to govern oneself

The wise Dutch statesman Hugo Grotius stated over two hundred years ago:

> A man [or woman] cannot govern a nation if he [she] cannot govern a city; he [she] cannot govern a city if he [she] cannot govern a family; he [she] cannot govern a family unless he [she] can govern himself [herself]; and he [she] cannot govern himself [herself] unless his [her] passions are subject to reason.[3]

The ability to govern oneself, to learn to have one's passions remain submissive to reason, is best taught in the home with a faithful and united father and mother as mentors.

Empirical study after empirical study bears witness to the increased opportunities for good health and happiness for children when they are living with their father and mother. Fathers and mothers that are actively and happily involved with their children positively affect a child's cognitive ability to problem solve, achieve academically and economically, deal with depression and to have a greater internal locus of control.[4]

To reach the goal of having societies capable of sustaining peaceful, kind communities that provide access to: justice, home, school or work, young people must be able to control their passions and appetites through an appeal to self-government and reason; their internal locus of self-control must be strong – and the role of stable fathers and mothers is key to this development.

Difficult questions from students

My own experience mirrors what international forums and empirical research reveal regarding the irreplaceable influence of faithful fathers and mothers. The ideal situation for children is to be in a home with their biological father and mother.[5] I teach the ideal taught at all levels of social policy: the biological parents should be the best choice for nurturing and caring for each other and their children. However, it would naïve to suggest that this ideal is being played out in every family situation. It is not.

But that does not mean the ideal should not be taught and sought.

I spend a great deal of time counseling, advising and encouraging students throughout each school year regarding their current academic status, their future goals, etc. For too many of my students, my words of encouragement are to help heal their hearts due to pain caused by problems in their homes. With tears in their eyes, they ask me very difficult questions:

- What do I do when I suspect my parents' marriage is falling apart?
- My father was unfaithful to my mother and it is tearing my family apart. How can I avoid something like this happening to me? I thought the family was the place I could feel safe and secure.
- How do I build a relationship with my father? We do not get along and I want to be close to him.
- My mother will not forgive my father for their divorce and her physical and mental state struggle because of her pain. What do I do?

Often these students are disenchanted by the idea of marriage and family due to the pain they have experienced. I exhort them, in spite of the injury they have received from their own family's struggles, to not give up on creating their as-close-to-the-ideal family of their own. I look them in the eyes and with great love and emphasis state: No success in this world, no matter how important it may seem, can equal the success of faithful parents in the home.[6]

Target 16.3 – Promote the rule of law

One of the key targets under Goal 16 is to "promote the rule of law at the national and international levels and ensure equal access to justice for all." The focus of this target, the rule of law, is by far the most important target of the sixteenth goal. Without laws that are universally accepted and respected, there is little hope for order at the individual government level, through family government and all the way to the level of international government. Laws must exist that protect essential rights of individuals and promote moral values and social stability.[7]

What is law? There are physical laws, laws of nations, moral laws and laws that govern personal behavior. Specifically, a law is an established or permanent rule that is intended to regulate social actions. They are either permissive or prohibitive. Laws tell people what they can and cannot do in order to ensure civil order. Laws encourage order and stability or invite disorder and chaos.[8]

Laws protect rights

Now, a critical question: Which came first, laws or rights? The renowned French statesman and economist Frederic Bastiat stated: "Life, liberty, and property do not exist because men have made laws. On the contrary, it was the fact that life, liberty, and property existed beforehand that caused men to make laws in the first place."[9] Laws exist to protect the rights of individuals.

Finally, the level of government best suited and most sincerely motivated to teach and exemplify laws that respect rights is the family. How is this taught? Parents teach this through moral education and religion. Religion and moral education prepare young hearts and minds to seek access to justice for all, and peaceful solutions to conflict.

The foundation of freedom, justice and peace

The preamble of The Universal Declaration of Human Rights states the "purpose of law is to protect the rights of individuals." Continuing in the declaration, "Whereas recognition of the inherent dignity and of the equal and inalienable rights of all members of the human family is the foundation of freedom, justice and peace in the world . . . . Whereas it is essential, if man is not to be compelled to have recourse, as a last resort, to rebellion against tyranny and oppression, that human rights should be protected by the rule of law . . . ."[10]

From the beginning of the United Nations, there is clear point of emphasis that fixed and permanent rules we call laws are to protect the rights of "life, liberty and security of person."[11] From the beginning, the United Nations recognized the family is the "foundation of freedom, justice and peace in the world" and the most effective government for teaching laws that protect rights through religious and moral education.

In Article 13-3 of the International Covenant on Economic, Social and Cultural Rights, a great trust in faithful parents teaching their children moral and religious law is codified, advocating:

> . . . respect for the liberty of parents and, when applicable, legal guardians to choose for their children schools, . . . and to ensure the religious and moral education of their children in conformity with their own convictions.[12]

This important message of family capital being properly used to produce just, peaceful and tolerant children must be recognized and respected if we are to achieve SDG 16.

The greatest moral influence on children – parents

Whether parents like it or not, they are the greatest moral influence on their children. Faithful fathers and mothers make moral education a priority – to mold and shape the character of their children. Through day-to-day teaching and example, such parents teach: honesty, empathy, compassion, kindness, gentleness, virtue, respect, honor and self-control to their children.[13]

The role of religious teaching is essential at the family level. Parents have the right to teach their children according to their own convictions. While there are differences (some quite vast) between the five major religions of the world (and hundreds if not thousands more), there is one religious tenet that appeals to the vast majority of human beings on the planet: The Ethics of Reciprocity or simply, The Golden Rule.[14] Families from the five major world religions (Judaism, Islam, Christianity, Hinduism and Buddhism) all teach this important law as recorded in their sacred writings:

- Judaism – "What is hateful to you, do not to your fellow man. This is the law: all the rest is commentary." Talmud, Shabbat 31a
- Islam – "None [truly] believes until he wishes for his brother what he wishes for himself." Number 13 of Imam, Al-Nawawi's Forty Hadiths
- Christianity – "Therefore all things whatsoever ye would that men should do to you, do ye even so to them: for this is the law and the prophets." Matthew 7:12
- Hinduism – "This is the sum of duty: do not do to others what would cause pain if done to you." Mahabharata 5:1517
- Buddhism – "One should seek for other the happiness one desires for oneself."[15]

Inalienable rights vs. human rights

The subject of laws (i.e. civil vs. moral, national vs. international, and absolute vs. relative) consistently contributes to heated debates in my classroom. As part of these discussions, we also spend quite a bit of time trying to understand what a right is and the difference between an inalienable right vs. a human right. Every year my students come to the conclusion that an inalienable right is a right one is born with and a human right may be a right provided from birth or a right granted by government. Ultimately, the students reason the purpose of government is to protect primarily inalienable rights, or rights from birth, and any other rights.

I remember one discussion in particular, that was transformational for myself and my students. We were discussing the basic rights of each person in the room and the limited list consisted of the right of speech, conscience, property, life, liberty and security of person.[16] Then the question was asked: If the role of government is to enforce laws and protect rights, what recourse does it have to fulfill this role? In other words, if I, or one of my students, violate a right of another person, what potentially can, and must, government do?

My students began to list what force or punishment government uses to protect rights: government can force a person to pay a fee or fine; government can imprison a person; or government can execute a person. Eyes began to increase in size as students realized rights are sacred and the rights directly protected by government should be limited. We reasoned together that if one advocates the existence of a right and then secures government force to protect that right, then the force to fine, imprison and even execute has been unleashed. I jokingly said to my students, "So, if some of you want to make it a right (protected by law and the force of government) to have interesting, entertaining and fun learning experiences in a classroom and to never be bored, what would be the consequence for me if I did not keep that law and honor that right?"

The students looked at each other and then at me and simply stated: "We could have you fined, imprisoned or killed." The conclusion – be careful when determining rights and the laws to protect them.

Target 16.2 – Reduction of violence and abuse of children

SDG 16 includes important targets that aim to "significantly reduce all forms of violence…end abuse, exploitation, trafficking and all forms of violence against and torture of children."[17] The vast majority of humankind would agree that protecting lives, particularly the lives of children, is the great responsibility of all. No decent person can simply sit back and allow the trafficking of women and children to occur without working to do something to stop it.

International, national and state governments are scrambling for solutions to these ever-increasing manifestations of the darkest side of human nature; solutions that primarily include using human capital and other resources in the form of increased police forces, security guards, politicians to pass more laws and controls, funding, etc., but until solutions begin in the hearts and minds of faithful mothers and fathers, the problems will continue.

Which level of government is really the key to "significantly reducing" these horrible actions towards the most vulnerable in our societies? The family government. Family capital must be the first solution, particularly the irreplaceable use of "father" capital.

Reducing violence in the world

The United Nations, through its various conference and commission documentation, has been raising the clarion call to eliminate all violence towards women,[18] sexual exploitation and abuse, child pornography, child sex tourism and trafficking.[19] Also, in its documentations, the UN has shown the world the way to reduce, if not eliminate, these horrific abuses – the role of parents in the home. Parents are recognized as the front-line experts in providing "optimum care, nurturing and protection,"[20] "strengthening the self-image, self-esteem, and status and in protecting the health and well-being of girls,"[21] and "proper regard for parental guidance and responsibilities."[22] Fathers are to "have responsibilities to participate in their children's lives" and to share in the responsibility within the household and the family.[23] But fathers must go beyond these general guidelines. Fathers are the important missing-link in reducing and solving the violence and abuse epidemic experienced throughout the world.

The role of the family

Pope John Paul II wisely reminded us, "As the family goes, so goes the nation and so goes the whole world in which we live."[24]

Research showing the role of the family structure in creating or solving many of society's ills is abundant. One study showed that family structure predicted five types of crime: drug offenses, violence, property offenses, traffic offenses and drunk driving. Taking into account other significant explanatory variables, the research study showed that a child's living in a broken home as the only independent predictor of all these types of criminality.[25] On the other hand, the reduction of criminal behavior is linked directly to faithful family and marriages.[26]

Yes, even in the best of homes with faithful parents, children may still exhibit criminal behaviors. But for the vast majority of humankind, the home is the front line for preparing children to be, and do, good in the world. It is in the home where children are taught by faithful parents to control passion, appetites, show kindness, forgive and to use reason and not force to solve problems.

It is in the home where fathers teach young men to defend motherhood, womanhood and children. As the father goes, so goes the home, the nation and the whole world in which we live. We need fathers to be faithful and take seriously their responsibilities.

In 1999 the US National Center for Fathering administered a poll to answer the following question: What is the most significant family or social problem facing America? (And I would include the world.) The answer was fatherlessness or the physical absence of the father from the home or the presence of a father who is absent emotionally and spiritually.[27] Now, many years later, is it better or worse? Last year (2015) a researcher published an article entitled, "The Plague of Fatherlessness."[28]

Research by the Children's Legal Foundation highlights some of the potential and perishing consequences fatherless boys may face individually. In the realm of anti-social behavior, fatherless boys seem to be masters of misery. Of these boys, 90% of homeless and runaways are fatherless, 70% of those in juvenile detention, 75% in chemical abuse centers, 85% of prisoners, 86% of psychotic delinquents and 80% of rapists come from fatherless homes. Finally, of fatherless boys, 85% have behavioral disorders; many struggle with sex-role conflict and gender identity issues and 63% of successful suicides can be traced to homes without Dad.[29]

One English proverb states: "One father is more than a hundred schoolmasters"[30] and I would add one father is more than any number of police officers and juvenile detention centers. Father capital is essential to meeting SDG 16 and its targets.

Comparing our day with Plato's time

One day in class, I took my students through a very interesting exercise. Using excerpts from Plato's classic book on government and law, *The Republic*, we compared the above heartbreaking statistics of the effects of fatherlessness on children with the description of the youth (particularly the boys) in the Republic as their nation moved from democracy to tyranny.

The following table was produced:

Fatherless – Our Day – 2015	Socratic Dialogue by Plato – 360 BC
90% of homeless and runaways	"eager for revolution"
70% in juvenile detention	"life of idleness of body and mind"
75% in chemical abuse centers	"focus on useless and unnecessary pleasures"
85% of prisoners	"hate and conspire against those have got…property"
Threefold chance of gang membership	"vulgar and miserly way"
86% of psychotic delinquents	"competing factions in their souls"
80% of rapists	"indulge in the appetite of the hour" "cease to care even for the laws, written or unwritten"
85% of behavioral disorders	"boys and men chafe impatiently at the least touch of authority
63% of successful suicides	"war with themselves"

Times have not really changed, have they? Now, to be fair, I told my students that the comparison focused on the young men and not young women, though some of the comparisons may apply to women; however, I reminded them that much of the abuse and violence in this world is by some men who were not taught by their fathers how to behave in a society.

A few years ago, I was working with my students in an international setting, laying a cement floor for a seventeen-year-old single mother. This young woman had been impregnated and left to her own devices for survival. The service organization we represented was attempting to give her a better living space with her baby. The area in which she lived was known for violence and an abandonment of law – to the point that local police officers often avoided it at night. As we were outside her tiny home holding her baby, two young men suspiciously walked past us. The look in their eyes and the feeling that we all felt when they passed loudly declared that they were up to no good. To me, they appeared to be wolves in search of prey. I remember thinking and even saying aloud, that these are the types of boys that most likely fathered this child and abandoned it and its mother. With my students, we asked the simple yet critical question: **Where are the fathers?**

Where is the father of the baby? Where was the father of this young lady? Where was the father of the father of the child? What is the story here? Where were the fathers that could remove the fear and failure of this community by simply, and faithfully, working with their wives to create a home of justice and morality? A home where respect for women and girls is lived and loved?

One student raised his hand and bravely shared the following: "Mr. Haymond, my father taught me that to respect and honor a girl's body and virtue is my duty. He told me that I should give up my life to defend her from anyone attempting to violate her." If only the boy who fathered this child and then abandoned both his child and its mother had been taught this by his own father!

Family Capital is the only sustainable solution

Family capital is the only truly sustainable solution to peaceful and inclusive societies that offer access to justice for everyone. Any other way may do much good, but it is too far from the sources to effectuate lasting change: the home and the hearth. International and national bodies can write and distribute laws to abolish violence, abuse and exploitation; charitable organizations can bring resources and education to suffering areas; men and women with the greatest of intentions can advocate for, and gather support for, women and children who are victims of terrible crimes; but until the laws protecting and honoring: life, liberty, conscience, morality, kindness, respect, honesty and courage are written upon the hearts of children raised and taught by their fathers and mothers, no substantial change will be realized. Truly, the "hands that rock the cradle" rule and save the world.

Father capital plays a key role in "rocking the cradle." In a world easily offended, faithful fathers teach their boys and girls how to forgive and understand; as permissiveness pervades hearts and homes, kind fathers lead young men and women in justice and order. Protecting, presiding and providing are the priorities of fathers who are about their families' business. Young men and women raised by such faithful heroes tend to live by, and according to, correct rules – they will be more likely to live by the best rule: the Golden Rule. Private and public virtue, the foundation of every sound individual and nation, are demonstrated consistently to boys and girls as they grow to manhood and womanhood. Such fathers teach their children that virtue is fulfilling the measure of their creation – the purpose for which they were created. As virtues such as humility, morality and fidelity are inculcated in the hearts and minds of young people, the sick are healed, the naked are clothed, the hungry are fed, the ignorant are educated and the captives are liberated.

Endnotes

1. United Nations Sustainable Development Goals, http://www.un.org/sustainabledevelopment/peace-justice/
2. World Declaration on the Survival, Protection and Development of Children, 30 September 1990, http://www.unicef.org/wsc/plan.htm
3. Hugo Grotius and the Origins of the Enlightenment in the Netherlands, http://www1.umassd.edu/euro/2007papers/truslow.pdf
4. The Effects of Father Involvement: An Updated Research Summary of the Evidence, 2007, http://www.fira.ca/cms/documents/29/Effects_of_Father_Involvement.pdf
5. Are Married Parents Really Better for Children? What Research Says About the Effects of Family Structure on Child Well-Being, 2003, http://www.clasp.org/resources-and-publications/states/0086.pdf
6. Home: The Savior of Civilization, 1924, https://books.google.com/books?id=fpeRGQAACAAJ&dq=home+savior&cd=1
7. The Universal Declaration of Human Rights, 29.2, http://www.un.org/en/universal-declaration-human-rights/
8. Online Oxford Dictionary and Websters 1828 Dictionary, http://www.oxfordlearnersdictionaries.com/us/definition/english/law?q=law, http://webstersdictionary1828.com/Dictionary/law
9. The Law by Frederic Bastiat, http://bastiat.org/en/the_law.html
10. The Universal Declaration of Human Rights (Preamble), http://www.un.org/en/universal-declaration-human-rights/
11. Ibid, Article 3
12. International Covenant on Economic, Social and Cultural Rights, 1976, http://www.ohchr.org/EN/ProfessionalInterest/Pages/CESCR.aspx
13. Character Training and Moral Education, http://www.growingfamiliesusa.com/new-page-2/
14. "The Golden Rule" (a.k.a Ethics of Reciprocity), http://www.religioustolerance.org/reciproc2.htm
15. Ibid
16. The Universal Declaration of Human Rights (Preamble), http://www.un.org/en/universal-declaration-human-rights/
17. United Nations Sustainable Development Goals, SDG Goal 16 Targets, http://www.un.org/sustainabledevelopment/peace-justice/
18. Transforming our World: The 2030 Agenda for Sustainable Development, https://docs.google.com/gview?url=http://sustainabledevelopment.un.org/content/documents/2125 2030%20Agenda%20for%20Sustainable%20Development%20web.pdf&embedded=true
19. World Declaration on the Survival, Protection and Development of Children, http://www.unicef.org/wsc/declare.htm
20. Ibid
21. Key Actions for the Further Implementation of the Program of Action, http://www.unfpa.org/resources/key-actions-further-implementation-program-action
22. Ibid
23. World Declaration on the Survival, Protection and Development of Children, http://www.unicef.org/wsc/declare.htm
24. Homily of Pope St. John Paul II, https://w2.vatican.va/content/john-paul-ii/en/homilies/1986/documents/hf_jp-ii_hom_19861130_perth-australia.html
25. "Childhood Predictors of Male Criminality: A Prospective Population-Based Follow-up Study from Age 8 to Late Adolescence," Journal of the American Academy of Child and Adolescent Psychiatry, 45 (2006): 578-586.
26. The Real Root Causes of Violent Crime: The Breakdown of Marriage, Family, and Community, Dr. Patrick Fagan, http://www.heritage.org/research/reports/1995/03/bg1026nbsp-the-real-root-causes-of-violent-crime
27. Fathering in America, (http://www.fathers.com/documents/research/1999-NCF-Poll-Fathering-in-America.pdf
28. The Plague of Fatherlessness, http://www.cnsnews.com/commentary/lynn-wardle/plague-fatherlessness
29. Effects of Fatherlessness on Children – Social Consequences, http://sondur.com/fatherlessness.htm
30. http://www.forbes.com/quotes/3491/

SDG 17 OUTLINE

Vincenzina Santoro is an international economist, consultant and former Vice President of JPMorgan and Co. She is a volunteer at the Charity Accountability Program of the New York Better Business Bureau, represents the American Family Association of New York at the United Nations and writes frequently about international economic and social issues. Ms. Santoro is a native New Yorker, a graduate of Hunter College, City University of NY (BA, MA in economics) and is fluent in five languages.

---

17 - Implementation

Vincenzina Santoro

Families as partners for development

According to the United Nations Secretary-General's Synthesis Report of December 2014, the SDGs are supposed to be people centered. What could be more people centered than the family? The first "partnership" a person experiences is as a child in a family. In the family a child learns about relationships, responsibilities and respect for others. Families are at the core of the shift from poverty to prosperity. They provide the initial formation of human capital that sets the foundation for future partnerships and development.

Families are often the starting point for entrepreneurial activity from a micro-undertaking in a small African village to a budding genius working on a technical idea out of the family garage to eventually create a global corporation. Parents inspire children to come up with ideas, unleash creativity, become involved in designing, developing, producing and marketing products and services that are new, unique, desirable or merely an improvement on an existing item. The initiative, talent, skill and versatility often lead to the startup of a successful family business, based on common purpose, passion and vision, often passed on from one generation to the next. As sales and success take over, family businesses sometimes morph into giant multi-nationals.

Formation of partnerships

Partnerships, of various kinds, probably did more to bring people out of poverty and enhance development during the 15-year duration of the MDGs. Goal 17 with 21 targets, the last SDG goal, is a rework and expansion of MDG 8 on global partnerships. The final goal is divided into four segments: finance, technology, capacity-building and trade. In addition, it covers systemic issues including policy and institutional coherence, multi-stakeholder partnerships and data, monitoring and accountability.

Partnerships are all about people working together to accomplish a common purpose, to make things happen. The origin, formation and development of human capital begin at the family level. Throughout history families have banded and bonded together to earn a living, commencing with the family farm to feed family members then to small businesses that help develop the local community. Many global enterprises have emerged from family-based startups, creating millions of jobs the world over. Family businesses are key partnerships for development.

> The importance of family businesses to the global economy is undeniable. They account for more than two-thirds of all companies around the world and 50%-80% of employment in most countries.[1]

Globally the vast majority of jobs are created by the private sector, whether sole proprietorships, family-owned businesses or major corporations. From the United States to Africa, there is evidence that small businesses are often started and run by women, from family-owned farms to family firms. Women play a dominant role in family-owned companies representing true economic empowerment. Given that three-fourths of the world's poorest people live in rural areas according to IFAD (the International Fund for Agricultural Development), the promise of a family business, perhaps with the aid of a microloan, can hold the key to a better future.

A survey in 2014 of 2,400 of the world's largest family-owned businesses in 21 major countries in all continents showed that the top 25 family-owned businesses in each market had an average of 12,000 employees, averaged sales of nearly $3½ billion, and averaged 8% growth per annum with 54% planning to add an estimated 100,000 employees. About 87% of companies had a succession plan and 70% were considering a woman for their next CEO.[2] According to one compilation:

> The world's top 500 family businesses contributed US $6.5 trillion to global GDP in 2013 – more than the French and German economies combined. In the same year they employed 20.9 million people, larger than the South African workforce.[3]

In the United States alone there were 216 private companies with combined revenues of $1.6 trillion in 2015 as reported by Forbes magazine. There are numerous examples of very successful family-initiated, owned and operated companies across the globe. There is the Walton family in the United States which founded Walmart in 1962 and today several family members have become top billionaires. Walmart employs over 2.3 million worldwide, including 1.5 million in the United States. In Sweden, there is Ingvar Kamprad who founded IKEA in 1943, which today is the world's largest furniture distributor and is present in over 50 countries. The Ferrero family of Italy began, and still owns, a confectionery company founded at the close of World War II (**see Box 1**).

Many new businesses are conceived, formed and nourished at the family level with family, human and financial capital. Some of today's technology giants originated in a family garage, received their first financial boost from family resources and then prospered exponentially to become corporate multinational giants. Such were the origins of Microsoft, Apple and Google. Moreover, each was co-founded

---

> **Box 1: A family business global success story**
>
> One very interesting family story is that of Michele Ferrero, an Italian pioneer in the sweets business. His father started a small confectionery shop in Northern Italy during World War II and due to the scarcity of chocolate mixed it with a hazelnut paste he developed. Michele Ferrero, who inherited the business at age 23, refined his father's product into Nutella, now sold the world over. He also created the world-famous Ferrero Rocher chocolate and other sweets.
>
> Michele Ferrero died on February 14, 2015, leaving a family fortune in excess of $20 billion. In his lifetime he showed extraordinary care for his employees and his fellowmen at home and abroad. He provided dedicated bus service for employees living in outlying areas; provided a crèche for women with small children; paid for employees' medicines; and provided centers for his retired employees where they could gather, share each other's company and engage in whatever activity they choose. He built these centers not only in Italy but in other countries where the company has manufacturing operations.
>
> Despite his immense wealth and fame, Mr. Ferrero never sought the limelight. He led an exemplary life as a faith-filled, kind and generous man who shared his good fortune with his employees, the local community and well beyond Italy's borders by investing in several social enterprises in poor countries. These investments promote businesses that provide a product or service, create employment and make a profit – without which they cannot survive.

with a partner: Bill Gates and Paul Allen, Steve Jobs and Steve Wosniak, and Sergei Brin and Larry Page. These are true partnerships that grew from the local to the national then international level.

Both family- and publicly-owned companies engage in voluntary social-responsibility endeavors, starting at the community level, either through philanthropic activities (as explained later) or through public-private partnerships to work towards a common goal, such as in education or health.

From employment, earnings and profits to revenues for public coffers

Without successful enterprises that produce and sell goods and services, enable employment and produce profits, there would be no revenues for public coffers as Target 17.1 calls for. To assist the fiscal authorities of developing and least developed countries in collecting needed revenues, there are several advisory bodies that can, and do, lend assistance to governments as to how to enhance revenues and monitor and assure compliance.

The Fiscal Affairs Department of the International Monetary Fund provides expertise when IMF missions visit various member countries. The OECD has taken a leading role in tackling international tax matters especially with reference to BEPS (base erosion and profit shifting), that has become a major issue involving the behavior of

---

very large multinationals who seek out ways of paying the least amount of corporate income taxes.

BEPS is at the core of the behavior of large multinational corporations that are based in countries with a high tax rate, such as the United States, which has a corporate tax rate of 35%. All other developed countries have lower rates, with Ireland having one of the lowest at 12.5%. With such a low rate, Ireland has been able to attract significant foreign investment. Low-tax rates and favorable tax treatment are legitimate measures countries employ to bring in the foreign firms to create industries and jobs.

Whatever tax rates a government chooses, to be effective they have to be prudent and not punitive and government budgets must be administered with integrity, strategy and intelligence. Many development projects never see the light of day due to mismanagement and corruption. Hence some of the poorest countries have inadequate public services and infrastructures that impede development. Just tax rates, tax compliance and efficient administration depend on good governance so that revenues are collected and used to finance the security and development of each country.

Scaling-up official development assistance

As with the MDGs, the SDGs also are promoting more official development assistance (ODA), both bilateral and multilateral – the latter including grants to international entities such as UN agencies. There is a reference in Target 17.2 for Development Assistance Committee (DAC) countries to re-commit 0.7% of their gross national income (GNI) to official aid, of which 0.15% to 0.20% is to be destined for the 48 UN-designated least developed countries.

No reliable or credible estimate can be made of funds needed to "eradicate poverty" from the world, but the UN insists that the 0.7% is part of the solution. The percent has no economic basis. It is completely arbitrary. The UN has never explained how a percentage – as opposed to targeted, specific and prudent spending – is supposed to solve poverty.

The 28 members of the OECD's DAC collectively have never met this target. The 2015 average was 0.41% of GNI (see chart). Net ODA amounted to nearly $132 billion in 2015, down from just over $137 billion the previous year, which was an all-time record. Six countries were at or above the target: Sweden, Norway, Luxembourg, Denmark, the Netherlands and the United Kingdom. Together they contributed $40.8 billion (31%) of total ODA. The United Kingdom scaled-up efforts in recent years and just barely reached the 0.7% mark in 2013 for the first time. The United States has always been the largest aid donor. In 2015 the United States gave $31 billion in ODA (over two-thirds more than second-ranked United Kingdom), and accounted for 23.6% of total ODA despite donating only 0.17% of GNI.

Certain ODA members often direct aid to countries with which they have a special, historical relationship. For example, the country that received the largest amount of aid from the United Kingdom was India, a former colony. Similarly, Portugal's ODA went primarily to those countries in Africa (Angola, Mozambique) that were once considered its overseas territories. Moreover, some ODA countries that have received vast numbers of refugees, such as Germany, Greece and Italy, diverted part of their ODA towards refugee assistance in 2015.

At times foreign aid comes with a modern "colonial" tinge: Aid is sometimes withdrawn from countries that do not adhere to similar social or secular standards of the donor, thus becoming foreign interference rather than foreign assistance.

Since the global economic crisis of 2007-2008, a few DAC members have experienced severe financial problems. Greece, Ireland, Portugal and Spain have scaled back on ODA, while they themselves needed international financial assistance to deal with soaring budget deficits and rising government debt. Despite development needs, some of the 148 countries designated by the OECD as eligible candidates to receive ODA have finances that are in better shape than developed countries. For example, at the end of 2015, the United States had a gross government debt-to-GDP ratio of 106%, the United Kingdom was at 89% and Japan 248%.[4]

Existing and new sources of financing for the SDGs

Existing and new sources of financing were explored at the United Nations Financing for Development Conference held in July 2015 in Addis Ababa. In addition to the usual exhortations relating to the 0.7% aid target, attendees looked for ways of increasing government tax revenues including various references to global taxes. Despite vociferous discussions, "global taxes" are non-starters. Not all 193 UN member states can agree to adopt a similar tax to fund whatever purpose. All taxes must be proposed by, voted on and adopted by, the legislature of each country.

Much discussion has been spent on a "financial transactions tax" – an idea that originated in the 1960s. Some countries tried it. They soon removed it. Sweden is one example: Applied to transactions in the equity market, that market nearly dried up as more and more transactions were executed elsewhere. The matter last was discussed at the European Union level in 2014, but the United Kingdom, home to the largest and most sophisticated financial markets, quickly had the idea pushed aside even though some EU members are still arguing in its favor.

Numerous development funds already exist, some based at the United Nations, which provide financing for various purposes. The Global Fund was founded in 2002 as a private foundation to finance medical solutions for AIDS, tuberculosis and malaria. It has grown to $4 billion in assets; 80% of resources go to Africa.[5] There is the SDG Fund (originally the MDG Fund), gifted by the government of Spain, that is based with UNDP (United Nations Development Program), and finances numerous projects in the least developed countries. There is a Green Climate Fund for financing environmental programs and projects. The Global Financial Facility exists to fund the Secretary-General's "Every Woman Every Child" program. All represent forms of partnerships.

CHART 1: NET OFFICIAL DEVELOMENT ASSISTANCE FROM DAC DONORS IN 2015

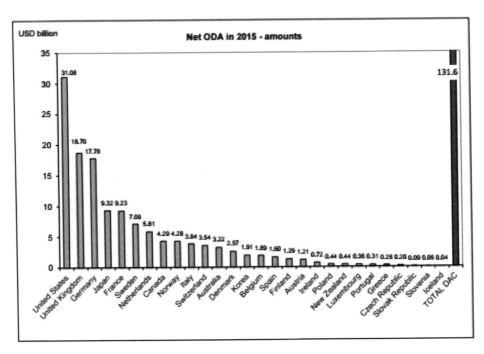

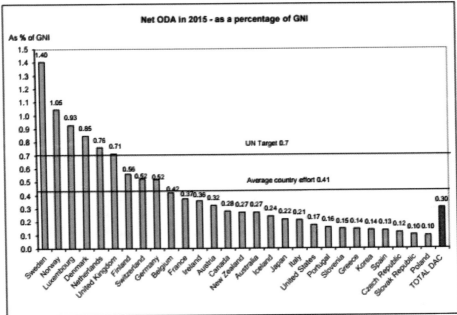

Source: OECD, 13 April 2016

There are many well-established international financial organizations already in place that provide ample financing to developing and least developed countries. Starting with agriculture, the International Fund for Agricultural Development (IFAD), a specialized UN agency, has lent or granted nearly $13 billion for various agricultural development programs in least developed countries since its founding in 1977.[6] Moreover, IFAD states that, "Partnerships are central to everything we do."[7] The World Bank and its affiliates are major providers of development finance. There are the regional lending institutions, such as the Inter-American Development Bank, the Asian Development Bank, the African Development Bank and even the European Bank for Reconstruction and Development to assist the countries of Central and Eastern Europe. (The latter commemorated its 25th anniversary in 2016.)

The Islamic Development Bank, based in Jeddah, Saudi Arabia, has been financing projects mostly in the Middle East for over four decades, offering financing in accordance with Sharia law. It reported having financed some $80 billion in projects during the MDG period, and pledged financing of $150 billion over the next 15 years. In 2015 China established the Asian Infrastructure Investment Bank, with an initial capital of $50 billion, to become a lending institution that will finance significant projects and counter the influence of the World Bank on the global stage.

In addition to special funds and development-bank lending, the capital markets have come up with several innovative forms of financing. There are now "Green Bonds" that are issued in various markets to fund projects related to environmental and other sustainable development activities. A few developing countries have established their own equity markets, known as frontier markets, that have attracted the attention of international investors. Moreover, each country has some sort of functioning banking system which will continue to supply credit and other financial services to businesses and government whenever and wherever there are opportunities.

After so many years, microlending has gone mainstream in the least developed countries, but borrowers at times need larger amounts than this system can provide. Some nonprofits, such as Caritas, have begun a program to encourage microsaving. When small amounts are pooled together as savings, they can provide the larger amounts needed by encouraging micro entrepreneurs to borrow, invest and take their business to the next stage.

In addition to the aforementioned development banks and financial innovations available in various markets, there are private funds available. One estimate of private financial assets globally put private financial assets at $200 trillion. Some of these funds could be mobilized for viable projects when opportunities arise.

While it is not possible to figure out how much is needed to wipe out poverty world-wide, ball-park estimates have been made by a daring few. UNCTAD, in its 2014 edition of the World Investment Report, estimated that five to seven trillion dollars per year would be needed for infrastructure projects alone:

The SDGs will have very significant resource implications across the developed and developing world. Global investment needs are in the order of $5 trillion to $7 trillion per year. Estimates for investment needs in developing countries alone range from $3.3 trillion to $4.5 trillion per year, mainly for basic infrastructure (roads, rail and ports; power stations; water and sanitation), food security (agriculture and rural development), climate change mitigation and adaptation, health, and education.

The SDGs will require a step-change in the levels of both public and private investment in all countries. At current levels of investment in SDG-relevant sectors, developing countries alone face an annual gap of $2.5 trillion. In developing countries, especially in LDCs and other vulnerable economies, public finances are central to investment in SDGs. However, they cannot meet all SDG-implied resource demands. The role of private sector investment will be indispensable.[8]

Foreign investment: A major development force

Globally, foreign direct investment flows reached $1.7 trillion in 2015 according to preliminary data assembled by UNCTAD (an annual increase of 36%, and a strong recovery from the year before when FDI flows had fallen 16%). A quadrupling of flows into the United States due to significant mergers and acquisitions deals produced a near-record inflow of $384 billion, as US growth outpaced very sluggish growth in most other developed countries. About 45% of FDI was directed to developing and least developed countries. China, India and Brazil ranked among the top ten FDI recipients in 2015 and together pulled in $251 billion. According to UNCTAD:

> **FDI will remain a critical source of finance for developing countries.** FDI continues to have important implications for a host country's balance of payments, savings, investment, the export-import gap, and overall macroeconomic management. It is seen also as a principal channel for the transfer of technology to developing countries and, through technology spillovers and enhancement of production and export capacities, as a boost to employment and economic growth.[9]

FDI includes cross-border mergers, acquisitions and new or "greenfield" projects where a foreign firm acquires at least 10% of a company in another country through equity, loans or reinvested earnings. In 2015, $721 billion flows were deemed to be greenfield projects.

> **A wide range of investors, domestic and foreign, are potential sources of external finance for development,** including commercial banks, state-owned banks, pension funds, insurance companies, MNEs, sovereign wealth funds, foundations, endowments, family offices and venture capital funds. The options are greater than ever before, but the challenge is to mobilize them, channel them to the SDG sectors and ensure their positive contributions to sustainable development and inclusive growth.[10]

Compared with foreign aid, the amount of FDI that was received by developing economies was more than quadruple the ODA amount in 2015 alone. Recognizing the importance of FDI, Target 17.5 calls for adopting and implementing "investment promotion regimes for the least developed countries." However, most of these countries already benefit from assistance given by the Multilateral Investment Guarantee Agency of the World Bank (MIGA). MIGA assists developing countries draft information materials, provides political-risk insurance and offers other advisory support to help countries market themselves as investment destinations. MIGA defines its purpose as follows:

> As a multilateral development agency, MIGA only supports investments that are developmentally sound and meet high social and environmental standards. MIGA applies a comprehensive set of social and environmental performance standards to all projects and offers extensive expertise in working with investors to ensure compliance to these standards.[11]

Furthermore, MIGA fulfills a number of functions as a go-between for investor and recipient, to assist both parties in moving a project ahead. MIGA states:

> We fulfill our mission by providing political risk insurance guarantees to private sector investors and lenders. MIGA's guarantees protect investments against non-commercial risks and can help investors obtain access to funding sources with improved financial terms and conditions. Our unique strength is derived from our standing as a member of the World Bank Group and our structure as an international organization with our shareholders including most countries of the world. Since our inception in 1988, MIGA has issued more than $28 billion in political risk insurance for projects in a wide variety of sectors, covering all regions of the world.[12]

Many countries (developed, developing and least developed) have a government entity such as an investment promotion agency to guide potential investors, domestic and foreign, to set up shop in a country. They offer information and advice on setting up a business, assist with location of a plant site, help to guide new investors through the regulatory process, explain any applicable fiscal incentives, and render follow-up assistance once a plant is up and running. There are 170 members from 120 countries in the World Association of Investment Promotion Agencies (WAIPA).[13]

Emigrants' remittances: The largest source of funds for the poor

In securing finance for development, emigrants' remittances are so important to some countries that they exceed merchandise exports, are larger than capital inflows and constitute a significant percentage of GDP. Remittances were mentioned in the SDGs towards the end of Goal 10 on migration, but only with reference to lowering transfer costs. Remittances to home countries are key components in the development process. Today they are more than four times as large as ODA and have generally been more stable than foreign direct investment in difficult economic times.

In 2015 the World Bank estimated that emigrants' remittances were $582 billion, a small decline from the previous year due to exchange-rate fluctuations (US dollar strength vis-à-vis the euro and especially against the Russian ruble, which declined 42%) but still up considerably (27%) from $460 billion in 2010. The true amount is probably underestimated given the existence of informal channels, such as couriers, to send money home.

The United Nations usually makes reference to remittances sent to the least developed countries instead of the global total. This gives an incomplete picture of developmental assistance because the poor reside in other countries, too. Indeed, "70% of the world's poor live in middle-income countries."[14]

Table 1: Cross-border financial flows – *in billions of US dollars*			
	2010	2015	% change
Foreign Direct Investment	1,328	1,700	+28.0
Developing countries	580	741	+27.8
Emigrants' Remittances	460	582	+26.5
Developing countries	332	432	+30.1
Official Development Assistance	129	132	+ 2.3
Source: UNCTAD, OECD and World Bank			

In 2014 the United Nations estimated there were 244 million persons (3% of the world population) living in a country not of their birth.[15] Undoubtedly, that number has swelled since then due to the massive flow of refugees, primarily from Syria and elsewhere in the Middle East as well as Africa. Some already may have found employment and are sending money home to desperate family members.

According to the World Bank, the largest migration corridors in the world are Mexico-United States, Russia-Ukraine and Bangladesh-India. The United States hosts the largest number of foreign-born residents and is the largest remitter with $56 billion sent abroad in 2014. Most of these outflows go to Mexico ($25 billion), China ($16 billion) and India ($12 billion).[16] The countries with the largest populations, China and India, also are the top two recipients of all global emigrants' remittances. Smaller countries, however, are much more dependent on remittances as a proportion of their GDP as indicated in Table 2.

Table 2: Top five remittance receiving countries			
In billions of US dollars, 2015		*In % of GDP, 2014*	
India	69	Tajikistan	37
China	64	Kyrgyz Republic	30
Philippines	29	Nepal	29
Mexico	25	Tonga	27
Nigeria	21	Moldova	26
Source: World Bank, Migration and Development Brief #26, April 2016.			

IFAD has estimated that remittances support about 750 million people worldwide, more than 10% of world population.[17] Money sent home to their families by migrants working in other countries goes directly into the hands of the poor and should be considered the primary financial resource in alleviating poverty. Once they receive the funds the families can decide for themselves how the money should be spent: food, clothing, medical care, education for girls who otherwise would be working in the fields, housing improvements or even community development projects. In countries where remittances make a significant contribution to GDP, often there are special savings and investment schemes, and even financial advice, for both the remitters and their families to obtain the most mileage from this vital income source.

According to IFAD, by 2030 migrants abroad will have sent an accumulated $7.5 trillion to their hometowns in developing countries alone,[18] a figure likely to be higher when middle-income countries' receipts are added in. In recognition of the importance of the work of migrants and their remittances to families, in 2016 the Governing Council of IFAD declared June 16 the "International Day of Family Remittances" and called on the UN General Assembly "to endorse the observance of this day."[19]

WTO: A partnership promoting exports and growth

World trade is another major contributor to development and its foremost promoter is the World Trade Organization. Founded in 1995 as successor to GATT (General Agreement on Tariffs and Trade), the WTO currently has 164 member countries – the last to join was Afghanistan in July 2016 – that account for 98% of global trade. Global merchandise exports, valued in dollar terms, were $16.5 trillion in 2015, equal to about one-fifth of global GDP.

Due to a sharp decline in commodity prices and the appreciation of the US dollar, the value of global exports declined 13% in 2015 although in the previous year exports had reached the record amount of $19 trillion.

China alone accounted for nearly $2.3 trillion (13.8%) of global exports in 2015. The country became the world's largest exporter in 2009, surpassing the United States and Germany. Several developing countries ranked among the top 30 exporters including India (#19), Brazil (#25) and Vietnam (#27). Over the past two decades, developing and least developed countries have increased their share in merchandise trade from 27% in 1995 to 43% today, although most of this growth is due to China.[20] African exports, excluding South Africa, accounted for only 1.9% of total world exports in 2015, but may benefit in the future from WTO programs described below.

Due to the efforts of the WTO, since 1995 global tariffs have been halved from 15% to 8%, while trade volumes have doubled. Merchandise exports by volume expanded only 2.8% in 2015, compared with an average annual growth rate of 5% since 1990, due to: weak economic growth in developed countries and China, falling commodity prices and exchange rate volatility. Exports of developing and least developed countries nonetheless continued to grow faster than the global average as indicated in Table 3.

Table 3: Volume of merchandise exports – annual % change

	2012	2013	2014	2015
Developed economies	1.1	1.7	2.4	2.6
Developing and LDCs	3.8	3.8	3.1	3.3
World	2.2	2.4	2.8	2.8

Source: World Trade Organization

The WTO's main function is "to ensure that trade flows smoothly, predictably and as freely as possible." To that end, the WTO promotes free and open trade practices, works to eliminate trade barriers, assists in settling trade disputes between countries, and helps the least developed countries to diversify exports and facilitate sales of their products to other countries.

Under WTO's auspices, nations enter into trade agreements that set the ground rules for international commerce. The organization plays a key role in assisting the least developed countries in expanding markets, especially for agricultural products in industrial countries where they must meet stringent phytosanitary standards. The WTO offers a number of programs, funded by developed countries, which offer technical assistance and training to help LDCs meet those requirements.

The *Standards and Trade Development Facility* was designed to help LDCs enhance food safety, animal health, and plant health so these countries can gain and retain access to more markets.

The *Institute for Training and Technical Cooperation* was set up to train trade personnel from developing and LDCs to participate more effectively in WTO negotiations and other trade-related activities.

The *Doha Development Agenda Global Trust Fund* runs programs in Geneva and other places to provide training and enable LDC's trade officials to participate more fully in trade negotiations, especially the WTO Ministerial Conferences such as the one held in Nairobi, Kenya, in December 2015.

The *Trade Facilitation Agreement Facility*, launched in July 2014, was created to assist LDCs in complying with the recently established Trade Facilitation Agreement that is intended to simplify, standardize and speed up global customs procedures. This facility is expected to have a significant impact given that the TFA:

> …is the first multilateral trade agreement concluded since the establishment of the World Trade Organization in 1995. The TFA represents a landmark achievement for the WTO, with the potential to increase world trade by up to US $1 trillion per annum.[21]

Box 2: ColaLife partnership

Simple solutions often can have far-reaching implications for the better. A case in point is ColaLife. Coca-Cola is ubiquitous. The beverage is produced, marketed and sold in the remotest corners of the world. The bottled Coke product has an extensive distribution network that reaches all points.

A British aid worker, Simon Berry, who was stationed for many years in Zambia, took note that Coke was available everywhere he traveled. Mindful of the dire poverty and high infant and child mortality particularly in rural areas, Berry developed an ingenious and effective method for getting simple, life-saving medications to the remotest villages: transport these medicines on the bicycles of vendors who delivered crates of Coke bottles.

Berry developed a special plastic packaging that would fit between the necks of the Coke bottles in those crates. The packages became known as "Kit Yamoyo" or Kit of Life, and contained oral rehydration salts and zinc supplements, anti-diarrheal medications essential to save the lives of infants and small children, and hand-washing soap. To engage communities, the locals in the various villages were asked to determine how the medications were to be made available. The kits could be sold, simply given away or distributed via a local health care facility. The package could be sold cheaply and those unable to pay benefit from vouchers funded by ColaLife from donations.

The ColaLife partnership network began in 2008, became a registered United Kingdom charity in 2011 and has received funding from various private donors and official aid sources to expand the program. The end result has been a noticeable decline in infant and child mortality in Zambia for the benefit of families. In addition, the distribution package designed by Mr. Berry received a design award!

Developing and least developed countries requested this facility so that they may receive the necessary support to expedite the movement of goods across borders.

Partnerships with philanthropy

Many charities and non-profits, including those that deal with children, youth and families in poor countries, rely on partnerships with family and corporate foundations to fund a good part of their activities. Many successful family-owned businesses form their own philanthropic foundations, such as the Ferrero family (see Box 1).

Individual- and private-sector generosity have contributed toward meeting various social needs, such as education (so essential for empowerment of children – especially girls), and health care facilities to provide essential medical services. Where governments are unable to meet critical needs, non-profits may step in to provide assistance, at times by forming partnerships.

An example of such collaboration is the non-profit *Pencils of Promise*,[22] established

---

in New York in 2008. They form partnerships with local communities to provide a portion of the funds needed for school construction so that both donor and recipient have "skin in the game." So far they operate in Guam, Guatemala and Laos, helping to build schools. The local community contributes 20% of the cost of building the school in the form of construction materials and labor. Outside donors provide the rest. In addition, donors help overcome the lack of sufficient books by introducing and donating technology that the children would not otherwise have access to, such as tablets. This is but one private-public partnership in a critical area. Education for all is a daunting task.

> There are 250 million children of primary school age in the world who lack basic reading and writing skills, and still 50 per cent of schools in Africa have few or no books at all.[23]

The philanthropic/charitable/non-profit sector generally operates more closely than officialdom to assist people in need or to solve specific problems. There are no global estimates for philanthropy but the United Nations has recognized philanthropic endeavors as a force in achieving the SDGs due to their funding availability, expertise and technical knowledge.

Data on giving is available for the United States, which has a philanthropic culture second to none. Historians recognize this benevolence as having started with the Marshall Plan after World War II. (Although previously sharing wealth became a hallmark of some of the richest men of the Industrial Revolution, including Andrew Carnegie, who is reported to have said, "The man who dies rich dies disgraced.")

Each year the Giving USA Foundation produces "Giving USA,"[24] a compilation of data on giving by individuals, family foundations, private bequests and corporations. In 2015 collectively they donated $373 billion, a statistically significant 2.1% of GDP, up 4% from the prior year and a record amount for the second consecutive year. Charitable giving in the past two years also exceeded the 40-year average of 1.9% of GDP despite weak economic conditions and low wage growth. Individuals, family foundations and bequests accounted for 85% of the overall amount. Individuals alone contributed $265 billion – approximately double the amount of global foreign aid.

Of the nine categories of beneficiaries, donations to religious organizations (including churches) accounted for approximately one-third. Some of these funds may have been channeled toward operations and programs in poor countries. Donations in the area of international affairs saw a 17% increase in 2015 due to funds collected for humanitarian crises, including disaster victims and the millions of refugees fleeing from the Middle East.

A few years ago in the United States, the Tuesday after Thanksgiving Day was designated as "Giving Tuesday" to encourage generosity on the day following "Black Friday" (when persons shop for Christmas presents and help stores turn their financial bottom-line from red to black), and "Cyber Monday" (when online shopping hits a peak). Many charities launch specific campaigns to maximize donations on this day.

Generosity occurs at all income levels and some of the richest persons have taken a great interest in alleviating poverty, especially in the context of the achievement of the MDGs and now the SDGs. The opportunities to exploit ideas and innovations in a relatively unfettered environment, especially in technology, have led many individuals to establish new industries that generated great prosperity which in turn has led to the accumulation of vast personal fortunes. Most billionaires have set up foundations to dispense part of their wealth to support various causes. Bill Gates not only established a foundation with his wife, but has encouraged all billionaires to commit to a "giving pledge" to donate at least half of their fortune to charity during their lifetime. To date, more than 150 individuals or couples from the United States and other countries, too, have taken the pledge.

Corporate contributions to achieving the SDGs

In the September 1, 2015 issue, *Fortune* magazine compiled its first-ever, "Change the World List."[25] The focus was on 50 companies and how they were attacking global problems in a significant way and having plenty to show for it, often by partnering. The top example given was the partnership between Vodafone of the United Kingdom and Kenyan-based Safaricom. Jointly they created a mobile-phone platform in 2007 called M-Pesa, enabling people without bank accounts to use their smartphones to transfer money, receive pensions and pay bills.

Today there are 17 million users in several countries on three continents. Its tremendous impact was noted best by World Bank economist Wolfgang Fengler: "It has changed lives, businesses, and the perception of Africa, and brought substantial flows into the financial system that would have otherwise been lying literally under mattresses." A staggering 42% of Kenya's GDP is transacted through M-Pesa.[26]

Fiftieth on the list was the French eyewear colossus Essilor. In 2013 it founded a separate division called the "2.5 New Vision Generation" to expand eye care among the 2.5 billion people in developing and LDCs with poor vision who cannot afford eyeglasses. This venture makes very cheap glasses (available for $6), and enables more optometrists to operate in underserved areas via use of mobile ophthalmological units in remote areas, an endeavor that yields a vast improvement in people's lives.

While problems are discussed at length in the United Nations, corporations are hard at work to find solutions for many of the world's most complex problems. Problems are transformed into opportunities and opportunities into profitable ventures with palpable accomplishments. According to *Fortune*:

> The first Change the World List is only a start. Many more companies that are transforming the planet will be recognized in future years, and we hope that still more will be inspired. Our goal here is to solve social problems. Every company, large or small, should strive to be on this list. Business can – and must – compete to change the world.[27]

Not on the *Fortune* list but making notable progress in enhancing the supply of potable water as called for in SDG Goal 6, the German-based chemical giant BASF is focusing on desalination. The technology already exists but is expensive. Through technology and innovation, the process is likely to become more affordable and more widely employed. Just as irrigation pipelines bring water to arid agricultural areas and oil pipelines distribute oil over long distances, so too, desalinated water could be made available over long distances.

The company gave a few recent illustrations of accomplishments:

> Over 70% of the Earth's surface is covered in water – most of it saltwater. Desalinating seawater makes this valuable resource available for consumption. One such plant is located in the Spanish [municipality] El Prat de Llobregat. This desalinating plant supplies drinking water to around a quarter of the population in the greater Barcelona area.
>
> In Nungua, about 12 kilometers from the Ghanaian capital of Accra, desalination will soon provide drinking water to roughly half a million people.
>
> Potable water is a scarce commodity on Cyprus, too. Water scarcity can, at times, mean drastic restrictions for the island's inhabitants: It has happened that, during periods of drought, the water supply was reduced to 36 hours per week. Here, too, people now count on seawater desalination.[28]

The corrosive effect of corruption

Some of the monies destined for projects, programs and services for poverty alleviation and economic development are siphoned off due to corruption. Several organizations have developed indicators to estimate the extent of the problem. Among them are Transparency International (TI), the World Bank and the Heritage Foundation. Every year, for about two decades, Berlin-based Transparency International has been compiling a list of countries from most honest to most corrupt. Their *Corruption Perceptions Index* continues to show that among some of the most corrupt countries are many LDCs. According to TI, "Poor countries lose US$1 trillion a year to corruption" while over six billion people live in countries having "a serious corruption problem."[29] Data for 2015 indicates that:

> Overall, two-thirds of the 168 countries on the 2015 index scored below 50, on a scale from 0 (perceived to be highly corrupt) to 100 (perceived to be very clean).[30]

The highest-ranking scorers (and therefore the most honest) in the 2015 survey were Denmark, Finland and Sweden with scores of 91, 90 and 89, respectively. The United States ranked 16th with a score of 76. Only 20 countries scored 75 or higher. At the other end of the scale, Somalia and North Korea were tied at rock bottom, each ranking 167th with a score of 8, preceded by Afghanistan with a score of 11. Among the LDCs, the best performer was Bhutan, which ranked 27th with a score of 65, followed by Rwanda with a rank of 44 and a score of 54.

Table 4: The 48 Least Developed Countries: Corruption and Development Global rankings

LDCs	TI	DB	HF	PCY in $
Afghanistan	166	177	n.a.	1937
Angola	163	181	156	7203
Bangladesh	139	174	137	3373
Benin	83	158	101	1870
Bhutan	27	71	97	7641
Burkina Faso	76	143	104	1682
Burundi	150	152	133	911
Cambodia	150	127	112	3263
Central African Rep.	145	185	168	607
Chad	147	183	164	2617
Comoros	136	154	141	1548
Dem. Rep. of Congo	147	184	163	704
Djibouti	99	171	124	3051
Equatorial Guinea	n.a.	180	170	32,266
Eritrea	154	189	173	1195
Ethiopia	103	146	148	1589
Gambia	123	151	119	1599
Guinea	139	n.a.	136	1313
Guinea-Bissau	158	178	145	1436
Haiti	158	182	150	1750
Kiribati	n.a.	149	165	1713
Laos	139	n.a.	155	4987
Lesotho	61	114	152	2764
Liberia	83	179	143	882
Madagascar	123	164	87	1437
Malawi	112	141	146	780
Mali	95	143	121	1729
Mauritania	112	168	128	4288
Mozambique	112	133	139	1174
Myanmar (Burma)	147	167	158	4706
Nepal	130	99	151	2376
Niger	99	160	129	1048
Rwanda	44	62	71	1698
Sao Tome & Principe	66	166	n.a.	3153
Senegal	61	153	111	2311
Sierra Leone	119	147	142	2027
Solomon Islands	n.a.	12	161	1895
Somalia	167	n.a.	n.a.	600
South Sudan	163	187	n.a.	n.a.
Sudan	165	159	n.a.	4267
Timor-Leste	123	173	167	4928
Togo	107	150	135	1450
Tuvalu	n.a.	n.a.	n.a.	n.a.
Uganda	139	122	102	2023
United Rep. of Tanzania	117	139	110	2667
Vanuatu	n.a.	94	89	2608
Yemen	154	170	n.a.	3774
Zambia	76	97	106	4064
Number of countries covered:	**168**	**189**	**178**	

n.a. = not available.
PCY for Equatorial Guinea reflects high oil revenues.
PCY refers to per capita income as determined by The Heritage Foundation.

Sources:
TI: Transparency International, *Corruption Perceptions Index 2015*
DB: *Doing Business 2016* published by the World Bank
HF: The Heritage Foundation, *2016 Index of Economic Freedom*

Another yardstick in measuring integrity in development is the report prepared jointly by the World Bank and its affiliate the International Finance Corporation, known as Doing Business. Published every year since 2003, the report now uses 11 indicator sets to measure the ease of doing business in 189 countries, with a focus on regulations and processes involved in establishing and running a business using data derived from the largest business cities in each country.

Coverage includes dealing with: construction permits, securing electricity, registering property, obtaining credit, paying taxes, treatment of minority investors, enforcing contracts, trading across borders and resolving insolvency.[31] The 2015 results showed 40 of the 48 LDCs featured in the bottom half of the rankings: Singapore, New Zealand and Denmark ranked as the top three, while South Sudan, Libya and Eritrea were last in ranking.

The Heritage Foundation's *Index of Economic Freedom* (22nd edition issued in early 2016) focused on economic conditions and government policies in 178 countries, in the context of economic freedom for individuals to engage in economic pursuits. Countries were ranked into five classifications. Only five countries were designated "free:" Hong Kong, Singapore, New Zealand, Switzerland and Australia. "Mostly free" countries numbered 33; there were 54 "moderately free" countries; 62 "mostly unfree;" and 24 "repressed" countries. The mostly unfree and repressed groups of countries included 32 of the 48 least developed countries.[32] Encouragingly, the 2016 edition reported that:

> Ninety-seven countries, the majority of which are less developed, gained greater economic freedom over the past year; 32 countries . . . achieved their highest economic freedom scores ever in the 2016 Index. Twelve of these 32 are located in Sub-Saharan Africa.[33]

Worrisome prospects for the world economy

The world economy in 2016 is at a difficult crossroads. Economic growth is faltering in the advanced economies after a very modest recovery following the 2007-2008 economic crisis, while middle income, developing and developed countries are experiencing a notable growth slowdown. However, poorer countries are continuing to grow faster than developed countries, thus narrowing the development gap.

World trade growth, a past motor of overall expansion, has slowed significantly with dim prospects following Brexit and its impact on trade in general, putting on hold major regional-trade proposals, such as TTIP (Transatlantic Trade and Investment Partnership) between the European Union and the United States, and TPP (Trans-Pacific Partnership) affecting 12 countries.[34]

The specter of: lingering public deficits, expanding government indebtedness, failure of many governments to make economic reforms and the exhaustion of monetary policy ease, weigh heavily on the national policy framework and on prospects for international collaboration on policy decisions.

While commodity price declines have contributed to near-zero inflation in developed countries, they have dampened prospects in resource-dependent LDCs. Low inflation is likely to persist as is sluggish wage-growth, which in turn will keep consumption in check. Productivity, too, has shriveled – perhaps reflecting the slowdown in innovation and new business formation.

Labor markets are in a state of flux, adversely affected by key demographic factors including: population decline, rapid aging and a stagnant labor force needing more skilled workers. Massive inflows of both economic and refugee migrants are not necessarily providing the type of labor required by today's complex industrial world.

Leadership, too, is lacking as global problems mount, suggesting a difficult road ahead for economic growth, as many forecasters have indicated. The April 2016 projections of the International Monetary Fund are fairly representative for world economic prospects – and the implications for poverty reduction.

Table 5: World economic outlook - % change in GDP

	2012	2013	2014	2015	2016	2017
Advanced economies	1.2	1.2	1.8	1.9	1.9	2.0
Emerging market & developing economies	5.3	4.9	4.6	4.0	4.1	4.6
World	3.5	3.3	3.4	3.1	3.2	3.5

Source: International Monetary Fund, World Economic Outlook, April 2016.

No prosperity without peace

Since the United Nations was created there have been (by one account) more than 200 conflicts of various degrees of intensity around the globe, both within and among nations. The UN was created out of the ashes of World War II to maintain peace, but the UN does not have a good track record of nipping in the bud nascent crises. Every time belligerencies occur, a country suffers destruction of: infrastructure, numerous victims, displacement of people and a setback for economic development. Given escalating conflicts in number, intensity and complexity, more UN efforts need to be channeled toward peacemaking and peace retention.

Statisticians have found a way to measure peace. The Institute for Economics and Peace has developed the *Global Peace Index*, which ranks 162 independent countries with 99.6% of the global population. Perhaps the results are not surprising given that conflicts form part of daily news accounts, but the *Index* does offer some perspective. The results show some of the worst performers on the peace front are also developing and least developed countries.

According to the *Global Peace Index 2015*, 9th edition, today Europe is the most peaceful region, although this was not always the case – given the bitter strife in Northern Ireland when the IRA held sway; the violence caused by Basque separatists in Spain; and the Red Brigades that terrorized Italy in the 1970s. However, terrorist activities in 2016 in France, Belgium, Germany and elsewhere may adversely affect subsequent results.

> **Over the past eight years** the average country score deteriorated 2.4 percent, highlighting that on average the world has become slightly less peaceful. However, this decrease in peacefulness has not been evenly spread, with 86 countries deteriorating while 76 improved. MENA has suffered the largest decline of any region in the world, deteriorating 11 per cent over the past eight years.[35]

Violence not only destroys peace, but halts and sets back economic progress. The *Index* makes an estimate of the extent of that significant loss.

> **The economic impact of violence** on the global economy in 2014 was substantial and is estimated at US$14.3 trillion or 13.4 per cent of world GDP. This is equivalent to the combined economies of Brazil, Canada, France, Germany, Spain and the United Kingdom. Since 2008, the total economic impact on global GDP has increased by 15.3 per cent, from US$12.4 trillion to US$14.3 trillion.[36]

MENA (Middle East-North Africa region) remains the most unsettled area, with Syria being in the direst condition. It is no wonder that the last three rankings in the index compilation, 160-162, are held by Afghanistan, Iraq and Syria. Of the 48 least developed countries, precisely half are in the bottom half of the rankings.

The input into the *Index* is rather extensive and includes not only wars or conflicts between countries but also: domestic guerrilla activities, sectarian divides, internal conflicts, societal safety, homicides as well as political stability, government legitimacy, respect for rule of law, degree of inequality and even the effects of urbanization.

The five most peaceful countries according to the latest data are: Iceland, Denmark, Austria, New Zealand and Switzerland.

Surprisingly, the United States ranks number 94 for the following reasons.

> The United States is the greatest contributor to military expenditure, accounting for US$1.3 trillion of the US$3 trillion global figure by IEP's PPP-based calculations. While this is the greatest component of US costings, the United States also has substantial costs associated with homicides, fear from violence, deaths from external conflict and security agency costs. The high per capita income in the US and the large population combine to boost its absolute expenditure.[37]

Data disaggregation and diffusion

Several monitors of the SDGs have asked for voluminous, detailed data to measure progress in order to hold governments and others accountable. Statisticians, faced with an enormous challenge, nonetheless have come up with a framework of 230 indicators for the 17 goals and 169 targets. Some observers have demanded detailed disaggregated data, especially on gender, in order to track women's empowerment and gender equality. However, the verbosity and vagueness of the SDGs have made the task difficult and generated criticism from many quarters, including the Copenhagen Consensus Center. Experts there questioned the validity of gathering vast amounts of disaggregated data. They posed the query as to how it is possible to "define the gender-disaggregated value of a cow owned by a family of five."[38]

In the least developed countries often very basic indicators simply do not exist and statistical collection methods may not be reviewed and updated with the frequency necessary to capture changes that occur over time, such as the creation of new industries. This is the case with gross domestic product, which should measure the output of new industries that arise over time in addition to those already well established. Thus, the true economic standing of many developed and LDCs may be underestimated.

While all advanced countries have civil registration, in many LDCs basic civil-status data is nonexistent, despite the longstanding presence of several United Nations agencies such as: UNFPA, UNICEF, WHO and even the UN Statistics Division, among others. "There is no single agency within the United Nations responsible for helping countries set up and manage civil registration."[39]

According to the WHO, about half of the world's children have no identity. There is no birth registration and there are no birth or death certificates to prove a person's identity. How can one speak of "gender disaggregated data" when people are not even counted?

Conclusion

At about the same time the UN General Assembly stamped its approval on the SDGs in late 2015, the World Bank decided to redefine and update the poverty threshold to $1.90 per day.[40] However, the United Nations retained the poverty line of $1.25 per day (previously adopted for the MDGs). Under the new World Bank standard, an estimated 13% of the world's population lived below the $1.90 poverty line in 2012, down from 37% in 1990. Over this period of time the number of people living in poverty fell from 2 billion to 897 million and may have declined further since 2012.

For development that truly lifts people out of poverty, countries must have: ownership, control and management of their development process, given that each country has its own: history, culture, beliefs, traditions and sense of perspective. A worthwhile effort would be to: examine economic development around the world to learn which countries have succeeded in pulling their people out of poverty, study the successfully adopted strategies, policies and incentives; and then select those elements that could be emulated. Botswana, Cape Verde, Maldives and Samoa have graduated from the LDC group and may offer some guidance.

China, to a certain extent, followed much of the Singaporean model in allowing a private sector to emerge and flourish, encouraging manufacturing and promoting exports. While many Asian countries followed this pattern, Africa has not. According to one African observer:

Capitalism has been the greatest creator of national wealth in world history, lifting billions out of poverty from Singapore to China, and from South Korea to Brazil. But Africa stands on the cusp of a lost opportunity because its leaders — and those who assess its progress in London, Paris and Washington — are wrongly fixated on the rise and fall of GDP and foreign investment flows, mostly into resource extraction industries and modern shopping malls.[41]

Sub-Saharan Africa in particular needs to put behind the "resource curse" and provide an enabling environment for entrepreneurship to thrive, starting with small- and medium-sized companies, some of which could move up to global scale. A prudent regulatory environment is necessary in all countries in order to assure a level playing field for all participants and especially to mobilize global resources to promote greater economic development that will not only lift people out of poverty, but permit them to flourish. A peaceful environment is a *sine qua non*: There can be no prosperity without peace.

Acronyms

DAC.............Development Assistance Committee
DB................Doing Business
EU................European Union
FDI ....Foreign direct investment
GATT...........General Agreement on Tariffs and Trade
GDP.............Gross domestic product
GNI..............Gross national income
HF................Heritage Foundation
IEP ....Institute for Economics and Peace
IFAD ....International Fund for Agricultural Development
IMF..............International Monetary Fund
LDCs.............Least developed countries
MENA ....Middle East North Africa
MIGA...........Multilateral Investment Guarantee Agency
MNEs...........Multinational enterprises
ODA ....Official development assistance
OECD..........Organization for Economic Cooperation and Development
PPP ....Purchasing power parity
TI.................Transparency International
TTIP ....Transatlantic Trade and Investment Partnership
TPP ....Trans-Pacific Partnership
UNCTAD ...United Nations Conference on Trade and Development
UNDP..........United Nations Development Program
WTO ....World Trade Organization

Endnotes

1. Ernst&Young and Kennesaw State University Coles College of Business, *Staying power: how do family businesses create lasting success?* 2015.
2. Ibid.
3. "Relative Success," Capital Insights from EY Transaction Advisory Services, Q3, 2015. (Based on information from Ernst&Young, *Family Business Yearbook 2015*.)
4. International Monetary Fund, *World Economic Outlook*, April 2016.
5. "Fund manager who saves lives," *Financial Times*, April 2-3, 2016.
6. https://www.ifad.org/who
7. "IFAD at a glance" (pamphlet published by IFAD).
8. UNCTAD, *World Investment Report 2014*, page xi.
9. UNCTAD, *Global Investment Trends Monitor*, No. 20, 5 June 2015.
10. Ibid.
11. https://www.miga.org/who-we-are/overview
12. https://www.miga.org/who-we-are/overview
13. http://www.waipa.org/why-waipa/
14. Dr. Margaret Chan, *Finding new financing is vital for sustaining health in the post-MDGs world*, 11 June 2015. http://www.un.org/esa/ffd/ffd3/blog/new-financing-vital-for-sustaining-health.html
15. United Nations, Department of Economic and Social Affairs, Population Division, Trends in International Migration, 2015," *Population Facts*, No.2015/4
16. World Bank, *Migration and Remittances Factbook 2016*.
17. https://www.ifad.org/documents/10180/a9322807-2129-49e3-9ad4-9309ad21f874
18. "Remittances bring economic stability to families and countries, says IFAD president on International Day," Press release No.: IFAD/39/2016
19. https://www.ifad.org/documents/10180/a9322807-2129-49e3-9ad4-9309ad21f874
20. WTO Director General Roberto Azevêdo, Lecture at the Graduate Institute in Geneva, 28 September 2015.
21. World Trade Organization, World Trade Report, 2015. https://www.wto.org/english/res_e/booksp_e/world_trade_report15_e.pdf
22. https://pencilsofpromise.org/
23. UNESCO, 2015 Annual Report, page 84. http://unesdoc.unesco.org/images/0024/002448/244834e.pdf
24. http://givingusa.org/giving-usa-2016/ Giving USA: 2015 Was America's Most-Generous Year Ever.
25. *Fortune*, Volume 172, Number 3, Change the World List, September 1, 2015.
26. http://fortune.com/change-the-world/vodafone-and-safaricom-1/
27. Michael E. Porter & Mark Kramer, Profiting the Planet, *Fortune*, September 1, 2015.
28. BASF at 150, brochure produced by BASF.
29. http://www.transparency.org/cpi2015
30. CPI_2015_Press_Release_EN.pdf
31. World Bank, Doing Business 2016: Measuring Regulatory Quality and Efficiency, 13th edition.
32. http://www.heritage.org/index/book/executive-highlights
33. Ibid.
34. The 12 countries are: Australia, Brunei, Canada, Chile, Japan, Malaysia, Mexico, New Zealand, Peru, Singapore, United States, and Vietnam.
35. http://economicsandpeace.org/wp-content/uploads/2015/06/Global-Peace-Index-Report-2015_0.pdf
36. Ibid.
37. Ibid. page 79
38. Matt Ridley, "Smart Aid for the World's Poor," *Wall Street Journal 'Review'*, July 26-27, 2014
39. http://www.who.int/mediacentre/factsheets/fs324/en/
40. World Bank, World Development Indicators 2016.
41. "Africa has to go through its own industrial revolution" http://www.ft.com/intl/cms/s/0/d68f27fe-1aad-11e6-b286-cddde55ca122.html#axzz4BC32dU5j

Sustainable Development Goals and Targets

2030 Agenda for Sustainable Development
https://sustainabledevelopment.un.org/?menu=1300

Goal 1. End poverty in all its forms everywhere

1.1 By 2030, eradicate extreme poverty for all people everywhere, currently measured as people living on less than $1.25 a day

1.2 By 2030, reduce at least by half the proportion of men, women and children of all ages living in poverty in all its dimensions according to national definitions

1.3 Implement nationally appropriate social protection systems and measures for all, including floors, and by 2030 achieve substantial coverage of the poor and the vulnerable

1.4 By 2030, ensure that all men and women, in particular the poor and the vulnerable, have equal rights to economic resources, as well as access to basic services, ownership and control over land and other forms of property, inheritance, natural resources, appropriate new technology and financial services, including microfinance

1.5 By 2030, build the resilience of the poor and those in vulnerable situations and reduce their exposure and vulnerability to climate-related extreme events and other economic, social and environmental shocks and disasters

1.a Ensure significant mobilization of resources from a variety of sources, including through enhanced development cooperation, in order to provide adequate and predictable means for developing countries, in particular least developed countries, to implement programmes and policies to end poverty in all its dimensions

1.b Create sound policy frameworks at the national, regional and international levels, based on pro-poor and gender-sensitive development strategies, to support accelerated investment in poverty eradication actions

Goal 2. End hunger, achieve food security and improved nutrition and promote sustainable agriculture

2.1 By 2030, end hunger and ensure access by all people, in particular the poor and people in vulnerable situations, including infants, to safe, nutritious and sufficient food all year round

2.2 By 2030, end all forms of malnutrition, including achieving, by 2025, the internationally agreed targets on stunting and wasting in children under 5 years of age, and address the nutritional needs of adolescent girls, pregnant and lactating women and older persons

2.3 By 2030, double the agricultural productivity and incomes of small-scale food producers, in particular women, indigenous peoples, family farmers, pastoralists and fishers, including through secure and equal access to land, other productive resources and inputs, knowledge, financial services, markets and opportunities for value addition and non-farm employment

2.4 By 2030, ensure sustainable food production systems and implement resilient agricultural practices that increase productivity and production, that help maintain ecosystems, that strengthen capacity for adaptation to climate change, extreme weather, drought, flooding and other disasters and that progressively improve land and soil quality

2.5 By 2020, maintain the genetic diversity of seeds, cultivated plants and farmed and domesticated animals and their related wild species, including through soundly managed and diversified seed and plant banks at the national, regional and international levels, and promote access to and fair and equitable sharing of benefits arising from the utilization of genetic resources and associated traditional knowledge, as internationally agreed

2.a Increase investment, including through enhanced international cooperation, in rural infrastructure, agricultural research and extension services, technology development and plant and livestock gene banks in order to enhance agricultural productive capacity in developing countries, in particular least developed countries

2.b Correct and prevent trade restrictions and distortions in world agricultural markets, including through the parallel elimination of all forms of agricultural export subsidies and all export measures with equivalent effect, in accordance with the mandate of the Doha Development Round

2.c Adopt measures to ensure the proper functioning of food commodity markets and their derivatives and facilitate timely access to market information, including on food reserves, in order to help limit extreme food price volatility

Goal 3. Ensure healthy lives and promote well-being for all at all ages

3.1 By 2030, reduce the global maternal mortality ratio to less than 70 per 100,000 live births

3.2 By 2030, end preventable deaths of newborns and children under 5 years of age, with all countries aiming to reduce neonatal mortality to at least as low as 12 per 1,000 live births and under-5 mortality to at least as low as 25 per 1,000 live births

3.3 By 2030, end the epidemics of AIDS, tuberculosis, malaria and neglected tropical diseases and combat hepatitis, water-borne diseases and other communicable diseases

3.4 By 2030, reduce by one third premature mortality from non-communicable diseases through prevention and treatment and promote mental health and well-being

3.5 Strengthen the prevention and treatment of substance abuse, including narcotic drug abuse and harmful use of alcohol

3.6 By 2020, halve the number of global deaths and injuries from road traffic accidents

3.7 By 2030, ensure universal access to sexual and reproductive health-care services, including for family planning, information and education, and the integration of reproductive health into national strategies and programmes

3.8 Achieve universal health coverage, including financial risk protection, access to quality essential health-care services and access to safe, effective, quality and affordable essential medicines and vaccines for all

3.9 By 2030, substantially reduce the number of deaths and illnesses from hazardous chemicals and air, water and soil pollution and contamination

3.a Strengthen the implementation of the World Health Organization Framework Convention on Tobacco Control in all countries, as appropriate

3.b Support the research and development of vaccines and medicines for the communicable and non-communicable diseases that primarily affect developing countries, provide access to affordable essential medicines and vaccines, in accordance with the Doha Declaration on the TRIPS Agreement and Public Health, which affirms the right of developing countries to use to the full the provisions in the Agreement on Trade-Related Aspects of Intellectual Property Rights regarding flexibilities to protect public health, and, in particular, provide access to medicines for all

3.c Substantially increase health financing and the recruitment, development, training and retention of the health workforce in developing countries, especially in least developed countries and small island developing States

3.d Strengthen the capacity of all countries, in particular developing countries, for early warning, risk reduction and management of national and global health risks

Goal 4. Ensure inclusive and equitable quality education and promote lifelong learning opportunities for all

4.1 By 2030, ensure that all girls and boys complete free, equitable and quality primary and secondary education leading to relevant and effective learning outcomes

4.2 By 2030, ensure that all girls and boys have access to quality early childhood development, care and pre-primary education so that they are ready for primary education

4.3 By 2030, ensure equal access for all women and men to affordable and quality technical, vocational and tertiary education, including university

4.4 By 2030, substantially increase the number of youth and adults who have relevant skills, including technical and vocational skills, for employment, decent jobs and entrepreneurship

4.5 By 2030, eliminate gender disparities in education and ensure equal access to all levels of education and vocational training for the vulnerable, including persons with disabilities, indigenous peoples and children in vulnerable situations

4.6 By 2030, ensure that all youth and a substantial proportion of adults, both men and women, achieve literacy and numeracy

4.7 By 2030, ensure that all learners acquire the knowledge and skills needed to promote sustainable development, including, among others, through education for sustainable development and sustainable lifestyles, human rights, gender equality, promotion of a culture of peace and non-violence, global citizenship and appreciation of cultural diversity and of culture's contribution to sustainable development

4.a Build and upgrade education facilities that are child, disability and gender sensitive and provide safe, non-violent, inclusive and effective learning environments for all

4.b By 2020, substantially expand globally the number of scholarships available to developing countries, in particular least developed countries, small island developing States and African countries, for enrolment in higher education, including vocational training and information and communications technology, technical, engineering and scientific programmes, in developed countries and other developing countries

4.c By 2030, substantially increase the supply of qualified teachers, including through international cooperation for teacher training in developing countries, especially least developed countries and small island developing States

Goal 5. Achieve gender equality and empower all women and girls

5.1 End all forms of discrimination against all women and girls everywhere

5.2 Eliminate all forms of violence against all women and girls in the public and private spheres, including trafficking and sexual and other types of exploitation

5.3 Eliminate all harmful practices, such as child, early and forced marriage and female genital mutilation

5.4 Recognize and value unpaid care and domestic work through the provision of public services, infrastructure and social protection policies and the promotion of shared responsibility within the household and the family as nationally appropriate

5.5 Ensure women's full and effective participation and equal opportunities for leadership at all levels of decision-making in political, economic and public life

5.6 Ensure universal access to sexual and reproductive health and reproductive rights as agreed in accordance with the Programme of Action of the International Conference on Population and Development and the Beijing Platform for Action and the outcome documents of their review conferences

5.a Undertake reforms to give women equal rights to economic resources, as well as access to ownership and control over land and other forms of property, financial services, inheritance and natural resources, in accordance with national laws

5.b Enhance the use of enabling technology, in particular information and communications technology, to promote the empowerment of women

5.c Adopt and strengthen sound policies and enforceable legislation for the promotion of gender equality and the empowerment of all women and girls at all levels

Goal 6. Ensure availability and sustainable management of water and sanitation for all

6.1 By 2030, achieve universal and equitable access to safe and affordable drinking water for all

6.2 By 2030, achieve access to adequate and equitable sanitation and hygiene for all and end open defecation, paying special attention to the needs of women and girls and those in vulnerable situations

6.3 By 2030, improve water quality by reducing pollution, eliminating dumping and minimizing release of hazardous chemicals and materials, halving the proportion of untreated wastewater and substantially increasing recycling and safe reuse globally

6.4 By 2030, substantially increase water-use efficiency across all sectors and ensure sustainable withdrawals and supply of freshwater to address water scarcity and substantially reduce the number of people suffering from water scarcity

6.5 By 2030, implement integrated water resources management at all levels, including through transboundary cooperation as appropriate

6.6 By 2020, protect and restore water-related ecosystems, including mountains, forests, wetlands, rivers, aquifers and lakes

6.a By 2030, expand international cooperation and capacity-building support to developing countries in water- and sanitation-related activities and programmes, including water harvesting, desalination, water efficiency, wastewater treatment, recycling and reuse technologies

6.b Support and strengthen the participation of local communities in improving water and sanitation management

Goal 7. Ensure access to affordable, reliable, sustainable and modern energy for all

7.1 By 2030, ensure universal access to affordable, reliable and modern energy services

7.2 By 2030, increase substantially the share of renewable energy in the global energy mix

7.3 By 2030, double the global rate of improvement in energy efficiency

7.a By 2030, enhance international cooperation to facilitate access to clean energy research and technology, including renewable energy, energy efficiency and advanced and cleaner fossil-fuel technology, and promote investment in energy infrastructure and clean energy technology

7.b By 2030, expand infrastructure and upgrade technology for supplying modern and sustainable energy services for all in developing countries, in particular least developed countries, small island developing States and landlocked developing countries, in accordance with their respective programmes of support

Goal 8. Promote sustained, inclusive and sustainable economic growth, full and productive employment and decent work for all

8.1 Sustain per capita economic growth in accordance with national circumstances and, in particular, at least 7 per cent gross domestic product growth per annum in the least developed countries

8.2 Achieve higher levels of economic productivity through diversification, technological upgrading and innovation, including through a focus on high-value added and labour-intensive sectors

8.3 Promote development-oriented policies that support productive activities, decent job creation, entrepreneurship, creativity and innovation, and encourage the formalization and growth of micro-, small- and medium-sized enterprises, including through access to financial services

8.4 Improve progressively, through 2030, global resource efficiency in consumption and production and endeavour to decouple economic growth from environmental degradation, in accordance with the 10-year framework of programmes on sustainable consumption and production, with developed countries taking the lead

8.5 By 2030, achieve full and productive employment and decent work for all women and men, including for young people and persons with disabilities, and equal pay for work of equal value

8.6 By 2020, substantially reduce the proportion of youth not in employment, education or training

8.7 Take immediate and effective measures to eradicate forced labour, end modern slavery and human trafficking and secure the prohibition and elimination of the worst forms of child labour, including recruitment and use of child soldiers, and by 2025 end child labour in all its forms

8.8 Protect labour rights and promote safe and secure working environments for all workers, including migrant workers, in particular women migrants, and those in precarious employment

8.9 By 2030, devise and implement policies to promote sustainable tourism that creates jobs and promotes local culture and products

8.10 Strengthen the capacity of domestic financial institutions to encourage and expand access to banking, insurance and financial services for all

8.a Increase Aid for Trade support for developing countries, in particular least developed countries, including through the Enhanced Integrated Framework for Trade-Related Technical Assistance to Least Developed Countries

8.b By 2020, develop and operationalize a global strategy for youth employment and implement the Global Jobs Pact of the International Labour Organization

Goal 9. Build resilient infrastructure, promote inclusive and sustainable industrialization and foster innovation

9.1 Develop quality, reliable, sustainable and resilient infrastructure, including regional and transborder infrastructure, to support economic development and human well-being, with a focus on affordable and equitable access for all

9.2 Promote inclusive and sustainable industrialization and, by 2030, significantly raise industry's share of employment and gross domestic product, in line with national circumstances, and double its share in least developed countries

9.3 Increase the access of small-scale industrial and other enterprises, in particular in developing countries, to financial services, including affordable credit, and their integration into value chains and markets

9.4 By 2030, upgrade infrastructure and retrofit industries to make them sustainable, with increased resource-use efficiency and greater adoption of clean and environmentally sound technologies and industrial processes, with all countries taking action in accordance with their respective capabilities

9.5 Enhance scientific research, upgrade the technological capabilities of industrial sectors in all countries, in particular developing countries, including, by 2030, encouraging innovation and substantially increasing the number of research and development workers per 1 million people and public and private research and development spending

9.a Facilitate sustainable and resilient infrastructure development in developing countries through enhanced financial, technological and technical support to African countries, least developed countries, landlocked developing countries and small island developing States

9.b Support domestic technology development, research and innovation in developing countries, including by ensuring a conducive policy environment for, inter alia, industrial diversification and value addition to commodities

9.c Significantly increase access to information and communications technology and strive to provide universal and affordable access to the Internet in least developed countries by 2020

Goal 10. Reduce inequality within and among countries

10.1 By 2030, progressively achieve and sustain income growth of the bottom 40 per cent of the population at a rate higher than the national average

10.2 By 2030, empower and promote the social, economic and political inclusion of all, irrespective of age, sex, disability, race, ethnicity, origin, religion or economic or other status

10.3 Ensure equal opportunity and reduce inequalities of outcome, including by eliminating discriminatory laws, policies and practices and promoting appropriate legislation, policies and action in this regard

10.4 Adopt policies, especially fiscal, wage and social protection policies, and progressively achieve greater equality

10.5 Improve the regulation and monitoring of global financial markets and institutions and strengthen the implementation of such regulations

10.6 Ensure enhanced representation and voice for developing countries in decision-making in global international economic and financial institutions in order to deliver more effective, credible, accountable and legitimate institutions

10.7 Facilitate orderly, safe, regular and responsible migration and mobility of people, including through the implementation of planned and well-managed migration policies

10.a Implement the principle of special and differential treatment for developing countries, in particular least developed countries, in accordance with World Trade Organization agreements

10.b Encourage official development assistance and financial flows, including foreign direct investment, to States where the need is greatest, in particular least developed countries, African countries, small island developing States and landlocked developing countries, in accordance with their national plans and programmes

10.c By 2030, reduce to less than 3 per cent the transaction costs of migrant remittances and eliminate remittance corridors with costs higher than 5 per cent

Goal 11. Make cities and human settlements inclusive, safe, resilient and sustainable

11.1 By 2030, ensure access for all to adequate, safe and affordable housing and basic services and upgrade slums

11.2 By 2030, provide access to safe, affordable, accessible and sustainable transport systems for all, improving road safety, notably by expanding public transport, with special attention to the needs of those in vulnerable situations, women, children, persons with disabilities and older persons

11.3 By 2030, enhance inclusive and sustainable urbanization and capacity for participatory, integrated and sustainable human settlement planning and management in all countries

11.4 Strengthen efforts to protect and safeguard the world's cultural and natural heritage

11.5 By 2030, significantly reduce the number of deaths and the number of people affected and substantially decrease the direct economic losses relative to global gross domestic product caused by disasters, including water-related disasters, with a focus on protecting the poor and people in vulnerable situations

11.6 By 2030, reduce the adverse per capita environmental impact of cities, including by paying special attention to air quality and municipal and other waste management

11.7 By 2030, provide universal access to safe, inclusive and accessible, green and public spaces, in particular for women and children, older persons and persons with disabilities

11.a Support positive economic, social and environmental links between urban, peri-urban and rural areas by strengthening national and regional development planning

11.b By 2020, substantially increase the number of cities and human settlements adopting and implementing integrated policies and plans towards inclusion, resource efficiency, mitigation and adaptation to climate change, resilience to disasters, and develop and implement, in line with the Sendai Framework for Disaster Risk Reduction 2015-2030, holistic disaster risk management at all levels

11.c Support least developed countries, including through financial and technical assistance, in building sustainable and resilient buildings utilizing local materials

Goal 12. Ensure sustainable consumption and production patterns

12.1 Implement the 10-Year Framework of Programmes on Sustainable Consumption and Production Patterns, all countries taking action, with developed countries taking the lead, taking into account the development and capabilities of developing countries

12.2 By 2030, achieve the sustainable management and efficient use of natural resources

12.3 By 2030, halve per capita global food waste at the retail and consumer levels and reduce food losses along production and supply chains, including post-harvest losses

12.4 By 2020, achieve the environmentally sound management of chemicals and all wastes throughout their life cycle, in accordance with agreed international frameworks, and significantly reduce their release to air, water and soil in order to minimize their adverse impacts on human health and the environment

12.5 By 2030, substantially reduce waste generation through prevention, reduction, recycling and reuse

12.6 Encourage companies, especially large and transnational companies, to adopt sustainable practices and to integrate sustainability information into their reporting cycle

12.7 Promote public procurement practices that are sustainable, in accordance with national policies and priorities

12.8 By 2030, ensure that people everywhere have the relevant information and awareness for sustainable development and lifestyles in harmony with nature

12.a Support developing countries to strengthen their scientific and technological capacity to move towards more sustainable patterns of consumption and production

12.b Develop and implement tools to monitor sustainable development impacts for sustainable tourism that creates jobs and promotes local culture and products

12.c Rationalize inefficient fossil-fuel subsidies that encourage wasteful consumption by removing market distortions, in accordance with national circumstances, including by restructuring taxation and phasing out those harmful subsidies, where they exist, to reflect their environmental impacts, taking fully into account the specific needs and conditions of developing countries and minimizing the possible adverse impacts on their development in a manner that protects the poor and the affected communities

Goal 13. Take urgent action to combat climate change and its impacts

13.1 Strengthen resilience and adaptive capacity to climate-related hazards and natural disasters in all countries

13.2 Integrate climate change measures into national policies, strategies and planning

13.3 Improve education, awareness-raising and human and institutional capacity on climate change mitigation, adaptation, impact reduction and early warning

13.a Implement the commitment undertaken by developed-country parties to the United Nations Framework

Convention on Climate Change to a goal of mobilizing jointly $100 billion annually by 2020 from all sources to address the needs of developing countries in the context of meaningful mitigation actions and transparency on implementation and fully operationalize the Green Climate Fund through its capitalization as soon as possible

13.b Promote mechanisms for raising capacity for effective climate change-related planning and management in least developed countries and small island developing States, including focusing on women, youth and local and marginalized communities

Goal 14. Conserve and sustainably use the oceans, seas and marine resources for sustainable development

14.1 By 2025, prevent and significantly reduce marine pollution of all kinds, in particular from land-based activities, including marine debris and nutrient pollution

14.2 By 2020, sustainably manage and protect marine and coastal ecosystems to avoid significant adverse impacts, including by strengthening their resilience, and take action for their restoration in order to achieve healthy and productive oceans

14.3 Minimize and address the impacts of ocean acidification, including through enhanced scientific cooperation at all levels

14.4 By 2020, effectively regulate harvesting and end overfishing, illegal, unreported and unregulated fishing and destructive fishing practices and implement science-based management plans, in order to restore fish stocks in the shortest time feasible, at least to levels that can produce maximum sustainable yield as determined by their biological characteristics

14.5 By 2020, conserve at least 10 per cent of coastal and marine areas, consistent with national and international law and based on the best available scientific information

14.6 By 2020, prohibit certain forms of fisheries subsidies which contribute to overcapacity and overfishing, eliminate subsidies that contribute to illegal, unreported and unregulated fishing and refrain from introducing new such subsidies, recognizing that appropriate and effective special and differential treatment for developing and least developed countries should be an integral part of the World Trade Organization fisheries subsidies negotiation

14.7 By 2030, increase the economic benefits to small island developing States and least developed countries from the sustainable use of marine resources, including through sustainable management of fisheries, aquaculture and tourism

14.a Increase scientific knowledge, develop research capacity and transfer marine technology, taking into account the Intergovernmental Oceanographic Commission Criteria and Guidelines on the Transfer of Marine Technology, in order to improve ocean health and to enhance the contribution of marine biodiversity to the development of developing countries, in particular small island developing States and least developed countries

14.b Provide access for small-scale artisanal fishers to marine resources and markets

14.c Enhance the conservation and sustainable use of oceans and their resources by implementing international law as reflected in the United Nations Convention on the Law of the Sea, which provides the legal framework for the conservation and sustainable use of oceans and their resources, as recalled in paragraph 158 of "The future we want"

Goal 15. Protect, restore and promote sustainable use of terrestrial ecosystems, sustainably manage forests, combat desertification, and halt and reverse land degradation and halt biodiversity loss

15.1 By 2020, ensure the conservation, restoration and sustainable use of terrestrial and inland freshwater ecosystems and their services, in particular forests, wetlands, mountains and drylands, in line with obligations under international agreements

15.2 By 2020, promote the implementation of sustainable management of all types of forests, halt deforestation, restore degraded forests and substantially increase afforestation and reforestation globally

15.3 By 2030, combat desertification, restore degraded land and soil, including land affected by desertification, drought and floods, and strive to achieve a land degradation-neutral world

15.4 By 2030, ensure the conservation of mountain ecosystems, including their biodiversity, in order to enhance their capacity to provide benefits that are essential for sustainable development

15.5 Take urgent and significant action to reduce the degradation of natural habitats, halt the loss of biodiversity and, by 2020, protect and prevent the extinction of threatened species

15.6 Promote fair and equitable sharing of the benefits arising from the utilization of genetic resources and promote appropriate access to such resources, as internationally agreed

15.7 Take urgent action to end poaching and trafficking of protected species of flora and fauna and address both demand and supply of illegal wildlife products

15.8 By 2020, introduce measures to prevent the introduction and significantly reduce the impact of invasive alien species on land and water ecosystems and control or eradicate the priority species

15.9 By 2020, integrate ecosystem and biodiversity values into national and local planning, development processes, poverty reduction strategies and accounts

15.a Mobilize and significantly increase financial resources from all sources to conserve and sustainably use biodiversity and ecosystems

15.b Mobilize significant resources from all sources and at all levels to finance sustainable forest management and provide adequate incentives to developing countries to advance such management, including for conservation and reforestation

15.c Enhance global support for efforts to combat poaching and trafficking of protected species, including by increasing the capacity of local communities to pursue sustainable livelihood opportunities

Goal 16. Promote peaceful and inclusive societies for sustainable development, provide access to justice for all and build effective, accountable and inclusive institutions at all levels

16.1 Significantly reduce all forms of violence and related death rates everywhere

16.2 End abuse, exploitation, trafficking and all forms of violence against and torture of children

16.3 Promote the rule of law at the national and international levels and ensure equal access to justice for all

16.4 By 2030, significantly reduce illicit financial and arms flows, strengthen the recovery and return of stolen assets and combat all forms of organized crime

16.5 Substantially reduce corruption and bribery in all their forms

16.6 Develop effective, accountable and transparent institutions at all levels

16.7 Ensure responsive, inclusive, participatory and representative decision-making at all levels

16.8 Broaden and strengthen the participation of developing countries in the institutions of global governance

16.9 By 2030, provide legal identity for all, including birth registration

16.10 Ensure public access to information and protect fundamental freedoms, in accordance with national legislation and international agreements

16.a Strengthen relevant national institutions, including through international cooperation, for building capacity at all levels, in particular in developing countries, to prevent violence and combat terrorism and crime

16.b Promote and enforce non-discriminatory laws and policies for sustainable development

Goal 17. Strengthen the means of implementation and revitalize the Global Partnership for Sustainable Development

Finance

17.1 Strengthen domestic resource mobilization, including through international support to developing countries, to improve domestic capacity for tax and other revenue collection

17.2 Developed countries to implement fully their official development assistance commitments, including the commitment by many developed countries to achieve the target of 0.7 per cent of gross national income for official development assistance (ODA/GNI) to developing countries and 0.15 to 0.20 per cent of ODA/GNI to least developed countries; ODA providers are encouraged to consider setting a target to provide at least 0.20 per cent of ODA/GNI to least developed countries

17.3 Mobilize additional financial resources for developing countries from multiple sources

17.4 Assist developing countries in attaining long-term debt sustainability through coordinated policies aimed at fostering debt financing, debt relief and debt restructuring, as appropriate, and address the external debt of highly indebted poor countries to reduce debt distress

17.5 Adopt and implement investment promotion regimes for least developed countries

Technology

17.6 Enhance North-South, South-South and triangular regional and international cooperation on and access to science, technology and innovation and enhance knowledge sharing on mutually agreed terms, including through improved coordination among existing mechanisms, in particular at the United Nations level, and through a global technology facilitation mechanism

17.7 Promote the development, transfer, dissemination and diffusion of environmentally sound technologies to developing countries on favourable terms, including on concessional and preferential terms, as mutually agreed

17.8 Fully operationalize the technology bank and science, technology and innovation capacity-building mechanism for least developed countries by 2017 and enhance the use of enabling technology, in particular information and communications technology

Capacity-building

17.9 Enhance international support for implementing effective and targeted capacity-building in developing countries to support national plans to implement all the Sustainable Development Goals, including through North-South, South-South and triangular cooperation

Trade

17.10 Promote a universal, rules-based, open, non-discriminatory and equitable multilateral trading system under the World Trade Organization, including through the conclusion of negotiations under its Doha Development Agenda

17.11 Significantly increase the exports of developing countries, in particular with a view to doubling the least developed countries' share of global exports by 2020

17.12 Realize timely implementation of duty-free and quota-free market access on a lasting basis for all least developed countries, consistent with World Trade Organization decisions, including by ensuring that preferential rules of origin applicable to imports from least developed countries are transparent and simple, and contribute to facilitating market access

Systemic issues
Policy and institutional coherence

17.13 Enhance global macroeconomic stability, including through policy coordination and policy coherence

17.14 Enhance policy coherence for sustainable development

17.15 Respect each country's policy space and leadership to establish and implement policies for poverty eradication and sustainable development

Multi-stakeholder partnerships

17.16 Enhance the Global Partnership for Sustainable Development, complemented by multi-stakeholder partnerships that mobilize and share knowledge, expertise, technology and financial resources, to support the achievement of the Sustainable Development Goals in all countries, in particular developing countries

17.17 Encourage and promote effective public, public-private and civil society partnerships, building on the experience and resourcing strategies of partnerships

Data, monitoring and accountability

17.18 By 2020, enhance capacity-building support to developing countries, including for least developed countries and small island developing States, to increase significantly the availability of high-quality, timely and reliable data disaggregated by income, gender, age, race, ethnicity, migratory status, disability, geographic location and other characteristics relevant in national contexts

17.19 By 2030, build on existing initiatives to develop measurements of progress on sustainable development that complement gross domestic product, and support statistical capacity-building in developing countries

Index